Architecture as Environmental Communication

Approaches to Semiotics
69

Editorial Committee

Thomas A. Sebeok
Roland Posner
Alain Rey

Mouton Publishers
Berlin · New York · Amsterdam

Architecture as Environmental Communication

Asghar Talaye Minai

Associate Professor
School of Architecture & Planning
Howard University

Mouton Publishers
Berlin · New York · Amsterdam

Library of Congress Cataloging in Publication Data

Minai, Asghar Talaye.
  Architecture as environmental communication.

  (Approaches to semiotics ; 69)
  Includes index.
  1. Architecture – Environmental aspects. 2. Signs and symbols in architecture.
  I. Title. II. Series.
  NA2542.35.T3   1984   720'.1   84-20695
  ISBN 3-11-009814-8

CIP-Kurztitelaufnahme der Deutschen Bibliothek

Minai, Asghar Talaye:
Architecture as environmental communication / Asghar Talaye Minai. – Berlin;
New York; Amsterdam: Mouton, 1984.
      (Approaches to semiotics: 69)
      ISBN 3–11–009814–8

This work is dedicated to all my teachers, specially those who taught me architecture and planning, including Russell Ackoff, Edmund Bacon, David Crane, Heydar Ghiaee, Romaldo Giurgola, Imre Halasz, Britton Harris, Louis Kahn, Gyorgy Kepes, Ian McHarg, Peter McCleary, Parviz Moayed-ahd, G. Holmes Perkings. Lloyd Rodwin, Houshang Sanele, and Houshang Seyhoon.

Contents

Acknowledgement

I should give my thanks to the following: Above and beyond acknowledgement, I would like to thank my wife, without whose encouragement and assistance this would not have been possible.

I would also like to acknowledge my appreciation for the reviews and comments made by my colleagues: Leland Allen, P. Kenneth Jadin, Jay Kabriel, and Sam Simaika on the manuscript at its final stage and the initial editing of the work by Robert Griffen.

I am also indebted to Harry Robinson, Dean of the School of Architecture and Planning, Glean Chase and Anthony Johns, Chairmen of the Department of Architecture as well as the faculty of the School of Architecture and Planning for their cooperation and support.

Preface

This is an output of an ongoing study begun 15 years ago. The origin of some of the ideas in the text can be traced back to the time I did my doctoral dissertation at the University of Pennsylvania. This volume was intended to cover the theme of communication approach from philosophy to application, but as material grew, it was decided to publish the application of this approach in another volume, *Design as Aesthetic Communication.*

Although this book is published in the series, *Approaches to Semiotics*, it does not directly deal with semiotics. However semiotics in its broadest sense is perceived as communication, the difference being, communication is everything that one can see or think about. All manifestations of culture and physical and natural formations, such as the structure of matter or genetic codes, could be considered communication. Semiotics on the other hand is that portion of communication in which something is signified to stand for something else. The emphasis in semiotics is on signification, whereas here it is on communication, i.e., on any exchange of information rather than on only those signified. The material initially was not prepared as a part of this series, but after the final form of the manuscript was proposed to Mouton it was decided to be published in the series.

One of the main areas of concern in this book is the issue of creativity and its relation to subjectivity, objectivity, intuition, and rational judgements. Throughout my architectural experience I have always been puzzled by the nature of creative acts and their dualistic characteristics. No doubt any architect or student of architecture constantly struggles with the same paradigm and wants to draw lines between right and wrong or good and bad in the judging of aesthetic experience. This attempt constantly leads to an open ended argument when it comes to subjectivity and objectivity. It is relatively easy to make definite judgements in the objective world, but not in the subjective one. The clue is that subjective behavior is tied to the unconscious activities and structure of the mind which until recently were little understood. In this quandary I have found no alternative other than looking into the two realms of creative activities, i.e, the conscious and subconscious. The concensus of recent discoveries in sociology and psychology show that the unconscious activities are in part personal/individual and in part universal and common to all men.

I believe first of all, that students of the Arts in general and Architecture and design specifically should be introduced to those disciplines dealing with the totality of man and his environment. Secondly, until we attain a better understanding of the nature of man and his individual unconscious behavior, it is a waste of time to constantly rely on something we have very little knowledge of. Thirdly, our most constructive artistic experiences entailing the part of knowledge dealing with the notion of creativity comes from the universal part of the unconscious which Carl Jung calls "the collective unconscious."[1] Regarding these activities, he suggests they represent "the living creative matrix of all our unconscious and conscious feeling, the essential structural basis of all our psychic life."[2]

The Arts and Architecture can no longer afford to merely hang onto some mysterious notion of "intuition," having been acknowledged to exist beyond question and doubt. Let us for once not look at intuition as a thing, but rather as a word and try to observe its origin and components from a phenomenological point of view. There we might find nothing but a complex world of structural and random matters following the laws of "change and necessity."[3]

Both the discoveries in the material sciences and psychological studies in the early part of the 20th century reach the same conclusion which suggests that "connection does exist between the psychic unconscious and the subject matter of physics."[4] The preconceived idea that man's psychic activities are "only subjectively expendable," different from those of the material world which is "objectively present in the outer world," has now been proven to be false. Jung points out that the activity in "the lowest collective level of our psyche is simply pure nature, 'Nature, which includes *everything,* thus also the unknown, *inclusive* of matter.'"[5] Similar structures manifest themselves "both in the unconscious psyche *and* in matter, the unity of existence which underlies the duality of psyche and matter becomes more comprehensible to us."[6] In assuming psyche and matter to be the prime components of any creative act in the paradoxical duality of human life, I then search for methods of bringing together these opposing characteristics of rational and non-rational man, namely the "morphic"[7] and "entropic". Where morphic tends to build up orders, entropic disturbs them in order to establish the organism's cooperative pattern of interaction with its environment.

Peirce was one of the first who emphasized the notion of chance in communication context. He held that "chance was not merely for mathematical conveniences but was fundamental to the universe."[8] He used the notion of chance as the "doctrine that absolute chance is a factor in the universe." This doctrine is in opposition to the deterministic philosophies of the 19th century of "universal necessity" claiming that everything is determined by fixed, mechanical laws. Moreover Peirce says that "The first and most fundamental element that we have to assume is a Freedom, or Choice, or Spontaneity, by virtue of which the general vague nothing-in-particular-ness that preceeded the chaos took on a thousand definite qualities."[9]

This text then, dealing with the above mentioned issues, is intended for those architectural students (at any level), faculty, and professionals in other design and communication disciplines who are interested in challenging the undertaking of creative phenomena, specially those who are open to alternative ways of looking at tomorrow's design and architecture. Some might find the arguments controversial because while this is a methodology-oriented theory of architecture, one might expect it to be rational and quantitatively oriented, but to the contrary it is found to challenge the idea that creative acts of design and Architecture are based on either of the two ends of the spectrum, namely the objective rational or subjective emotional.

Regarding the use of scientifically oriented design methods in architecture, I find that since the late 50's architects have started questioning the international style, looking for alternatives, both at the level of cultures and subcultures and historical methodology. In the 60's, in the objective orientation to Architecture,

Christopher Alexander's book, *Notes on the Synthesis of Form,*[10] was an excellent introduction to this field. Significant analytical methodologies were presented, yet his application of these methodologies in *Community and Privacy* was premature, especially at the end of this text when painted aftermaths of image drawings of neighborhoods were rushed. After Alexander there grew a tendency to overuse the capabilities of such techniques, i.e., the objective analytical method was used as the sole means of designing the built environment, ignoring the other side of this dualism, namely the random, nonrational irregularities of the human environment subject to unpredictable patterns of individual behavior. Because of such hasty conclusions and lack of enough momentum to support these general notions and concepts in the 70's, there was a move back to the drawing boards. Parallel with this some of those on the frontiers, such as Alexander in *The Timeless Way of Building,*[11] took a 180 degree change of direction into a romantic view of appreciating the mysterious spontaneity of pluralistic participation in the design of the complexity of a dynamic community. I do not question this approach; as a matter of fact when I suggest emphasizing the unpredictability of random patterns as an important part of aesthetic patterns and thus the creative qualities of environmental communication, I am referring to those rich qualities of irregular patterns that Alexander has perceived as "being rich." Nevertheless my departure from his approach is that individuals' participation in the shaping of their environment can no longer be done in the fashion of medieval times. Our knowledge and technological means today has enabled us to introduce new levels of complexities in our creative forms by considering random uncertainties a part of cosmic and human order. For example, whereas in the past our *a priori* techniques allowed us to determine the localities of billiard balls on a pool table, today we are able to see the information process regarding instantaneous configurations of pattern relationships of all balls moving in synchronization. I believe this is the technology we have to use to bring together a coherent "ordered disorder." We should design these new complex orders rather than just leaving their fate uncertain.

I even go to the extent of saying that post modernism, just like the above romantic movement, has not been anything more than a reaction to previously mentioned formalism and rationalism. My justification for post modernism goes to such an extent that I appreciate the followers of this movement for questioning the preceding emphasis on formalistic rationalism in Architecture. In this regard I also see some common ground between this work and the movement, because I have reacted to the solely rational approach to design and adhere to the notion that nonrational, random, and irregular patterns as contrasts to the logical and rational are necessary to produce a harmony of aesthetic information systems. What I react to in post modernism is the view that reaction alone is insufficient. We have to come up with alternatives to replace the questioned past in a constructive way' There is a difference between "chaotic" and "random;" whereas chaos is any haphazard event pattern or isolated reaction such as replacement of misplaced or misused pieces of history, random is another form of order organized in higher levels of complexity. As patterns of mind's activity behavior, random patterns conform to higher levels of orderliness. Post modernism has highly subjective views of aesthetic criteria. This I very much question because following this attitude brings us back again to another period in which design was characterized as individualistic trial and error.

As previously stated the intent here is to address the student of architecture as well as those dealing with various forms of human communication, specially those dealing with creative symbols and aesthetics. In addressing these groups, the aims of this book are: one, to introduce the notion of need for theories of Architecture, not notions of aesthetic criticism and judgement in the traditional sense, but theories which could encompass the findings of other related disciplines such as the physical sciences, natural sciences, psychology, anthropology, sociology, communication, and pure and applied science and technology; two, to suggest one such alternative, the communication approach. This approach is believed to be capable of bridging the gap between the aesthetic qualities of artistic values held by architects and the material and technological considerations espoused by other relevant disciplines. It is genuine to the nature of the communication approach to see everything in a structural context, i.e., as patterns of entities and relationships, whether they be the regularities of logical patterns, e.g., the geometry of environment, or the irregularities of random pattern behavior in the order of man and his environment, i.e., the "hidden dimensions" of sociocultural patterns.

Adapting the notion of information and communication to Architecture, I believe, encompasses potential descriptive values which can be useful in describing the order of environmental components and relationships, the entropic potential of which not only measures rational and logical objective order in qualitative terms, but also measures random patterns and organization in qualitative terms. It also enables architectural students to capitalize both on the wide spectrum of scientific discoveries and the increasing capability of computer science and information processing systems in defining architectural elements and relationships through new mathematical representations and techniques.

In measuring the order of a communication field or information system, it is assumed that its component conceptions and images *"are in themselves ordered* and therefore lawful, *they participate in a world of number and can be grasped in a numerical procedure.* In others words, they enter the playfield of number and can, as legitimate subject of theory, be numerically structured."[12]

This numerical structure is found to be the laws of probability and the notion of entropy formulating the basis for Information and Communication theory. Information theory is adapted to measure the regularities and irregularities or commonalities and unique characteristic patterns with which we defined aesthetic order.

Notes to Preface

1. Carl G. Jung, referred to by Marie-Louise von Franz, *Number and Time. Reflections Leading Towards a Unification of Psychology and Physics.* Rider & Company, London, 1974, p. 4.
2. C. Jung, referred to by Marie-Louise von Franz, *Number and Time*, p. 4.
3. Erich Jantsch, *The Self-Organizing Universe. Scientific and Human Implications of the Emerging Paradigm of Evolution*, Pergamon Press, 1980 p. 8.

4. Marie-Louise von Franz, *Number and Time*, p. 5.
5. *Ibid.*, pp. 7-8.
6. *Ibid.*, p. 8.
7. Lancelot L. Whyte, *The Universe of Experience. A World View Beyond Science and Religion*, Harper & Row, Publishers, 1974.
8. C. Peirce, quoted by A. Bork, "Randomness and the Twentieth Century", in *Antioch Review, Vol. 27*, 1967, p. 57.
9. *Ibid.*
10. Christopher Alexander, *Notes on the Synthesis of Form*, Harvard Univ. Press, Cambridge, 1964.
11. C. Alexander, *The Timeless Way of Building*, Oxford Univ. Press, New York, 1979.
12. Marie-Louise von Franz, *Number and Time*, p. 10.

List of Illustrations

Introduction

Architecture as environmental communication is an outgrowth of the author's response to two concerns. The first is a concern for the absence of architecture from the general stream of knowledge and the lack of interaction between architecture and other disciplines, particularly over the past hundred years. During this period profound changes and advances have occurred in many sciences, most notably the physical and natural sciences as well as the computer sciences and cybernetics, from which architecture did not fully benefit.

The second concern deals with problems facing architectural practice and education. Here, again, the absence of a common language linking all research-oriented activities and theories has left architects in isolation and unable to communicate with other scientists.

Following is a glance at some aspects of these two concerns, which have led to the development of this theoretical work.

I. Historical change in man's viewpoint

Changes that have occurred in man's conception of the cosmic order, nature, and life since the turn of the century have had a fundamental impact on attitudes regarding the arts and sciences. These changes hold great implications for education in art, architecture, and planning. This new philosophical outlook manifests itself in various intellectual endeavors. It finds expression in numerous disciplines dealing with different aspects of nature such as: the physical sciences (physics, chemistry, biology, and other life forms), the pure sciences (mathematics, logic, and geometry), as well as the social sciences, humanities, and the arts.

With regard to the physical sciences, at the turn of the century, physics witnessed a breakdown of the mechanistic view of classical physics. The new concept of reality, relativity, based on "uncertainty principles," took over and provided a foundation for the theories of thermodynamics and field physics. In chemistry, similar theories were developed. Moreover, in biology, the *ad hoc* dualism of "life principle" was replaced by the law of integrated wholes. Hence the key principle in all sciences became, in Warren Weaver's words, the "science of organized complexity."[1]

For example, instead of the constituent elements of a substance serving as a basis for the differentiation and classification of materials, the arrangement of the structure of the constituent materials assumed prime importance in determining the set nature of a substance or organism. That finite particle, termed an atom, was not seen as the basic building block of the universe, nor was the universe thought of as a great machine reflecting a ". . .world picture. . .that is reducible to such relationships in all essential respects."[2] Rather, it was contended that the focal point of investigation should be the structure and organization of the parts and building blocks; i.e., the fundamental way in which they are tied together into a totality.

A similar reorientation occurred in the pure sciences when the classical view of the world, based on the concept of finite numbers, was replaced by one based on infinite numbers. Thus deterministic and absolute orders, previously thought to be perceptible in nature and expressed in terms of real numbers and Euclidean geometry, were pushed into a corner in favor of relative orders. Subsequently, the laws of probability were expressed in terms of unreal numbers. Inherent within this change in outlook is the realization than man can no longer expect to find absolute and unchanging relationships. On the contrary, he must search for dynamic, changing, momentary, relative orders and their inherent interrelationship properties and interaction and, thus, communication.

In the social sciences a similar movement developed. The view of Rousseau and Locke that the association between isolated individuals exists in and of themselves, as well as Darwin's theories, were replaced by the school of realism—represented by Marx—which emphasized essential relationships formed by man's social nature. However, this school was subsequently overshadowed by Spencer's philosophy which regarded society as a total unit rather than a composite of collective individuals. Consistent with the latter, Lévi-Strauss, the French social anthropologist, later viewed culture as the manifestation of underlying structures that reflect patterns of the subconscious mind; language is an externalized form of such structures.

Parallel movements were also apparent in the arts and humanities. In the plastic arts, these changes signaled the emergence of such schools of thought as Structuralism, Constructivism, Cubism, and Futurism—each emphasizing a unique philosophical train of thought. Here also the trend was toward perceiving the world not individualistically but rather through communal laws inherent in humanity and based on common cultural values. The artist was trying to make a strong claim for the existence of universal art dimensions—form, color, shape—which communicate messages rooted in cultural values common to all men. In other words, these dimensions that can be universally interpreted characterize all art forms. The artist can create order from universal dimensions to communicate unique messages. Once again, the key is the structure and organization, as well as order and harmony, in works of arts.

These changes in man's view of nature and life fall into three major categories;

A. INSEPARABLE INTRA- AND INTERRELATIONSHIPS AMONG THE ELEMENTS OF NATURE AND ITS COMMUNICATION.

As a consequence of the above mentioned changes in man's understanding of the inherent laws of nature, his comprehension of relativity, the transformation of "life forms" into one another, has increased.

B. FUNDAMENTAL SOCIAL ORGANIZATION AND CHANGE.

The new sociocultural outlook appears to be the result of recent developments in numerous disciplines (including biology and psychology) characterized by mobility, rapid expansion, and population growth. New formal, verbal, and rational organizations and institutions replace the traditional hidden structures of cultural organization and unity. These changes would have been impossible without technological advancements and mass communication. Environmental planning and design are no exceptions to this new outlook.

Art and architecture are no longer confined to the elite as they were in the 18th and 19th centuries. As a result, the artist or architect must respond to the masses, as well as to a select few. Consequently, today's environmentalist must be made cognizant of group sociocultural attitudes and of problems related to all human population growth and change. He must also be informed of those media available to him and their potentials. Dealing with the arts and sciences—and thus architecture and planning—on such a wide horizon must be individually, as well as socially, oriented.

Architecture and the arts are sociocultural and biological in nature and thus constitute much more than merely dealing with crafts or creating artifacts. The messages to be transmitted are cultural and biological as well as personal in nature. Since the sum of human experience constitutes the base of the arts and sciences, architectural education must correspond to physical, biological, and sociocultural factors. It is only through a knowledge and understanding of all these factors that one is able to catch the subtleties of intra-and interrelationships and structural properties involved in life patterns.

C. NEW CONCEPTS OF PHYSICAL REALITY – TECHNOLOGICAL DEVELOPMENT.

In addition to a phenomenological change in man's view of nature and the social sciences, as discussed above, an even greater development in the physical sciences, particularly in the creation of tools, has become apparent.

In the physical sciences the concept *field physics* not only drastically attacked the Newtonian deterministic view of the universe, it even questioned the concept of quantum theory developed at the beginning of the century. Notions of physical field do not look at events within the frame of reference of any preconceived coordinate system, but rather as changes of state in a field. They also state that any change of a state at any point

x of a given field is dependent on the structure of the total field. So in such a context everything is conceived of as a change of some state of a field in a given unit of time.

In Newtonian mechanics and closed systems, deterministic and predictable processes relate any action to its reaction. Such interactions are viewed in a mechanistic manner and result in causal relationships. However, within field communication, viewed as open systems, not only are action and reaction remote from being simultaneous, they are completely independent of one another's behavior. The behavior of any action or reaction is conditioned by total field characteristics and structure. So the intended messages an architect has in mind to form and transform are not solely conditioned by and tied to his initiation and action, but rather they are conditioned by total environmental interactions.

In this century, an even greater development in man's creation of tools and techniques has become apparent—in a form we call technology. Technological advancements have greatly expanded the human horizon and have added so many new dimensions to human experience that it is impossible to estimate their long-term potential, magnitude, and depth. Technology has become the current means of achieving knowledge and experience. Technological development has a tremendous impact on the first two factors related to environmental design and planning. Technology conceivably can be the key to human growth. It can prevent war, but it can cause war as well. It can serve as a common reference point for all disciplinary knowledge and is thus a factor in the communication and unification of the main scope of human knowledge and experience. Although technology does not unify in the sense of true integration, it indirectly affects human knowledge by employing a common denominator as a means. Technology has its own unique laws and principles which are at the disposal of all disciplines,—the arts as well as the sciences.

Thus if environmental design and planning are to deal with the concept of forms and the form-making process, formation and transformation of activities, and finally, creation of new orders, these disciplines should recognize and deal with all these changes. There is an external and internal structure of the environment, messages, and media, as well as a changing form. Environment as "ordered complexity" has been found in art, sociology, biology, botany, physics, psychology, and, in fact, all the arts and sciences. Within each of these fields there are different ideas of what constitutes environmental form and structure.

II. Problem identification–shortcomings in architectural practice and education

The problem with architectural practice and education is that historically it has been developed as a profession responsible for the production of buildings and has addressed itself to the issue of how to build better rather than what to build. Up to the 17th and 18th centuries, when other professionally-oriented disciplines, such as medicine, still followed this course of action, such an approach would have been accepted. But, as already sketched out, scientific advancements resulting from research-oriented discoveries in the 18th, 19th, and 20th centuries in the physical and natural sciences have greatly affected the education and practice of these disciplines. However architects are still dealing with the same notions involved in 18th and 19th century educational philosophy; i.e., *beaux arts*-oriented subjectivity originated at the dawn of industrial development. Moreover, recent emphasis on a solely rational and analytical approach to architecture as a function of "scientific methods" dealing with environmental systems is just as wrong as either of these two.

It is unfortunate that the environmental holistic approach, which was primarily initiated by artists and architects during the early 20th century, has not been followed by architects themselves. Although an increasing number of scientists in many disciplines are beginning to take this *Gestalt* approach, the principles addressed by scientists and the holistic intuitive approach used by traditional architects are different. Scientists, following Aristotle and Hegel, attempt to incorporate the whole of human knowledge into a gigantic complex, capable of analysis and cooperation, whereas the traditional intuitive holistic view shared by architects views the whole in personal and intuitive form.

Karl Popper[3] has some reservations about the use of the holistic approach. He argues that phenomena such as society are so complex that each part is related to every other part. When one tries to incorporate the inputs of various disciplines into one complex system, the attempt fails because with each input the change resulting from that particular point of view affects all other inputs as well.

Much of today's architectural education is geared to teaching architecture with "architecture," form with "form;" that is to say, teaching essential infinite experiences with the finite "architectural conventions" or forms and "styles" of the past. The vocabularies of the past can only be used to stimulate and extend the horizon of study, imagination, and creativity. Learning skills are useful in the solution of today's problems. To perform with the architecture of tomorrow does not mean, ". . .playing the same old games with new rules in preference to new games altogether, not only the rules must be changed but the games as well."[4]

Architecture as isolated individual artifacts or rational assemblages of "mechanical" parts reached through quantitative methods has no value. Medicine, as well, was taught and practiced in accordance with the same approach as architecture in the 17th and 18th centuries and yet is quite different today. Medical schools now approach the teaching and practice of medicine from both a practical and experimental, theoretical and research-oriented point of view. Had it not been for the discoveries of research institutions, medicine would have been practiced in the same manner as architecture, i.e., through an individualistic approach of trial and error.

There are numerous reasons why architecture has not involved itself in research. One is that the final step in the architectural design and implementation process—making the building—takes a large portion of the effort. Since its final appearance provides the yardstick for public judgement, it has absorbed all available human resources in order to improve relevant craftmanship to perfect certain shapes and appearances. The development and mastery of various architectural styles is the output of such efforts; each style begins with new ideas; then during its development almost all available energy and talent is put into improving practical mastery of that particular style, such as Gothic architecture.

The second reason why architecture has avoided research is lack of a tradition in this area. With the exception of brief periods of historical and practically-oriented efforts, there has been no tradition of architectural research. Literature is likewise generally deficient in theories and concepts that could serve as a base for the classification and organization of spatial order in various cultural contexts.

In recent years it has been common practice to bring in researchers from fields outside of architecture—physics, psychology, sociology, economics, etc. But this procedure has created more problems than it has solved existing ones. One problem is that these specialists come to architects with fixed views and methods regarding issues related to the fields of their particular groups. Another problem is that owing to the preconceptions on which their disciplines are based, as well as unfamiliarity with the field, they do not fully see the problem as do architects. And finally, even the simple addition of various fragments of theories, techniques, and methods brought into architecture could not solve our problems. Thus there is a demonstrative need for fundamental changes in architectural education and theory:

1. There must be a change in architectural attitude so that architecture is seen as a conglomeration of all these forces rather than as a creator of artifacts. This could not be simply reached without a great amount of energy and resources channeled into this direction.
2. Research-oriented theories must be developed, leading to the creation of a framework within which various imported theories and techniques of different disciplines could fall into place. Architecture, or environmental design, which is not so broad in scope and which actually includes any human experience cannot be treated as a subdiscipline, nor can it be studied within a single prefabricated approach. Due to the above characteristics, i.e., multidimensionality, a great number of disciplines are involved in molding environmental form. Thus a move toward the development of any architectural framework should be initiated from within architecture; only then would the inputs from other disciplines into such a framework be useful.

There must be a development of specialized experimentation and research in specific areas which runs the least risk of overlapping with other disciplinary efforts.

A certain communication language must be devised, capable of incorporating meanings related to sociocultural and physical environmental symbol systems.

Behaviorally-oriented studies must be undertaken, focusing on spatial context as a means of incorporating such results into unified theories of environmental communication.

Physically-oriented studies must be carried out focusing on the nature of material substances and their inputs into architectural communication.

And finally, there must be development of forms of architectural education and practice which encompasses all the above inputs.

As a response to the concerns and needs outlined above, the material which follows has been developed into a thesis defining architecture as environmental communication. The notion behind this study is to seek a philosophy of environmental design responsive to the important issues and problems that are raised.

Architecture is seen here as a totality of man's experience, including man in the midst of nature and natural forces; among fellow human beings and their sociopolitical and cultural value systems; within an energy pattern or restless matter; and finally, it is man by himself alone as a being carrying a unique space-time experience and potential.

A concept used here to incorporate such total experience is *environmental field concepts.* Although the origin of this concept can be traced to the physical sciences, it is broadly used by various disciplines. So, here architecture is expressed through superimpositions of varous fields; i.e., sociocultural, physical, natural, etc. *Fields are seen as patterns of energy in space and time.* But what we see, what we sense, what we comprehend and/or rationalize is only grasped through apparent similarities and differences of structure, order and form, and through the law of probabilities. Could such probabilistic behavior of energy pattern be anything but communication? A negative answer explains why man's total experience must be called environmental communication.

1. Cultural communication: A framework for environmental planning and design

1.0 Introduction—Abstract

The attempt is made in this chapter to define a philosophical framework within which environmental planning and design activities can operate. On the conceptual side, such a framework relates to the philosophical boundaries of man's view of the cosmos, seen and interpreted by various disciplines; i.e., the natural, physical, and social sciences.

On the more concrete side, cultural communication is thought to provide a framework for man's activity patterns and, consequently, planning and design activities. Culture is man's adaptation to and utilization of universal environmental space-time energy patterns and their attributes as communication systems. The medium is man's total universe; the messages are in the form of *symbols* and *values*; the values being the social interactions, and the symbols being the dispositional characteristics of matter in space and time.

In this framework four major characteristic constituent behaviors are defined; namely, conscious and subconscious (metaphysical) and organic and inorganic (physical). Environmental planning and design activity is then considered to fall within this framework and can thus be analyzed and studied via relevant synthetic criteria.

Structure and order represented in any planning and design activity is considered to be a structure of structures reflecting the order of the four system components and the universal system. Individualistic versus universalistic views regarding cultural values and change are to correspond to the four sets of determining factors or be conditioned by environmental communication systems.

Cultural communication

Let us for the present define culture as man's adaptation to and utilization of universal environmental resources and their attributes as a communication system in space and time. The medium is man's total universe. The messages disseminated through this medium are formulated through the interaction of the physical and metaphysical[1] (nonphysical) in the form of symbols and values. The *values* are the manifestation in social interactions either on a conscious or subconscious level, and the *symbols* are the disposition of matter in space and time in physical or biological forms. Whereas values are of individual as well as social origin, symbols take on either tangible physical form, e.g., the environmental symbol system, or intangible form, e.g., language.

Using this definition of culture, we must first define cultural communication and its constituent components, then draw a framework within which environmental communication could be based. It is also necessary to analyze the impact of technological development and industralization on cultural change and cultural identity, in general, and its relation to environmental values specifically. In so doing, the above definition of culture will be used as a starting point and philosophical perspective, whereupon, in an effort to complement this broad definition, a *general framework of man's relation to this universe* will be defined. Having defined the structure of the universe and culture, *communication systems* are proposed as a reflection of the structure of man's concept of the universe.

1.1 Man's Concept of the Universe and its Building Blocks

With regard to the conceptual definition of the universe, Fuller, reflecting the general consensus of views which has appeared throughout history, defines the universe in physical and metaphysical terms, including both objective as well as subjective elements.[2]

The division made by Fuller and others, owing to its generality, seems to lack concrete applications.[3] However, upon reflection, it appears that in addition to Fuller's analysis, it is definitely possible to distinguish between the *a priori* and *a posteriori* behavior of man; that is, behavior that is "pure," rational, and objective, as opposed to behavior that is driven by a total experience, by the conscious and the subconscious. It is also not too difficult to separate the living and nonliving elements of the universe and define their characteristics beyond the above mentioned generalized principles. Accordingly, the author suggests the following classification of the universe, and outlines the advantages of such expansion and theoretical development.

Although the totality of man ideally should be dealt with holistically in its total form and without any subdivision, let us for the minute discuss the physical[4] and metaphysical[5] aspects distinctly, and examine the major characteristics of each. As has been discussed throughout history by scientists and poets, the conscious and subconscious behavior of man follows different paths, yet they counterbalance one another. The differences between the organic and inorganic aspects of the universe has also been explored sufficiently in the last hundred-and-fifty years to enable us to distinguish their specific and unique behavioral patterns and characteristics.

The physical/metaphysical definition of the universe may be further subdivided as follows: 1) physical: inorganic and organic (physiobiological); and 2) metaphysical: conscious and subconscious. The building blocks of culture are based upon these universal constituent components, which have been reached by an aggregate of all humanity over time and are expressed consciously through subconsciously apprehended and communicated experiences.

The subdivision of the universe's constituent components as proposed above can be further described in detail:

i. Physical: 1) inorganic and 2) organic (physiobiological)

1) the *inorganic* component reflecting only the physical aspect of experiences following the law of the conservation of energy, which states that energy is neither created nor destroyed.

2) the *organic* component reflecting the physiobiological organizations and the evolution of life forms.

ii. Metaphysical (nonmaterial): 3) conscious and 4) subconscious

3) the *conscious* components reflecting "objective reality" as ascertained from the outside. In this regard, Foucault has described man as being one with a universal system based on a pattern-logic structure with which man as well as the rest of nature acts in accordance. The law governing the structure of the universe, and thus man's basic thought processes, transcends the individual conscious self. What society consciously perceives as its order and the way this order does indeed conform to reality and subconscious elements are two different things.

4) the *subconscious* component reflecting the immeasurable innate dynamics of life, including psychological and emotional drives, as well as other qualitative and subjective values; i.e., the pattern and structure indirectly observed (e.g., the structure of language as pointed out in studies by Lévi-Strauss). In social terms, one might say the subconscious behavior of members of society is reflected in "social structures." Whereas social relations reflect empirical reality, social structures are those models derived from this reality. In contrast to the above three categories, no common ground can be found among different disciplines in discussing subconscious behavior.

The nature of the above four components has been analyzed by various disciplines. The physical sciences, natural sciences and policy oriented social sciences have all developed theories searching for a better understanding and ability to predict more accurately the behavior of three of the components; i.e., the inorganic, organic, and conscious behavior of the universe. The one constituent component left relatively unknown is the subconscious dimension of the metaphysical world which is directly linked to the qualitative nature of life and to cultural communication and thus to environmental aesthetics and design. The higher degree of abstraction of the qualitative aspect of this phenomenon has not left much room to enable man to follow empirically the formations and transformations involved. As a result, to understand this phenomenon man has been forced to use the methodological principles reached through the analysis of the other three components. In most cases, the materially oriented schools of thought basically tend to identify this last component with the first three components. Hence the following discussion is intended to throw light on some of the critical issues entailed, and to stress the need for concern for the quality of life, and especially to emphasize the subconscious dimension of cultural structures[6] as a basis for cultural communication and environmental planning and design activities.

Relative to these four components, four sets of order can be defined which control our surrounding universe:

1) the laws of entropy measuring "order and disorder" in the material world and the "increase of random elements" and therefore disorder;
2) the laws of entropy measuring the evolutionary process of organic forms by moving from "high to low entropy" and consequently ordered complexity;
3) the laws of "centropy" measuring the "elimination of chaos" through conscious behavior and the intellect and therefore increased order; and
4) the laws of "entropy-centropy" measuring the ordered-disordered behavior of the subconscious mind through the non-directional circumstantial changing patterns of the qualitative aspects of culture and environment.

Thus both areas of man's reliance (namely, perceived behavior which is in accordance with the laws of nature; i.e., the laws of the natural sciences) as well as man's intellect and rational behavior formulated into man's knowledge, can be conditioned by past circumstances.

In other words, they follow a directional evolutionary process, and so are meaningful as far as the knowledge of any maximum probability (nearly constant) and are therefore concrete and applicable.

On the other hand, the nature of matter and therefore the material world, has been experimentally proven to be probabilistic and is thus viewed in terms of disordered realities. This is also expandable to the natural sciences. However, in regard to the physical world, there exist two schools of thought. One adheres more to logic and philosophy, believing that experimentally observed and proven disorder is one facet of a higher complex of ordered systems, uncomprehended by man and beyond the reach of his insufficient tools and knowledge. It is interesting that Einstein, founder of the theory of relativity and such "disorder," was himself a follower of this school. He has said that "God does not play dice," meaning that there is a superorder above and beyond which is inadequately observed. The second school, more pragmatically oriented, might accept the above statements only in the form of philosophy, with the qualification that it is only experimentally proven theories which can be thought of as scientific knowledge; meaning, only that which has been experimentally proven (that is, the probabilistic behavior of matter) can be accepted.

The hidden dimensions and qualities of life, culture, and environment, on the other hand, can be conceived in terms of an unpredictable picture which operates more in terms of a probabilistic pattern rather than a set of preconditioned forms. The artistic and creative behavior of man is a rich, indescribable phenomenon which is instantaneously shaped in a generic way, the origin of which can only be found to be that special moment and that specific circumstance; any event is unique in itself, never having preexisted, never to be succeeded by an identical form.

From a compositive interaction of the four components, one could conclude by saying that the structure of a culture, as well as environmental pattern, as a consequence of man's concept of the universe's constituent components, follows an ordered-disordered pattern of forms. Such forms are not directional, leading into the future, nor do they thrust into the past. Rather they are part of the flow of probabilistic events, originated in various space-time circumstances determined by the future, as well as the past. A comparative analysis would show more similarity between these patterns and the structure of matter and the material world than with biological and rational thought processes. The conscious rational man seeks predictable, simplified, ordered paths into the future. But the subconscious, irrational man seeks rich, complex, diversified, and unexpected unique patterns, in order to attain the highest degree of freedom, and consequently to achieve the highest potential for creativity. No doubt these subconscious patterns certainly do have order too, but a different order formed at a different level, in the subconscious mind and tied to the structure of culture and its unknown hidden dimensions. It is an order that cannot be comprehended by the logical process of the human mind.

1.2 Communication Systems as a Structure of the Universe, Culture, and Environment

In order to arrive at a unified system which could integrate the universe's four constituent components, and thus environmental planning and design activities, one might suggest communication systems within which each of the four constituent components could be conceived as a subcommunication system, in which formation and transformation of events are regarded as the discharge of information. Whereas ordered-disordered patterns express timeless formations of information occurring irrespective of any preconceived subsequent states, which are therefore rich and unexpected in nature, ordered patterns are specific areas in the system where predicted changes are presented with zero information. With this approach then the entire universal system, as well as culture and environment, can be described as one complex communication system consisting of all constituent components.

Within such a communication system, information is transmitted via *ordered-disordered pattern systems of messages*[7]: ordered-disordered patterns are measured against the laws of *entropy* and *centropy* to be information or noise, to be meaningful or meaningless; and the messages are shaped through material media, as well as sociocultural (and individual) content symbols and value systems.

There is a difference between the term communication as used in this sense and that employed in scientific literature. The communication used in cybernetics is based on principles of information theory and deals solely with the material world and messages which can be transferred through electronic channels and picked up by instrument technology. *In this type of communication, nonmaterial qualitative symbols and values are not included.* Therefore it is two-dimensional as a system and incapable of taking into consideration the multidimensional activities and thought patterns of human beings. However, in the context within which we are employing the term, communication is applied to a much larger system encompassing both material and nonmaterial interactions. Such a system then would include all dimensions and activities as related to culture and the arts. Whereas art in the general communication system is a subsystem related to specific behaviors of subgroups and individuals, within the framework of this larger definition of communication, the arts are also included.

Defining culture and environment as a communication system involves the notion of *field theory* which can be used as a model reflecting and describing the structure of the universe, and thus communication behavior. In terms of field principles, any question regarding the relationships of the parts relative to the whole and vice versa, as well as any circumstantial comparison of the past, present, and future state of any culture and environment, is termed "field". Any individual or group behavior in any space-time circumstance is conditioned by the very nature of its own state relative to its past and present. Based on such a framework, only field principles could hold true and be a fit methodological model.

It would seem that the basic principles of field theory are applicable to the totality of universal systems, as well as to each individual universe. That is to say that through the transformation of states in the system, each state is originated (its origin-state) and at the same time generates the others (either past or future). The laws of each state are of optimum usefulness for that state and of relative and probabilistic usefulness to the others.

The logic behind this proposal is that since the ordered components—i.e., the conscious logical and natural elements (physiobiological), due to the directionality of their function—are time-bound phenomena, they cannot perform according to the pattern displayed by ordered-disordered elements (the second two components, i.e., material and subconscious).

With regard to time, whereas the first component groups (1 & 2) hold n degree of freedom, the second component groups (3 & 4) hold $n + m$ degree of freedom and therefore include a more timeless flow of unpredictable events. Therefore to find a common framework within which the structure of the universe can be formulated would necessitate a model capable of incorporating and being responsive to order-disorder principles. Using his model then, it is the overruling principles of the latter group of components which will be expanded to the others rather than vice versa. Therefore field principles are suggested as a methodological framework (model premise) since it is built on the premise of describing an independent and probabilistic state of events which could easily describe deterministic predictable states as well.

CULTURAL RELATIVITY AND ENVIRONMENT

Cultural relativity and cultural identity, either in space dealing with different cultures at different locations or in time dealing with the evolution of cultures, can be found to correspond to the four components of the universe. As demonstrated by the natural sciences, in terms of natural forms, evolution moves toward complexity, higher order, and progression. On the conscious side, this corresponds to the development of knowledge, the accumulation of fact, the development and application of tools, and technological advances. However both the laws of matter and the subconscious behavior of man are everchanging and subject to their own states. Concerning relativity in culture and environment, the totality of man's behavior is ever changing, subject to its own states. The totality of the four components in a unified form and not as a sum of all are involved. In other words, in making cultural and environmental comparisons, all four components in unified form must be dealt with, not just one or a few of them. Some see cultural advancement in terms of the first two components which entail conscious experience as manifested through the accumulation of knowledge, the advancement of technology, and the availability of abundant and higher quantity and quality natural resources.

However the above two components are merely that which constitute the *quantitative side of life, culture, and environment,* whereas the intrinsic value of life and the very essence of culture and environment are geared toward the other components (in the nature of matter and the subconscious) which deal with the *quality of life.* Whereas the first two components are involved in the process of making quantitative judgements of various cultures, in the second component no such judgements and definite comparisons can be made. Each culture has values inherent and relative to its own state. For example, in the case of art forms, especially in the modern movement, the individualistic approach to art forms and beauty has been personalized to an extreme, demonstrating that personal expression and communication channels have been developed in a unique form by individuals. In other words, beauty relates to the particular state of an individual's being and his circumstances. A similar situation exists in the case of societies and cultures. Hence, in putting the four components together, one should not be misled into thinking that the essence of man and the innate nature of matter changes in the sense of progression. Rather, its state is changing and therefore any comparison made should be relative to specific states. The major question then is this: *to what extent is a culture composed of elements common to all cultures and what aspects are unique to each culture and subculture?*

Before answering the question of whether or not cultures are composed of common elements which lay the basis for a common value system, the concept of cultural relativity must be examined. This theory states that there is no way to determine the moral superiority of one culture and its environmental system over another, that each culture is equally valid for its own inhabitants and their values, and that there is no common value against which the achievements of separate cultures can be measured.

Furthermore, the theory of "cultural relativity" based on man's individualistic behavior as a response to his material and subconscious nature, postulates that no culture, and its environmental values, in its totality can be judged to be morally superior to another. This presupposes that there is no ultimate value for man against which different societies can be compared and ranked.

But it has already been shown that biological and conscious man has a basic nature which he must fulfill toward adaptation to nature and environment, and part of this nature involves cooperating and the full development of his fellows. *Hence cultures can be ranked according to the degree to which they allow and foster this sense of personal involvement in the total society* or, in other words, whether or not their institutions make it possible, and desirable, for a man to actively aid in the development of others.

Benedict was the first to look at societies within this framework. That society in which the social structure allows for an individual to follow his own interests while at the same time benefitting other members of his society is termed "good," while that which allows for the individual to pursue his own interests at the expense of the whole is termed "bad." Benedict placed all societies on a continuum between the two extremes. With respect to this gamut which she calls "synergy," she refers to cultures with low synergy ". . .where the social structure provides for acts that are mutually opposed and counteractive" and to cultures with high synergy ". . .where it provides for acts that are mutually reinforcing."[8] Hence a good society is one in which the existing social framework allows for and reinforces the individual's tendency to serve the corporative whole while at the same time benefitting himself.

Maslow[9] speaks of such an ideal situation among the Blackfoot Indians where an institutionalized system of redistributing wealth among all sectors of the society through the Sun Dance was developed. During this dance, a wealthy man places all his possessions at the disposal of those in his society who are in greatest need, thereby making himself at one and the same time the poorest and most respected man in his society. Hence his amassing of wealth functions as a mechanism for bringing material support to the poorest sectors of the society, while at the same time fulfilling his need for self-esteem and social recognition. Due to the man's own personal qualities and skills, he would probably be able to repeat this same ceremony by the next year.

Just as there is no definite norm which can be applied to all dimensions of culture, or the individual, and used as a basic standard of evaluation, the constituent components of culture

have also proved to have different and even opposite social manifestations depending on the cultures in which they appear. Hence
there are varying yardsticks employed according to which man
is measuring a particular culture and its environmental qualities.
Therefore, the only sound basis for evaluation is acceptance of
the same principle of diversity within unity; meaning, that at the
same time that individual and social cultural identity is required,
unity is also required. While diversity provides that restless changing freedom within which individuality (3 & 4) can be maintained,
unity acts as a framework within which continuous evolutionary
directional forces (1 & 2) can operate.

Finally, the basis for identical cultural and environmental
values which societies hold in common lies in the ground between
two major characteristic components of the universe, or, as
Weisskoff says, in the common ground of being itself:

On the level of concrete actuality, historical conditions, society
and culture determine the content of values. The ultimate ground
of values, however, is rooted in the ultimate ground of being.
Values have an ontological source. Even those who reject metaphysical arguments can learn from history that all cultures derived
their ultimate values from a basic concept or symbol which
stood for the ground of being. . . .[10]

Having analyzed and found a logical base for cultural identity,
cultural relativity, and environmental qualities, it is now appropriate to address ourselves to the question of the communication
and transmission of the arts, experience, knowledge, technology,
etc. from one culture to another. Considering the foregoing
discussion *we find that it is easier to transfer these experiences
reached by the natural sciences, consciously developed experiences
and knowledge, and quantitative learning from one culture to
another than the subconscious behavior and qualitative values
inherent in any particular culture.*

In analyzing this transfer of cultural elements, one common
technique employed in communication and development (i.e.,
preparation of future plans and projection) is that involved with
deterministic models which are equated with linear models. This
approach could be used for the first two components which deal
with the quantitative aspects of life, because these are the only
parts of life which have processes similar to those found in linear

problem solving. The third and fourth constituent components have high complexity, variety, and entropy and they cannot be regarded as progressive sequential phenomena capable of being pinned down for the prediction of future behavior. Whereas the sequential changes of the first two components are dependent on one another and from the behavior of one, the behavior of the other can be predicted, there is no sequential relationship with the other two components. Rather, each element depends on its own state and no state can be measured in order to allow for the prediction of the other. In a work of art or cultural and environmental form, each state stands unevaluated on its own.

Linear problem solving is the most accepted approach for dealing with problems in science and technology, and furthermore is justified by Aristotelian logic and the structure of Western languages.[11] Even when it has been recognized that particular problems were not linear in nature (e.g., social planning, environmental planning, and design) linear approximations have often been used with the assumption that the results would closely approximate the real solution. But Nature, life, and sociocultural and environmental systems are seldom linear; only in very simple problems are linear approximations realistic. The complex systems that comprise physical and social environments have proven to be resistant to such approaches. The use of linear planning in such areas of human life has often been disastrous, producing results which were more complex than the original problem.

Hence the transfer of models dealing with such endeavors from one culture to another is impossible. Rather, in such areas, *methods for treating each culture and environmental qualities should be developed which intrinsically generate analytical insights from within its own system.*

One of the quantitative aspects of culture and environment related to the first two universal components is economic advancement which in part, owing to its *a priori* nature, has nothing to do with the inherent qualitative values of culture and human life. However it is used as a qualitative measuring stick to evaluate a society's standard of living or quality of life and environment at the disposal of its members. In economics, for example, evaluations have always been based on the idea that "growth" is not only good for the economy, but is moreover an absolute necessity.

Due to the finite limitations of our planet's recourses, this has been shown to be a physical impossibility over an unlimited time horizon.[12] Because of this, many economists have turned away from such an oversimplified view of the world and are now proposing realizable alternatives.[13]

Thus, according to economic principles concerning communication and development, the current understanding of what constitutes "wealth" corresponds to a society's exploitation of its finite resources and the growth of total production. However such yardsticks must not be allowed to obscure the fact that another dimension of such wealth is the human aspect of "know-how" which is, in the final analysis, the crucial factor. This is an inherent part of human conscious and subconscious involvement in economic activities. This type of wealth is grained through "both social cooperation and individual enterprise"[14] which acts to produce increased wealth. It would be disastrous to assume that the motivation were solely material gain with a disregard for the human values involved. Such values cannot be easily predicted in terms of quantitative measurements and techniques alone, but rather in terms of a qualitative approach.

Before one can say whether it is possible to deal effectively with nonlinear systems and organic problems involved with economic growth, it must be recognized that current problem solving techniques are, for the most part, linear. *It must also be noted that these techniques are not only inadequate, but are potentially disastrous (especially in the long term) if used in areas other than linear functions.*

In order to make this position clear, and to bring it to the fore of thinking and planning, a new nonlinear vocabulary is needed. It is suggested here that, based on proposed communication systems and field principles and based on a philosophy of interdependence, integration, and intercommunication among all elements of nature, the term "synergy" could serve as the basis for such a revised terminology. By definition it is a nonlinear ideological scheme. Use of this term will serve as a reminder that linear solutions are in fact no solution at all, but instead result in the creation of feedback loops which aggrevate the original problem.

1.3 Cultural Change and Environmental Communication

One of the disadvantageous effects of industralization on human culture lies in its tendency toward homogeneity of symbols and values in predominately industralized cultures. *The more the similarity existing between value systems and symbol systems, the less the complexity, diversity, originality. And consequently there appears less originality and richness in cultural and environmental values.*

In contrast to the days when the majority of the world's population was scattered over the countryside, in this age of the emergence of cities, our children are progressively being deprived of an opportunity to develop their aesthetic and intuitive sensitivities. Hence their capability for grasping the significance of things or even the possibility of forming different attitudes and potentialities has been severely dimmed.[15]

A reflection of this tendency toward uniformity and increased insensitivity to cultural differences and environmental relativity and related human factors is found in architecture. According to Fuller,[16] yesterday's aesthetic qualities and values, and therefore architecture, dealt promisingly with what he terms the six "S's": "the sensorial, sensual, symbolic, superstitious, symmetrical, and superficial." He adds that the architecture of today involves itself with the "invisible, intellectual integrity manifest by the explorers and formulators operating within the sensorially unreachable, yet vast ranges of the electrochemical and mathematical realm of the physical and metaphysical realities." However the form which the architecture flowing from this invisible thought process takes is quite visible, though in a way different from earlier architecture. An emphasis on basic structural lines, developed by individual architects as trademarks of their style, emerged in the midnineteen-twenties. Later in the 30's and persisting into today's architecture, there arose an interest in *function,* with architectural "form following function" to the extreme of exposing the basic structure of the building.

Whereas today's architecture is an integral part of the drive toward self-expression and the continuation of definite functional structures, *tomorrow's architecture will strive toward the nonexistential on the visual level as a result of the realization that the purpose of architecture is to serve humanity and, as such, accomodate itself to its dictates and necessities.* Such a situation is analogous to a box emitting electronic concerts.[17] By looking at the outside of the box one cannot detect that it contains a battery of gadgets which perform a tremendous variety of tasks. As the newer generation seeks to achieve a deeper understanding of the secrets and meaning of the universe, new values and attitudes will emerge which could only be integrated in new communication models which are responsive to qualities as well as quantities.

No doubt new communication channels would consist of a much greater number of diversified elements. In the past, although culture and, accordingly, communication and environmental systems consisted of fewer elements or a much smaller set of dimensions, there still existed a greater complexity and richness which was assembled in a harmonious and unified manner. However today, although there exist many more possibilities for combining a greater number of elements and thus symbols, the effort is diffused into the production of meaningless similar parts answerable to the economic factors set forward by the world of intellect and its by-product, technology, and hence a less rich whole is produced. For example, if one examines a European or Middle Eastern city of the Middle Ages, the background and foreground elements of the townscape are so meaningfully put together and given form that there are no misleading messages conveyed to anyone; the church or the mosque stands out absolutely and clearly as the main point of reference. The social spaces are organized in a way that clearly transfers the hierarchical order of spatial sequences to which a person need orient himself. The relationship and scale of public spaces and buildings are so individually treated that no other message could possibly be transferred to the users other than that expressed by the unique design and locational fitness of its origins.

The beauty of communication channels between builders and users is due to common values having resulted from the unity of culture and the social system. The basis for values, and consequently for the communication language, is not transferred from outside and is not originated *a priori* by predefined academic or professional jargons or clichés, but is intuitively assimilated from life and cultural experiences. Furthermore, *in traditional society, the subconscious laws inherent in the totality of subconscious behavior of the individual is the ruling factor.* It is not the predictable behavior of the parts of a system which dictates the future direction of a community, but rather the whole unity of communal desire. In such situations, it was the strength of social norms that exerted an influence upon the behavior and thought patterns of members of any one social community. In a sense, individual behavior was subordinated to the unspoken dictates of the larger whole, the whole being a sum of individual norms, immutable characters. One born into a system with such well defined unwritten boundaries and characteristics was under strong pressure from the hidden properties of unspoken cultural clues to pursue a way of life in conformity with the total aggregate. At the same time, with the individual systems which constituted humanity, there existed a richness and diversity of cultural patterns which, paradoxically, allowed individualism itself to develop into a harmonious universal whole similar to integrated patterns.

In our urban environment today, not only are there not enough meaningful symbols, but furthermore those that do exist are only unclear statements which generate nothing but meaningless symbols. Several reasons exist for this:

1. There is a lack of cultural unity and social values, and thus communication language, to which all can relate.
2. The values and symbol systems employed by intellectuals, scientists, and artists who lead society are very different from those exercised by laymen; even between members of different disciplines, gaps exist. Moreover there are no common unifying theories maintained by various disciplines which tie together the findings of different groups.
3. Owing to the population explosion, on the one hand, and the development and expansion of human knowledge and technology, on the other, conscious order, which by its very nature must be organized, is replacing the unorganized, communal principle. Owing to the innate nature of predesigned *a priori* laws, the new order is not sensitive to the qualitative aspects of human life and environment.
4. With regard to the transfer of technology to developing so-

cieties, the subsequent pace of change in the sociocultural value system of these societies does not usually keep up with the growth of the material and technological side of life. Consequently, the one which is sacrificed is the former.

5. Even those who delve into history for new ideas and those who search for sound bases in the roots of past cultures, face problems in uncovering basic values through a maze of surface facades. Unfortunately, some confuse the two and superfically copy the past, not realizing that traditionalism is in itself erroneous.

What we actually need is a search for the essential principles of our past cultural values which cannot merely be found empirically in the physical world and logically through the rational intellectual world, but rather in the immeasurable, vivid dimensions of the subconscious pattern of cultural values as well. We need a value system which is common to the past and the future, as well as a unity of historical development. We need a totality of time and space which can respond to individuals, as well as to society as a whole.

1.4 Intercultural Communication

It could easily be demonstrated that the world's nations are to a greater or lesser extent heading in the direction of technological advancement. The universal goal is to achieve a better way of life through industrialization. Western countries, especially the United States, are being looked to as models for such growth. However industrial advancement in those countries was paralleled by a socioeconomic and intellectual evolution which took material form in the Industrial Revolution. *The main question is how industrialization and its by-products, which in the Western countries was the result of an evolutionary process, can be effectively transferred to the developing countries.*

In the developed world, two types of society are found. One is that dominated by technology and the material world: the forces of materialism are so strong that to a great extent they dominate the life of the society as a whole, as well as the life of its individual members. The second type of society is exemplified by Japan. This country has a rich cultural heritage, but is moving toward high industrialization. However the strength of the traditional culture and the socioeconomic and political climate of the country are strong enough to counter-balance the negative effects of industrial growth and technology. Therefore those values imported along with technology could, to some extent, be transformed and absorbed. Therefore repercussions of the evolution of cultural change in Japan were not as critical as in the case of the so-called developing countries. Most Asian, African, and Latin American countries, because of separate sets of circumstances and sociocultural backgrounds, are mistakenly striving to duplicate the material and economic advancement of the West as far as material gains are concerned, with a disregard for the basic facts related to their sociocultural situations.

Based on man's new orientation to nature and the cosmos, and the consequences of industrialization and mass production, the world's nations can be divided into three categories: 1) Western industrialized countries, 2) the Eastern communist industrialized bloc, and 3) the Third World.

The direction taken by the cultures of the Western industrialized countries has been determined by socioeconomic factors. Economically they are very much influenced by quantitative values and raising the *per capita* income of their nations. Socially the people are constantly pushed into isolation, on the one hand, and mass contact, on the other. The social unifying factors have become increasingly under the control of predefined common law, rules, and regulations based on anticipated predefined norms, rather than qualitative values and thus environment.

The Eastern communist bloc countries, as well, economically strive for higher production *per capita*. Socially, owing to a socialistic philosophy, the State has been favored at the expense of individuals. Freedom of choice and individual values are fostered as long as they fit in with society's predefined plans and objectives. So like the Western industrialized world, the beauty of life and richness of culture which could have emerged out of an organization of individuals into a total whole is now being doomed by a predefined and *a priori* set of objective values and thus environment.

The Third World, on the other hand, fortunately or unfortunately, has not had the opportunity to prosper materially and achieve industrial growth. So, while it may be left far behind economically, these countries will have a chance to consciously see the consequences of material growth and evaluate their stand so that they can plot their way through before being caught in the industrial stream. They still have a chance to retain some of the finer qualities of life, and to utilize their material and nonmaterial resources in such a way as to better their quality of life and environment. In fact, in this regard, Africa has been named the "Continent of the Future."

Based on information theories and suggested communication models, sociopolitical systems can be identified by two features: *unity* and *diversity*. The more totalitarian the system, the greater the temporary success it should exhibit, because all the forces and energy in that society are being expanded in one direction. However in the long run such one-sided development could be dangerous. According to the laws of entropy, the laws of the natural sciences, and "the survival of the fittest," variety in society imparts a greater chance for survival. The similarity of functions in a totalitarian culture provides those cultures with low entropy and information exchange. Consequently, if such a mass society were to face an unexpected internal or external threat, no new lines of resistance would be open, since diversity and alternative life styles had previously been sacrificed to the attainment of those goals associated with an "ideal" industrialized state. A parallel to such a situation can be found in the world of nature: because the mammal species is diversified and the way of life of its members is based on a complex system of interdependencies, if one member of the species is faced with extinction by attack from the outside, the remainder of the total organism can survive. In other words, take away the energy-distributing networks and the industrial machinery from America, Russia, and all the world's industrialized countries, and within six months over two billion swiftly and painfully deteriorating inhabitants of these countries would starve to death.

Emphasis on material values is an outcome of the technological approach. The question is whether such new values can be compatible with values of traditional societies, and whether they can be saved. Recent history demonstrates that the confrontation and conflict between these two sets of values, each based on the basic characteristics of the universe's distinct constituent components, is inevitable. While it is true that traditional values are not always of great advantage for a nation, they are no doubt proved and tested values which have gone through an evolutionary process and have been filtered by social and cultural processes. They are thus those with which the country is identified. A great number of such values without question must be maintained and protected from external threats. It is a manifestation of man's ingenuity that he is able to make unique values in his culture distinguishable from those found in other societies.

As pointed out earlier, without such a rich accumulation of complex symbols and values, there would be no communication and thus no culture. A good example of an element of culture is language, without which the world would have been far less colorful. Various languages have been developed in different circumstances, each of which gives a great new input to the dynamics of world culture. It is not actually the totality of cultural values which must be preserved, but rather their dynamic essense.

Knowledge can be transferred. Even in the area of technology, pure *a priori* techniques can be transferred, although the experience of these techniques for the use of technology again falls into the sociocultural behavior of each society. The structure and behavior of the nature of matter is relatively unordered and probabilistically constant over space and time. Again, *a priori* pure knowledge developed by man's rational intellect is verified through unified logic and rational thought processes. Therefore it is relatively uniform over space, but the relation of matter to the other constituent components, and therefore the role of matter in the totality of the universe and environment, is uniquely perceived by different cultures.

That which has been geared to the material and natural components of the universe is definitely measurable in terms of the development and advancement of the physical sciences. Therefore it can be readily evaluated, filtered, and transferred. The development of intellect and knowledge is also measurable against philosophy, intellect, and logic which are tied, on the one hand, to the physical world and its principal laws of nature and, on the other hand, to the immeasurable dimensions of the qualities of life and, therefore, subconscious behavior. That part related to subconscious behavior has no yardstick or standards by which it can be measured. So this is the crucial part which cannot be analyzed by means of any logical process but rather must be evaluated through society as a whole. The only measurement for such an evaluation is the dynamic process involved in the entire cultural process, in which every individual consciously and sub-consciously plays a vivid and active role. As part of this last component, the qualitative aspects of environment and its aesthetic values should definitely be mentioned as one of the most significant indicators of man's sense of creation and change. They embody all cultural values expressed through the active participation of a culture's creative participants. Within such qualitative and quantitative boundries of environmental communication and among its activities, different virtues and qualities related to the ordered-disordered senses of the participant are represented in such dispositional potentials of material form as color, form, proportion, and finally, beauty.

So if our cultural heritage is to survive, *we have to be cognizant of the dangers inherent in advanced technology and the obvious move toward cultural similarities.* The timeless elements of cultures and their environments are those that give beauty to life, those which reach through the active participation and expressions of each member of society. These are properties of life and culture and the qualitative "hidden dimensions" of the environmental communication system which cannot be predetermined and set up in an *a priori* manner by the organized, formal, selective members of society.

To be sure, no culture or environmental communication system could survive without the great inputs and dynamic variety of contributions made by all participating members in different art forms. In various aspects of knowledge, it has already been demonstrated how important the role of this input on cultural development and environmental communication is. Based on the principles reached by the natural sciences, it has been proved that the advancement of any natural form is altered by the complexity and variety of its active elements. According to the theories of communication and information principles, *in any communication system, including environmental communication systems, it is through the complexity, diversity, and variety of its component elements that a greater number of bits of information and therefore a more advanced communication system can materialize. It is through the arts that the noblest, most lasting, timeless expressions, and information are produced.* No civilization from any time or space can be conceived in which artistic creativity is not a major element. It would be a very sad situation for any culture if technological advancement became a danger to its artistic creativity.

Notes

1. Fuller has defined physical and metaphysical as follows: "Universe consists of both the *physical* and *metaphysical*. Every phenomenon which science can weigh, measure and identify as energy, i.e., *energy associative* as *matter* and *energy disassociative* as *radiation* is a part of *physical reality*. Any and all of our thoughts are unweighable. They and their comprehensive family concepts, generalized principles and our awareness of the inter-relatedness are altogether weightless and constitute what we speak of as the metaphysical part of reality." R.B. Fuller, "Architecture as Sub-ultra-invisible Reality," unpublished paper, p. 2.
2. Fuller speaks of "all *voluntary experiences,* experiments, as well as all *involuntary experiences,* i.e., all happenings." He states that it can be seen that the metaphysical is to the physical as anti-matter is to matter, i.e., as the electron is to the position: "*Metaphysics* and *physics* are thus seen to co-function, to progressively conserve the self-regeneration of non-simultaneously evolving universe." While he defines the laws of man to be entropy, he says: "Man's function in the universe is metaphysical and anti-entropic. He is essential to the conservation of the universe, which is in itself an intellectual conception." R.B. Fuller, "Letter of Doxiadis," *Main Currents in Modern Thought,* March/April, 1969, vol. 25, no. 4.
3. As Fuller says, "the universe, both physical and metaphysical, is resolvable into a set of principles which are ever more accurately (but never exactly) described by the scientists' weightless intellectual generalizations. And generalized principles which are weightless cognitions of intellect have no inherent beginning or end (nothing in human experience has ever suggested the beginning or ending of a generalized principle)—ergo, the 'beginning' of universe concepts together with all axioms are experimental or unproven and only superficially obvious functions," *ibid.*
4. Fuller defined the physical part of the universe as follows: "Universe inherently includes all the ponderable, i.e., weighable, instrumentally detectable, associative and disassociative, material and radiation energy behaviors of the physical sub-

division of the universe." Fuller argues that he as well as Norbert Weiner independently reached the conclusion that man is the anti-entropy of the universe, *ibid.*

5. Fuller defined "metaphysical as being all the weightless experiences of thought, which includes the mathematics and the organization of the data regarding all physical experiments; science, both first and last, being metaphysical. The metaphysical includes the mind-extracted, definitely concentrated and consciously formulated anti-entropic generalizations, in a hierarchy of progressively contracting degree, which most economically describe the workings of the metaphysical subdivision of universe," *ibid.*

6. Lévi-Strauss states that it is easier to study subconscious than conscious behavior: "Those social structures which are most deeply embedded in a cultural pattern are more frequently totally unconscious and, therefore, easier to get at since there have not evolved false theories or conceptual categories to explain their existence. On the other hand, those patterns which are closer to the surface are usually found to be more difficult to ascertain due to the fact that, in most cases, inaccurate explanations for them exist in the collective consciousness." G. LeBaron, unpublished paper on structural anthropology, p. 6.

7. Asghar T. Minai, *Art, Science, and Architecture: Architecture as a Dynamic Process of Structuring Matter-Energy in the Spatio-Temporal World,* University Microfilms, Inc., Ann Arbor, Michigan, 1969.

8. Ruth Benedict, "Synergy: Patterns of the Good Culture," *Psychology Today,* (June 1970) pp. 54-55.

9. A.H. Maslow, *Eupsychian Management: A Journal,* Richard D. Irwin, Inc., Homewood, Ill., 1965.

10. W.A. Weisskoff, *A New Knowledge in Human Values,* ed. by A.H. Maslow, Henry Regnery Co., Chicago, 1971.

11. A. Korzybski, *Science and Society,* 4th ed., International Non-Aristotelian Library Publishing Co., Lakeville, Conn., 1958.

12. D. Meadows et. al., *The Limits of Growth: A Report for the Club of Rome's Project on the Predicament of Mankind,* Universe Books, New York, 1972.

13. P. Bunyard, "How Much Growth is Possible?" *The Ecologist,* (March 1973, vol. 3, no. 3).

14. H.E. Daly, "The Stationary-state Economy," *The Ecologist,* (July 1972, vol. 2, no. 7).

15. H.V. Hodson, *The Diseconomies of Growth,* Ballantine Books, New York 1972.

16. Buckminster R. Fuller, "Letter to Doxiadis," *Main Currents in Modern Thought* (March/April 1969, vol. 25, no. 4).

17. *Ibid.*

2. Environmental Planning and Design

2.0 Introduction–Abstract

In this chapter the notion of planning and design is developed based on the conceptual universal framework outlined in chapter 1. That is to say, the objective of this chapter is to outline the relationship of environmental planning and design relative to the sum total of human activities. In viewing man's total activity pattern, a three-level breakdown is defined: namely, *ethics and values, planning and design,* and *sociophysical realities.* Planning and design is here considered to be that part of man's activities that constantly tries to restructure sociophysical realities to conform with ethics and values which are also preconditioned by sociophysical realities. While sociophysical realities are "what they are" and ethics and values "what they ought to be," planning and design activities constantly readjust realities to ethics and values in the form of "what can be."

Planning and design are defined as man's activities which are designated to change the "environment" either in substance or structure, quality, or quantity. Planning and design overlap in activity. Whereas planning is more involved with sociocultural, economic, and administrative issues, design deals with the physical environment. Whereas planning is more objective, quantitative, and rational in approach, design is more intuitive and deals with qualitative matters as well. Conscious, subconscious, organic, and inorganic types of behavior are also defined as universal planning and design components of the metaphysical and the material world. To plan or design, one deals with the characteristic behavior of these four universal components. Without a full knowledge of such behaviors, those activities fail to conform to universal functions and communication.

The total scope of human activities, whether metaphysical or physical, including the arts and sciences, the subjective and objective, conscious and subconscious, organic and inorganic, and *a priori* and *a posteriori,* are all seen as subcomponents of the above four universal components, and thus the domain of planning and design activities.

2.1 Environmental Planning and Design

The same universal components previously outlined, i.e., conscious, subconscious, organic, and inorganic types of behavior, are used as planning and design components. Adaptation of communication systems as the structure of the universe, and thus culture and environment, provides planning and design activities with a general framework system which unifies all human endeavors. As shown in figure 1, human involvement in worldly activities could be divided into the following three major subdivisions:

2.2 Ethics and Values

These endeavors deal with matters regarding WHAT OUGHT TO BE (fig. 2–1); that is, where man is going, what his goals are set for, and finally, what he wants out of life. Such endeavors are usually defined within the domain of the religious, philosophical, and sociocultural objectives and value systems of different societies.

Value systems do not necessarily always have a rational justification. Rational and logical methods are better tools for dealing with that part of life and planning and design, termed here WHAT CAN BE. "(That) rational knowledge cast into the form of internally consistent, logically constructed and closed models of science constitutes a useful but by no means sufficient, tool for dealing with matters of human design and for a human world."[1]

Norbert Wiener emphasizes the need for an orientation of human knowledge in reaching for a kind of knowledge revealing "know-where-to" rather than solely "know-what."[2] Ideological views formulating directions of change would be Utopias unless they are shaped with regard to consideration of the Forces of Reality. In other words, unless one has both an idea of the directions of life and the direction of growth and change, planning or design or the formulation of any policies in this regard does not mean anything. If such questions are answered then the issues of how and what and by what means could be confronted more easily. Then we could shape our future environment and its dynamics of human life patterns and its complexities of interrelation with cosmic order.

Finally, if we address the issues of change and direction of change which are actually built into the environmental system characteristics—order, structure, and process of change, we can expect global continuity, balance, and equilibrium in the system.

Concerning man's relation to nature, in the history of Western science which followed the basic views of Christianity, a great deal of responsibilities and burdens were put on human shoulders when man was placed in a separate category from the rest of nature and in control of the environment. A modern interpretation of such an orientation would mean that man on the top of the pyramid of creation stands alone against increasing randomness and entropy having resulted from the total pyramid.

New developments in Western knowledge, particularly in the areas of the physical and biological sciences, indicates the existence of nonequilibrium in nature. These developments not only disprove the above notion and Newtonian mechanics, but also the recently considered thermodynamics equilibrium which is the source of such an orientation. The discoveries of Ilya Prigonine formulating principles of "order through fluctuation"[3] are known to be the origin of such revolutionary changes in recent scientific orientation.

Besides the above discoveries in the physical and biological sciences, there are also indications of a verification of the same principles in the sociocultural sciences. As a matter of fact, this is the very same principle man has been searching for to explain the issue of man's (or any organism's) interaction and adaptation to his surroundings environment as an open system, i.e., the Principles of Systems theory in a nonequilibrium state assumes that the environment of any organism forces him constantly to interact with his surroundings, changing its state of energy via entropy producing activities.

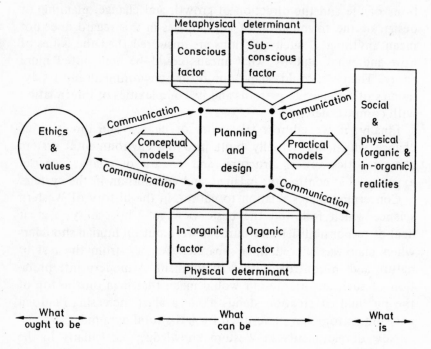

Figure 2-1
Planning and Design Processes

There have been claims that these recent views of development have similarities with Eastern philosophy. Eastern philosophy sees man as an indistinguishable part of nature and thus equal with and not superior to the rest. The two views rendered above, the "Western" and the "Eastern," stand on the opposite extremes of a spectrum. Thus if these recent theories are proved to hold true in various disciplines, a major change and thus challenge confronts man. This consequently would be reflected in the philosophy of human knowledge, and finally, planning and design activities.

2.3 Sociophysical Realities

These endeavors deal with matters regarding WHAT IS, that is, how things are, how the facts represent reality. These realities would, of course, include knowledge of the formation of man's past goals and objectives, the means by which his problems were approached, and finally, what, where, and how everything stands now and was in the past.

Philosophies of the sciences and the arts in various space–time reflect how man has perceived these realities. An historical accumulation of knowledge represented in varying modes of inquiry often shows how man and his environment and planning and design have been considered throughout history.

Erich Jantsch[4] proposes three different modes of inquiry based on the assumptions an inquirer makes about his relation to the object he is studying:

–The "rational approach" is based on the assumption that there is a distinct separation between the observer and observed. The objectivity of the observer prevents him from involvement in the behavioral characteristics of the object. Logic is the principle source of inquiry. The results are reflected as either quantitative or a representation of linkage systems or structures of components. The dynamic part is perceived "as change."

–The "mythological approach" is a kind of inquiry where a linkage feedback is established between the observer and the observed. To some extent, the subjectivity of the observer makes him involved in the life of the object. Feeling is the principle source of inquiry. The results are reflected in qualitative form. The dynamic part is perceived as "process, or order of change."

The "evolutionary approach" is a type of inquiry in which a union exists between the observer and the observed. It focuses in on either both the observer and the observed or the interacting forces involved in the process between the two. "Tuning-in" is the principle source of inquiry. The results are reflected in the form of "sharing" in a universal order of process (i.e., evolution).

No doubt the first approach is constantly used by the physical sciences. The second approach is used by the arts and humanities. Architects and designers have used both of the first two ap-

proaches and in various planning and design states from conceptualization to implementation. Problems have always arisen
when these sets of distinct approaches have come into contact in
comprehensive planning and design processes.

The third mode of inquiry has shown significant potential since
the development of Systems theory, communication, Information
theory, and cybernetics, where a two way feedback process is
essential. In planning and designing, wherever man and his environment are seen in a highly integrated way, neither the objectivity
of the physical sciences nor the subjectivity of the arts alone are
sufficient. Rather I believe there is an urgent need for new modes
of dynamic processes of inquiries which could contain both the
ordered characteristics of the logics of science and the random
behavior of the arts.

2.4 Planning and Design

These endeavors deal with matters relating to WHAT CAN BE
(fig. 2–1); that is, how man alters things from the way they are
to the way he wants them to be, and how he goes about changing
them from their state of being to their state to be (from 2 to 1).

Design and planning is most concerned with this third matter,
with WHAT CAN BE.

Design and planning generally cover the totality of man's activities which are designed to change our "environment," either in
substance or structure, qualitatively or quantitatively. Planning
and design are two activities with broad scope, both dealing with
phenomena ranging from sociocultural to natural and physical
matters. Although planning and design each has a specific domain
of deeper involvement, each extends over the other's territory.
Thus there is a great deal of overlap in their activities.

*Whereas planning is more involved with sociocultural and
economic development, design deals with the physical environment. While planning is more objective, quantitative, oriented,
and rational in approach, design is more intuitive, dealing with
qualitative matters.*

2.5 The Universe – the Domain of Planning and Design

In addition to the above three major human endeavors influencing the domain of planning and design activities, there are also other dynamics involved. One process involved is time and the other is entropy, resulted from a complex set of interconnecting factors presented in fig. 2–2. As has already been pointed out, man's view of nature and life changes with time, both due to an accumulation of knowledge and an understanding of nature; i.e., life forms and their function. To present these two major component factors influencing planning and design, time has been eliminated on fig. 2–2, and only a picture rendering a change interval is shown. To present framework processes in this picture, two principle characteristics, i.e., the metaphysical and material, predominantly shape the image. The complex interaction of the two complementary sets and the resulting entropy is what sets the world into activity. The nature of processes is actually where "impulses"[5] of life forces push and pull the world, and that has to do with the issue of order and structure of the cosmos.

The main issue related to the notion of ordering principles is the concept of "autopoisis." "Autopoisis refers to the characteristics of living systems to continuously renew themselves and to regulate this process in such a way that the integrity of their structure is maintained. Whereas a machine is geared to the output of a specific product, a biological cell is primarily concerned with renewing itself. Upgrading (anabolic) and downgrading (catabolic) processes run simultaneously."[6]

Where these upgradings of constructive metabolism and downgradings of destructive metabolism are simultaneously continuous, "change and necessity now appear as complementary principles."[7] In this regard Waddington states that "Evolution consists of nothing more than random utilization and natural selection."[8]

Planning and design are man's efforts to bring "order" to the pattern properties of the conscious and subconscious mind, as well as to organic and inorganic matter, directing them from their state *now* to their state *to be,* reaching ethics and values (sociocultural) (fig. 2.–1). However, these orders are very different in nature, following different processes, as well as different

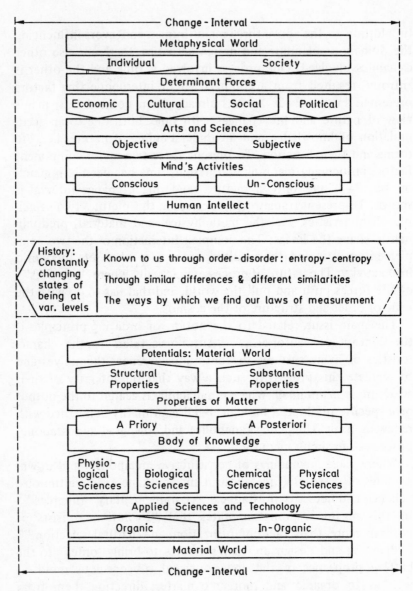

Figure 2—2
Universal Determinant Factors, Components of Planning and Design

courses of action. They are conscious (rational thought processes and cognition), subconscious (feelings, instinctive behavior) and conscious-subconscious (perceptions, i.e., encompassing most of the artistic and qualitative properties of life).

Let us now discuss the breakdown of these different components of the total environmental system, reflected in fig. 2–2.

As shown in fig. 2–2, the determining factors of our environment at any given time (t_o) are shown on numerous boxes abbreviated in this figure. The material factors on the one side and the metaphysical on the other are apt to condition the future of our environment. The change of state within change-interval (dt) would bring us to a different state at $(t_o + dt)$.

In any given moment (time interval), different individual factors presented on the matrix follow their own probabilistic random behavior while being influenced, and thus conditioned, by others, as well as the combined complex interaction of all. In such circumstances, the governing laws and principles of all phenomena at different levels, under different conditions, at different space-time circumstances vary.

In such a condition, our only reliable reference in this ever-changing flow of events is the principle of similar differences and different similarities; i.e., the laws of probability, Information theory, and the principles of entropy and centropy. These principles could enable us to measure "order" and "disorder" in the perceived pattern-behavior of various events within a certain degree of accuracy. The results would provide us with an ever-changing accumulation of relative and probabilistic information rather than a compilation of historically conditioned preconceptions of environmental-event-pattern. Let us now define the universe in terms of physical and metaphysical elements, i.e., "all *voluntary experiences,* experiments, as well as all *involuntary experiences,* i.e., all happenings." Or, as Fuller states, "It can be seen that the metaphysical is to the physical as anti-matter is to matter, i.e., as the electron is to the position: *metaphysics* and *physics* are thus seen to co-function, to progressively conserve the self-regeneration of non-simultaneously evolving universe."[9] While he defines the laws of man as centropy, he says, "Man's function in the universe is metaphysical and anti-entropic. He is essential to the conservation of the universe, which is in itself an intellectual conception."[10]   Below, the two characteristic worlds are discussed in detail.

2.6 The Material World

Erich Jantsch has summarized the commonalities of findings of the 1970s as breaking the walls and boundaries drawn around various components of the universal systems and introducing the notions of "openness," "plasticity of structures" and "their freedom to evolve."[11] He is specially fascinated and influenced by the break through during this period, particularly by the works of Ilya Prigogine and his colleagues who presented the theory of so called "dissipative structure"[12] in chemical processes. The new ordering principle, called "order through fluctuation," is a theory which overshadows the notion of equilibrium in existing theories of thermodynamics.

Erich Jantsch used "paradigm of self-organization"[13] as a new means of *"synthesis,"* or what we might call ordering of the universe, of what he calls an "emergent unifying paradigm." He defines adaptation and survival as the underlying aspects of evolution where "survival of the species" is framed within the game of evolution, a game in which the only reward is to stay in the game."

By adaptation of course he refers to two-way adaptation where the environment also adapts itself. He suggests that to understand this paradigm is to be able to deal with "self-transcendance, the reaching out beyond the boundaries of one's own existence" and that is possible when "emergent paradigm of self-organization permits the elaboration of a vision based on the interconnectedness of natural dynamics at all levels of evolving micro- and macro systems."[14]

In this theory he sees man as an inseparable part of the universal system. "The rising consciousness of an indivisable unity with nature - and even of human existence as an integral aspect of nature - has transformed the esoteric notion of an esosystem into an immensely practical notion."[15]

Within this unity two basic characteristic forms are identical:

A. Inorganic Matter
B. Organic Matter.

A. INORGANIC MATTER

New discoveries in the physical sciences of the early 20th century have drastically changed man's view of matter, the material world, and consequently, the entire cosmos system which is reflected in all human activities and thought processes. In physics and mechanics, classical theories have been overthrown by both the laws of thermodynamics and an atomic view of nature. In mathematics, modern algebra and the laws of probability have set new perspectives for man from which to view the world, not with definite, finite eyes, but rather with the eyes of relativity and uncertainty. The keystone of chemistry, which traditionally was atoms and molecules, has also been replaced by the ordering structure and interrelationships among particles rather than basic units.

The change over from adherence to Newtonian laws to the doctrine of relativity at the beginning of the century and the advancement of the laws of thermodynamics and quantum theories in the 1930–1960's, shifted the commonly held view of the world from a deterministic one to a view based on uncertainty, embodying the probabilistic realities of our century. The atomic view of the world, which emphasized complex finite numbers of fixed ultimate material units, was replaced by the quantum mechanics school which worked in terms of "elementary particles." On the basis of this change in viewpoint, the predictive behavior of matter and thus the world to be planned and designed was overshadowed by unpredictable structures of quantum behavior. Previous philosophies adhered to by scientists, as well as religious leaders, holding that the coincidence in direction of life forms and nonliving matter toward an ultimate state (in the religious sense) and a deterministic evolutionary future (in a scientific sense) were overturned by the new doctrines. As previously discussed, a distinction is now evident between the conscious and subconscious, as well as the living and nonliving parts of the physical world.

Having asserted that for the first time in history man has entered upon an "entirely new philosophical era . . . on earth."[16] Fuller argues that man has the ability to play a conscious, active role in his own evolution and therefore to make himself a complete success in his environment. According to Fuller, this dazzling prospect was opened to us by Einstein's concept of energy as the basis of the universe. "Einstein shattered the Newtonian cosmos," he was quoted as saying recently. "In the famous first law of dynamics, Newton had said that a body persisted in a state of rest or constant motion except as it was affected by other bodies. He was assuming that the normal condition of all things was inertia. Einstein realized that all bodies were constantly being affected by other bodies though, and this meant that their normal condition was not inertia at all but continuous motion and continuous change."[17]

The world of the nonliving environment is directed toward increasing entropy[18] and randomness, whereas life systems never experience this trend. This very philosophical change in the physical sciences has necessitated a new outlook which requires new tools for measurement, planning, and design. *Accordingly, the laws of entropy have become the ordering principles; thus it should be the case in planning and design as well.*

B. ORGANIC MATTER

In this issue of biological order Waddington refers to discoveries in the 1940's to elaborate on the role of change in evolution. He says during this period two major developments altered man's interpretation of evolution.

The first development rejected the idea that in a population of organisms most of them have almost the same genes and there are only small variants; thus almost no room exists for evolutionary change unless a new and suitable gene turns up. However this actually proves that in a population most individuals are different. This theory then postulates the idea that any population shares a "large pool of highly diverse genes" and each individual has a small sample of this pool, or if for some reason some changes are necessitated, "genetic potentialities to meet the new needs are almost certain to be already available within the pool."[19]

Finally, Waddington states that here "the role of mutation is not to be a fundamental constraint, so that evolution is always waiting on an appearance of the appropriate mutation. Rather what random mutation does is to feed into the pool a continuous supply of new minor variants, so that there is always a rich mix available, from which natural selection can pick out those which suit its purposes at the time."[20]

He asserts that the second development is as follows: Earlier theories suggested that the choice of future offspring is from among the genes. However, it is not the genes which are the agent of offspring to the next generation, but rather the relevant organism. He further argues that "the environment in which development occurs has an effect on the character of the phenotype which will be produced."[21] This idea in fact increases the indeterminateness of the total system. This means that the same genes may produce different phenotypes in different environments, or various characteristics of genetypes may disappear or reappear if they are produced in different environments. There is "no one-to-one correlation between the genotypes which will be inherited, and the phenotype on which natural selection will occur. The theory that one can reduce natural selection to the simple notion of 'necessity' is thus completely untenable."[22]

In one of his last articles Waddington concludes by saying, while we think of evolution as the selection of phenotypes produced from genes drawn from a gene pool under certain environmental conditions accepted by the organism and vice versa, we have to conclude that "biological evolution, even at the subhuman level, is a matter of interlocking series of open-ended, cybernetic, or circular processes."[23]

Concerning the evolution of organic components of the universe, naturalists have reached the conclusion that creation might be defined as movement or evolution from a lower to a higher order, characterized by a gradual change from simplicity to diversity. In the words of Ian McHarg, "Evolution is then seen as a creative process, retrogression as reductive."[24]

McHarg[25] has compared the case of two environmental situations—a sand dune and a forest—to support his basic thesis. In looking at the physical make-up and life processes constituting a sand dune, it is clear that its basic state is a premature one in which simplicity, uniformity, and instability are its overriding characteristics. The interplay of physical factors involved in a sand dune, which has only relatively recently emerged from the sea, are the sand itself and a few grasses and insects, all of which are subject to the pressures of sand and sun. The low number of species is correlated with a low number of symbiotic relationships and high occurrence of entropy. The number of species is limited and the interrelations among them are few and basic.

However, upon examination, a forest will be found to be in an advanced state of complexity, diversity, and stability with a high number of species, as well as a high number of symbiotic relationships characterized by low entropy. The forest is the product of millennia, during which time scores of organisms have evolved and adjusted to their environment, while at the same time adjusting the environment to themselves within a complex symbiotic relationship. The sand dune though is strongly subject to the influences of outside natural forces and has nothing from within with which to protect itself, other than scanty vegetation to help keep the sand down when the winds blow. The forest, which was once a sand dune, has become nearly complete and self-sufficient in itself, dependent on its own processes which provide stability and low entropy. The forest is able to utilize the sunlight it receives to a great extent, whereas vegetation in the sand dune can only absorb a small amount of it.

Thus creation involves increase in the order of a system and retrogression reflects a reduction in order from higher to lower. A higher order of complexity is accompanied by a greater ability on the part of organisms within that system to survive in the face of outside pressures, such as disease. This is due to the fact that more life forms have evolved, and thus the chances of one or more of these forms being able to halt the influences of an external threat is great. A sand dune however gives way very quickly to outside pressures since its species are limited in number, thereby effectively reducing its success in combating varied outside influences.

McHarg extends this concept to man's sociocultural environment, noting that the creative environment requires that it be made more varied and complex while at the same time, the inhabitants of a total environment must adapt themselves to that environment. The mechanisms and tools involved in cultural change are the same as those embodied in physical changes as found in nature, i.e., mutation and natural selection, though the rate of change is greater.

> The creative test is to accomplish a creative fitting. This involves iden-
> tifying those environments intrinsically fit for an organism or process,
> identifying the organism, species or institution fit for the environment,
> and inaugurating the process whereby the organism and the environment
> is adapted to accomplish a better fit.[26]

Although the material world follows its own laws of nature independent of human desires, the use of matter by man as "social objects" adds new dimensions to its flow of life. These new dimensions as a product of the human mind are sociocultural, thus conscious and subconscious in nature. Man utilized matter in two ways; one is due to a mechanistic view based on physical specification, the second is due to the symbolic values and meanings conveyed because of its form, color, and the manner in which it is used in the larger context of human communication systems. Whereas the physical and natural sciences deal with the first characteristic, planners and particularly designers deal with both. In the past some visionary architects neglected the first.

More comprehensive designers such as Louis Kahn however talk of the organic and generic interrelation between these two dimensions of matter; he highly recommends that the proper use of materials be based on their potentials. In other words, the use of different materials for a social qualitative and artistic expression is not the matter of an architect's arbitrary choice. On the contrary, matter has inherent potential dictating its use based on "what it wants to be" or "what it is supposed to be doing." Finally, it is artists and architects who are to understand the laws of nature and inherent potential which exists in different forms of matter. This knowledge then enables them to use various material forms properly. The two aspects of object systems are discussed below.

1. *Substance of Matter*—Matter presents two characteristics:
(1) the *objective and universal,* dictating from within through the nature of material formation and its substances, and
(2) the *subjective and qualitative* which it acquires as a result of the way different individuals use or experience it. Moreover,

both are even combined; i.e., art forms also create their own meanings independent of the objective and subjective preconditions or objects they represent. As Henry Moore states, the sculpture he makes is "self-supporting" and "has a life of its own, independent of the object it represents."[27] These subjective attributes vary from individual to individual, thus from architect to architect. Understanding and knowledge of both the qualitative and quantitative aspects of matter are vital to architectural studies.

2. *Structure of Matter*—In addition to the substance of matter, the structure of matter also plays a great role in shaping our environment. This characteristic of matter involves structural properties which have to do with the shape and reshape, formation and transformation of matter under different structural conditions and environmental circumstances. That is to say, the structural properties of matter are also capable of creating additional characteristics and potentials due to organizational changes wich would enable them to form different quantitative material, as well as qualitative aesthetic functions. In other words, the structural properties of matter are also capable of providing it with addtional qualities enabling it to carry respective messages and meanings.

2.7 The Metaphysical World

To my knowledge, in regard to the metaphysical world no consensus yet exists which resolves the question of the existence or nonexistence of directionality of human purpose and orientation. Some scientists and anthropologists, more geared to the material aspects of our world measurable by empirical experiments, have indirectly included the metaphysical aspects of man in the evolutionaly process of the physical world. Within such terms they actually see man from a physiobiological viewpoint.

Although this orientation is not the total picture of our metaphysical world, owing to practical reasons this behavioral branch of the social sciences attracted a great deal of our human resources in recent years. The experimental orientation of scientific philosophy in this era has necessitated that recent studies of man be geared more to the conscious rather than the subconscious behavior of man, to the rational, logical rather than subconscious behavior of man and finally, to man's objectivity rather than subjectivity and individuality. In the following pages we review some of these issues as a means for seeking a better understanding of factors influencing man and his environment and planning and design activities.

A. CONSCIOUS AND SUBCONSCIOUS

The very nature of the conscious and subconscious activities of the human mind involves two different phenomena. While conscious, rational thought processes are linear-two-dimensional in character, the subconscious is holistic n-dimensional. A rational thought process as a conscious behavior of the mind is predictable, transferrable, and restorable since it can be divided into isolated parts and sequential processes. It can be carried out by teams and at different places and times by its creator or any one else. This does not hold true in the case of the subconscious: its dimensions in space and time are quite different (discussed in chapter 4). It can be understood only through a system which is similar to it in character, and in a holistic way. Conscious space and time are quite different. Conscious behavior could be considered as a momentary concrete, finite snapshot of a subconscious behavior pattern, separated from the dynamic flow of events thrusting into unlimited space-time (past/future). Actually, when a painter paints or a designer designs, he always tries for ideas; he moves back and forth at levels of consciousness and subconsciousness. He constantly attempts to grasp what might slip into the focus of consciousness from the flow of formless patterns that are unconscious messages. To produce conscious pictures he always looks to subconscious stimulti patterns of the past or future which might crop up as design ideas. The artist always seeks something which is on the point of breaking into consciousness, not necessarily from experiences of the past, but also from future situations, or as Carl Jung states,

We find this in everyday life, where dilemmas are sometimes solved by the most surprising new proposition; many artists, philosophers, and even scientists owe some of their best ideas to inspirations that appear suddenly from the unconscious. The ability to reach a rich vein of such material and to translate it effectively into philosophy, literature, music, or scientific discovery is one of the hallmarks of what is commonly called genius.[28]

On the issue of consciousness and unconsciousness, Poincaré and Freud share a similar orientation which is simply descriptive of two minds when it comes to consciousness and subconsciousness, "each governed by its own dynamic laws, each able to carry out different functions with severely limited access to the other's activities."[29] Poincaré is especially fascinated with the relationship between the conscious and subconscious activities of the mind; i.e., when and how sudden thoughts bring to the focus of consciousness some answers to the problems contemplated in the past which have been consciously phased out and fused into the subconscious vocabulary of the mind. Ideas and forms reached by the unconscious are more dynamic and alive than those produced by consciousness. One of the reasons for this is that forms, shapes, colors, concepts, and ideas experienced by the subconscious are vivid, colorful, rich messages free of constraints, whereas the conscious-"controlled" thoughts are restrained within the boundaries of space-time limits, as well as conventional knowledge dictated by the limited vocabulary of rational thought processes and its language. So they are much less colorful than the source (unconscious) from which they have been stripped.

Logical analyses are the consequences of consciousness. We select with reason and knowledge, meaning, and information. Information filtered through this process into the focus of consciousness necessarily falls into the domain of conventional, accepted forms of knowledge. In other words, some messages experienced by the subconscious are a nuisance to the consciousness because they cannot be formulated in a way that is satisfactory to the intellect and logic.

If we more fully want to understand the role of the subconscious mind in the design of environmental quality and the creation of art forms, we can look at some vernacular architecture, some of the old urban and rural patterns and indigenous architecture of the past—when consciousness and rationality had not yet so overwhelmed the subconscious spirit of man. Most architects and art historians praise the dynamic and vivid qualities of the rich and picturesque architecture of the past. Without a doubt, everyone loves the irregular pattern of alleys and shopping malls, or the bazaars of medieval and baroque towns. But we hardly realize the fact that its beauty lies in its organic irregularities, which in themselves create an unpredictability of forms and shapes and flow of unique spatial sequences. It is the unpredictable, probabilistic occurrence of events which plays upon the language of the subconscious, which makes it pleasing and rich. It is chance arrangement which gives depth to works of art; it points to an unknown but active principle, order and meaning, which corresponds to the subconscious dimensions of man's mind. The random organic patterns of indigenous architecture are compositions of chance. And it is with an understanding of these considerations that planners and designers should start their work.

For a man who comes in contact with them, meanings conveyed through such patterns are absolutely different and conditioned by the receiver's history, heredity, and environment. What then are the "secret codes" of chance arrangement insofar as man can even understand them or, more fittingly, experience them?

If we want to see and characterize this type of spirit, we shall certainly get closer to it in the sphere of past vernacular, organic architecture than in the products of conscious modern man. I should clarify that I do not, by any means, deny the great gains which arise from the history of scientific development and the evolution of man's rational thought process. But I am afraid that these gains, unfortunately, have been made at the cost of other qualitative aspects of life; namely, aspects of the subconscious. To most science-oriented architects and planners, it is annoying to deal with materials that cannot be completely or adequately grasped. The trouble with these phenomena is that they are undeniable and yet cannot be formulated into intellectual terms. This group is probably not aware of the fact that the beauty of life and aesthetic experience is very likely not to be totally consciously grasped.

In contrast to the subconscious activities of the mind and man's intellect, Fuller suggests that his rational behavior follows the laws of what can be termed centropy, which is the reduction of disorder. The conscious part of human behavior, based on a factual body of knowledge and development of a higher logical order in man's ordering of his environment, is moving toward advancement and evolution.

The hypothesis made by Fuller is that the intellect follows the laws of centropy:

> By *centropy,* I refer to the omni-accelerating - acceleration of the clarifyingly differentiated and inter-communicated, experience derived, pattern cognitions of the human mind, which progressively disclose the orderly complex of omni-interactive, pure, weightless and apparently eternal principles governing the intellectual design and operation of the seemingly and 'suggestively' only infinitely self-regenerative universe.
>
> We may call this metaphysical phenomenon - which continually *simplifies* and *contracts* the generalized description of principles apparently operative in all special case experiences: 'The Law of Decreasing Confusion,' or the 'Law of Intellectual Conservation,' or the 'Law of the Contracting Universe,' or the 'Law of Diminishing Chaos,' or the 'Law of Progressive Order,' or the 'Law of Contractively Orderly Generalizations.'[30]

This hypothesis may (though not necessarily) be relatively true over a short span of time because if we accept the random behavior of a combination of physical systems and if we assume that subconscious behavior does not follow a deterministic path, the whole state which rational thought processes and intellect addresses is unpredictable, and so probabilistic. In other words, Hisenberg's uncertainty principle used in the physical sciences is valid here too. That is to say, knowledge of a previous state of being does not exactly hold true for its changed state in the next moment in time. Of course the relativity of time spans has a lot to do with the usefulness of knowledge of each state either in the past or future—in other words, a perceived past, whereas the past no longer exists. So it is our mind preconditioned by previous states, which sees advancement.

It could be stated that no one has yet proved that over time man's subconscious behavior is changing in a directional way, or as Lévi-Strauss has suggested, that the mind of primitive man is on the same level as that of modern scientific man. The obvious difference in emphasis on the two types of thought is not one of kind, but rather one of a directional application of logic which is universally inherent in human thought processes. Lévi-Strauss contends that,

> . . .the improvement lies, not in the alleged progress of man's mind, but in the discovery of new areas to which it may apply its unchanged and unchanging powers.[31]

Furthermore, Polanyi states,

> It is obvious, therefore, that the rise of man can be accounted for only by other principles than those known today to physics and chemistry. If this be vitalism, then vitalism is mere common sense, which can be ignored only by a truculently bigoted mechanistic outlook. And so long as we can form no idea of the way a material system may become a conscious, responsible person, it is an empty pretense to suggest that we have an explanation for the descent of man.[32]

B. OBJECTIVITY AND SUBJECTIVITY, RATIONALITY AND INTUITION

I have used objectivity, cognition, logic, and rationality synonymously with consciousness; and subjectivity, intuition, and feeling with subconsciousness. This does not necessarily imply that any conscious act is logical or vice versa or that any subconscious act is intuitive.

Any theory dealing with man's experiences, including environmental planning and design, tends to stand somewhere between the two extremes in regard to rationality. At one extreme, we deal with economics, engineering, and the technological sciences in which a rational view of man is a principle on which the theory is built. At the other extreme, we deal with artistic expressions which deal with issues such as the psychological and sociocultural which are based on man's motivations, emotions, feelings. In this case scientists try to explain man's behavior as being an integral part of his sociocultural structure.

To discuss these issues, I first present a very contrasted view regarding the nature of the two sets of the above characteristic functions of the mind.

The two sides of this controversy are seen most clearly in the debate surrounding "thinking machines." One side takes the position that man is nothing more than a cybernetic machine, the actions of which are predictable, given enough information about the control system. If this position is certain, they contend, it is theoretically possible to create a machine which can mimic man's actions completely. Quite simply, then, they believe there to be nothing unique in intelligence or creativity.

Herbert Simon, representing this group, in his theory of Problem Solving asserts that "thinking can be explained by means of information processing theory,"[33] where he considers humans as an information processor. He describes "artificial intelligence"[34] as machines in which the mechanical world takes in some properties of the human mind and activities of the environment, as determind or predicted by their structure and probabilistic performance.

The only difference between man as an adaptive organism and man-made machines is that in machines "the behavior of the individual parts can, in fact, be so unique and irregular that it bears no sign of relevance to the order of the whole system. This order is achieved by coordinating activities that do not rigidly constrain the parts but leave room for variation and flexibility, and it is this flexibility that enables living organisms to adapt to new circumstances."[35]

The opposing viewpoint is supported by Mumford, Polanyi, and Taube in the following quotation:

> The view being advanced here, in contradiction to the prevalent view, is that there are radical and basic discontinuities between digital computers and living organisms; that the essential characteristics of living organisms cannot be simulated, copied, imitated, or surpassed by machines.[36]

Geoffrey Vickers argues that because our culture has supported the idea that everything real is describable, it has not been fully capable of identifying the existence of intuition, and whenever it has not been able to do so, "it tends to confine it to the area where the creative process is least constrained and most in evidence—namely the narrow contemporary concept of Art."[37] He does not like the creation and appreciation of any act of "artistry" by the human mind whether it be an artifact, scientific model, machine, sonata, or plan of a city. He would rather see and prove that in all of these acts of artistry both intuition and rationality play a rôle both in the creation and criticism of the artistry.

Geoffrey Vickers states that "knowing and designing are not separate or even separable activities, since our whole schema for knowing is a design, a model of reality consciously and unconsciously made, and constantly revised."[38] Although I agree with him, I would like to draw a stronger line here distinguishing the overlapping activities of knowing and designing. I would not like to lead readers to believe that while schema present a model of reality, perceived reality and known reality are two different things. Thus I would say that although knowing and designing are both activities of the conscious-subconscious mind, knowing is attainable in complete form to the consciousness, whereas designing activities are never completely reached by the consciousness alone. After certain selection is made by our consciousness in regard to our concerns, from the patterns in our subconsciousness, then the selected one becomes the focus of our consciousness and its snapshots present knowledge.

Although I agree with Vickers that aesthetic experience is a judgement based on certain norms, I do not necessarily believe that the criteria are only norms; they are also unique personal experiences. Thus I question his statement, "I shall postulate, as the basic fact in the organization of experience, the evolution of norms by which subsequent experience is ordered, and which are themselves developed by the activities that they mediate."[39]

I disagree with him, based on what he himself says in the following: "The recognition of form is an exercise of judgement made by reference to criteria which are not fully describable because of the subtle combination of relationships in which they reside and equally because of their dependence on context."[40] That is, if we eliminate the value judgement attached to the definition of norms they could be considered the communality.

In the creation of art forms, intuition plays a great rôle. Intuition as a consequence of conscious-subconscious activities of the mind is a rational-nonrational function. Thus the exercize of judgement as based on intuition is not the product of a voluntary act; it is rather an involuntary event which depends upon different external or internal circumstances instead of an act of judgement.

I believe that art forms—communication messages—are for the most part manifestations of the subconscious which extend beyond the control of the conscious mind. As Carl Jung states,

> 'Deeds' were never invented, they were done; thoughts, on the other hand, are a relatively late discovery of man. First he was moved to deeds by unconscious factors; it was only a long time afterward that he began to reflect upon the causes that had moved him; and it took him a very long time indeed to arrive at the preposterous idea that he must have moved himself—his mind being unable to identify any other motivating force than his own.[41]

As stated previously, it is the law or order in diversity reached through random organic patternings which creates richness and beauty. And to satisfy man is to satisfy his rational need to reason through preplanned logical order, as well as his nonrational fervent desires, through the golden properties of random probability and change.

One should admit that vernacular architects and primitive artists were much more governed by their instincts and feelings which were deeply rooted in the organic flow of nature's energy pattern, than are many more "rational" artists. Their art work was actually a chunk of their life, not an appendix to it. The whole pattern of their environment, their neighborhood, was not preconceived, preplanned at one time by another person; but rather, it was brought into unity and purposefulness by the totality of a neighborhood and a town. It was created individually through a summation of subconscious behavior of individuals sharing a common culture. And that is the way beautiful diversity within unity was conceived. Diversity is provided by richness of unique individual inputs, and unity through hidden dimensions of the incomprehensible culture of the society. Culture resulted from an integration of patterns of conscious and subconscious behavior of members of society which was, itself, the ordering factor of discrete individual behavior. Thus those men were much more governed by instincts and the subconscious than are their "rational" modern descendents who have learned to "control" themselves.

As Carl Jung says,

Modern man does not understand how much his rationalism (which has destroyed his capacity to respond to unconscious symbols and ideas) has put him at the mercy of the psychic 'underworld.' He has freed himself from 'superstition' (or so he believes), but in the process he has lost his spiritual values to a positively dangerous degree. His moral and spiritual tradition has disintegrated, and he is now paying the price for this break-up in world-wide disorientation and dissociation.[42]

So as scientific, rational, logical understanding has grown, the world in contrast has become dehumanized. Man feels more and more isolated in the universal continuum, because he is no longer involved in nature and has lost his emotional "unconscious identity," "his madness" or "his rage for chaos" and relationship with natural, organic phenomena.

On the issue of the duality of rational and intuitive processes of experience I would also like to raise the issue in Vickers' words where he sees it as a long controversy "whether the mind identifies the familiar by checking a list of characteristics which defines its identity or recognizes it by fitting some kind of perceptual gestalt to some kind of mental template."[43] I agree with Vickers that we do not know whether it is either of the above two processes or a combination of both, but I tend to believe in the following.

If we accept the fact that for a picture to be transformed into a schema it must be a model of reality to be consciously and subconsciously made, I would then say this model has two choices of pattern. The first is associations based on information communication through the substantive nature of matter. The second is the associations based on information made relative to the structural properties of combinational linkages of matter.

Both of the two alternatives Vickers proposes fall into this first category; i.e., both of the forms put forward by Vickers are based on the notion of identified sets of entities (messages) or information as predefined criteria for judgement.

The idea of more contextual message systems based on dynamics and fluidity and the nature of "field experience" at all times, based on the second criterion, is missing in his suggestion.

I believe that the mechanisms of the mind do not stop with templates or lists. Accepting the ideas of template and criteria list is accepting a momentary stop for comparison, whereas a template with constantly changing patterns seems to be more appropriate. Cybernetics has combined the analogue and digital process and has already provided us with knowledge of how a mechanical device such as a computer could check these types of lists or templates against some stored information. But the reason we do not know enough about the human brain is due to the complexity of the dynamics of constant change or as G.H. Lewes states, "the new object presented to sense or the new idea presented to thought must also be *soluble in old experience* and be recognized as like them, otherwise it will be unperceived, un-comprehended."[44]

Environmental planning and design are not to be a response to man's rational needs alone, but also to his nonrational inspirations and feelings. For the sake of the stability of these two, the subconscious and conscious must be totally integrated. If they are apart, "ugliness" follows. In this respect an understanding of subconscious meanings and the communication of universal symbol systems is indispensable. Such communication language and symbol systems are the actual essential message carriers from the instinctive subconsciousness to the rational consciousness of the human mind; and their understanding enriches the consciousness so that it learns to understand again the forgotten language of instincts and feelings.

There are always differences among natural-organic forms, man-made forms, and *a priori* pure forms; there are differences among subconscious instincts, conscious–subconscious experience, and conscious behavior and acts. Thus emerges the creation of various environmental forms. While the second and third categories in both examples are always less than the concepts, forms, and factors they represent, the first categories always stand for something more than their obvious meanings; they are natural and spontaneous.

Polarization of these views of man at either end of the two extremes is viewed to be inadequate in architecture. Here planning and design is claimed to be a syntactic process enhancing both the rational and nonrational aspects of the human mind. In this regard I should say I have gone to the extent that I supposed these two sets of patterns to run in opposite directions and suggested that aesthetic behavior should not be sought only in the laws of ordered rationality, but also in random nonrationality. (This will be discussed later in detail.)

C. INDIVIDUAL VS. SOCIAL ENVIRONMENT

All preceding discussion suggests that man is not an isolated entity, and there are no boundaries between man and his environment. A line cannot be drawn indicating where individual ends and sociocultural, political, and economic environment or material environment begins. It is easier to see conscious man (logical-rational) stand out, distinguished from his surroundings, than subconscious man.

To understand man's sophisticated languages of unconscious communication and interaction with his surroundings, it is vital to try first to see what part of such meanings are common and universal "basic behavior" and what is unique to personal experiences. Thus a tremendous amount of study is needed in psychology, anthropology, the social, physical, and natural sciences to discover answers to some fundamental questions in this area.

Unique individual artistic contributions to human experience and knowledge, the creator's experiences and art works, ideas and concepts are directly connected to the subconscious mind, and thus to culture. So they are actually pieces of life itself—images that are integral parts of living individuals which are manifested through emotions. These experiences are unique to the whole life situation; past and future circumstances created the environment of individuals who relate to it. They are not to be understood in terms of simple causal relationships to their immediate surroundings. They have generically grown to their present state as they have been moved by forces from within the individual, by stimuli from without and through their interactions with past and future dispositional properties of space-time.

Symbolism and communication involved in man's interaction with his sociophysical environment is also an adaptive system developed in time and through a continuous feedback process.

No genius architect or artist has ever sat down with a pen or brush in his hand and thought, "Now I am going to invent a symbol," but as Kahn said their designs might later become symbols." "A symbol. . . .is not what you invent, but what it becomes. I cannot build symbolically. But I hope the new synagogue does become symbolic."[45] Thus he refutes the statement that "it is the symbolic content which gives the concrete things their social meaning." And there is always the question of what a church wants to be rather than what it is. No one can take a more or less rational thought, reached as a logical conclusion or by deliberate intent, and then give it "symbolic" form. No matter what is done to it, it will remain an *a priori* pure form or applied man-made form, linked to the conscious thought behind it.

Vickers, like McLuhan, tends to believe the message system interacting among individuals and their environment is contextual. We receive messages to learn from the media and contextual patterns disregarding whether those messages are intended for us or not. We observe repetitions and regularities versus dissimilarities in the physical world before knowing their causal behavior. These messages are inseparable from the context within which they are operating.

One of these contexts is ethics and values manifested in sociocultural norms which furnish everybody with certain frames of reference and render those dimensions of planning and design which are assumed here as *ought to be* (fig. 2–1). Belief systems "serve two opposing sets of functions. On the one hand, they are Everyman's theory for understanding the world he lives in. On the other hand, they represent everyman's defense network, through which information is filtered in order to render harmless that which threatens his ego . . . a belief system seems to be constructed to serve both masters at once; to understand the world in so far as possible and to defend against it in so far as necessary."[46]

This system can be interpreted in biological terms. The schemata are interconnected systems where a change in one will result in a change in the others. Each change also creates a reaction or resistance which is proportional to the relevant change and creates a chain of interactions just as the change did. Some resistance is offset by the benefit which had been expected to be received by the change. These are notions dealt with in field theory.

In dealing with fields methodology, one would have to deal with the structural properties of the environment. This would also entail shifting the emphasis in planning and design from isolated deterministic factors to syntactic issues reached through a realization of the comprehensive interrelationship of all those factors involved.

Consequently, in planning and design the essential problem exists in the area of synthesis where the material and nonmaterial, rational and nonrational, organic and inorganic, feelings and thoughts, conscious and subconscious come together. One should know that thinking and feeling are two opposing phenomena. It is to the very nature of both that thinking almost automatically throws out feelings and vice versa. In design and planning, in contrast to other disciplines, one deals with directing and shaping the future environment, and thus the life of individuals as well as societies. Planning and design consequently must deal with values and feelings.

In the recent past, architecture has been extremely criticized by its very fact-oriented or pragmatic, technologically-oriented colleagues for not being scientific. However, its critics fail to understand the scientific and practical necessity of giving due consideration to feelings.

In our time, everything that once bound man to the human world—earth, space, time, and energy—and to organic and inorganic life forms, seems to be gradually pushed aside by rational conscious acts. But unless the unconscious is balanced by an experience of consciousness and logical quantitative dimensions of rational thought processes, and the pattern of life is enriched by the colorful, vivid qualities of unconscious life characteristics, there cannot be survival. The wealth of a creative experience is the only power on earth which could bring harmony to the two spheres.

The problem then is a search for a far-reaching concept of "oneness" between the physical and nonphysical spheres, qualitative and quantitative aspects of life. It is true that both the conscious and subconscious behavior of the mind are completely pairs of opposites. Each new content that emerges from the unconscious is altered in its basic nature by partial integration into the conscious mind of the observer and vice versa. The unconscious as part of nature, follows the laws of nature. It acts as material world, following the laws of entropy. Therefore the psychic field of the unconscious is the background from which consciousness springs forth.

It seems that ultimate oneness of the material and nonmaterial world boils down to oneness of conscious and unconscious phenomena. This is because unconscious and inorganic universes have common characteristics; i.e., they both follow the laws of entropy. This has also been pointed out by Carl Jung: "the unconscious somehow links up with the structure of inorganic matter—a link to which the problem of so-called 'psychosomatic' illness seems to point."[48] This is the concept of a unitarian idea of reality—in his words, "The World, within which matter and psyche are not yet discrimated or separately actualized."[49]

The conscious mind, on the other hand, focuses on areas of the unconscious mind, the conscious explanation of which is in harmony with some preconscious constellation of contents in our unconscious. If we call something rational or objective in our conscious mind, and accept it as satisfactory, it is because it matches the characteristics of our conscious mind.

Imagination and intuition are necessary and basic to our lives. Although it is generally understood that these characteristics are only valuable to poets and artists, they are indeed as important to scientists as well. Here they play an increasingly vital role, which complements that of rational intellect.

As was suggested in the previous chapter, in order to arrive at a unified system which could integrate the universe's four constituent components one might suggest the use of communication systems as a tool for planning and design within which each of the four constituent components could be conceived of as a sub-communication system. Through this communication system synergy is a measure for the qualitative, as well as quantitative, aspect of universal behavior. Within these channels of communication it is not only the disposition of matter, transformation, and thus the energy behavior of matter, which provides us with information, it is also unmeasurable synergetic patterns which provide us with quantitative measures. That is, mechanistic synergy[50] deals with material chemical and biological behavior, and phenomenal synergy[51] deals with sociocultural descriptions as well as the qualitative and quantitative values of man and his society.

Notes to Chapter two

1. Erich Jantsch, *Design for Evolution*, George Braziller, New York, 1975 p. xiii.
2. Norbert Wiener, quoted by E. Jantsch in *Design for Evolution*, p. xiii.
3. Ilya Prigonine, "Order through Fluctuation: Self Organization and Social System," in *Evolution and Consciousness*, ed by E. Jantsch & C. Waddington (Addison-Wesley Publishing Co., 1976) p. 95. Hereafter cited as "Order Through Fluctuation."
4. E. Jantsch, *Design for Evolution*, p. 84.
5. Lancelot L. Whyte. "Organisms," in *The Universe of Experience*, Harper & Row, Publishers, New York, 1974 p. 80.
6. E. Jantsch, *The Self-Organizing Universe*, Pergamon Press, Inc., New York, 1980, p. 7.
7. *Ibid.*
8. Conrad H. Waddington, "Evolution in the Sub-Human World," in *Evolution and Consciousness. Human Systems in Transition*, Addison-Wesley Publishing Co. New York, p. 12.
9. B.R. Fuller, "Letter to Doxiadis," *Main Currents in Modern Thought*, p. 3.
10. *Ibid.*, pp. 2-3.
11. E. Jantsch, *The Self-Organizing Universe*, p. 1.
12. I. Prigogine, "Order through Fluctuation," in *Evolution and Consciousness*, p. 93.
13. E. Jantsch, *The Self-Organizing Universe*, p. xiii.
14. *Ibid.*
15. *Ibid.*, p. 2.
16. Calvin Tomkins, quoted by A T. Minai, Cultural Change: Man's Concept of Nature and Total Environmental Communication," paper for *World Congress on Black Communication*, Nairobi, July 26-31 1981.
17. *Ibid.*
18. Fuller states, "By entropy, I refer to the experimentally demonstrated physical behaviors covered by the Second Law of Thermodynamics and the latter's disclosure of the diffusion of physical energy patternings of universe spoken of by the mathematical physicist as the "Law of Increase of the Random Element, "which may also be called the 'Law of the Expanding Universe." As the stars are all in complex motions, the radiations given off by them are ever more diffusely dispatched. "Letter to Doxiadis," p. 3.
19. C.H Waddington, "Evolution in the Sub-Human World," in *Evolution and Consciousness*, p. 12.
20. *Ibid.*
21. *Ibid.*, p. 13.
22. *Ibid.*
23. *Ibid.*, p 15.
24. I.R. McHarg, *Design with Nature*, Natural History Press, Garden City, New York, 1969, p. 125.

25. *Ibid.*
26. *Ibid.*
27. Henry Moore, quoted by Erich Newmann, *The Architectural World of Henry Moore*, p. 18.
28. Carl Jung, *Man and His Symbols,* Doubleday & Co., Inc., Garden City, New York, 1964, p. 310.
29. Judith Wechsler, ed., *On Aesthetics in Science* (M.I.T. press, 1978) p. 108.
30. B.R. Fuller, "Letter of Doxiadis," p. 3.
31. Claude Lévi-Strauss, *Tristes Tropique,* Atheneum, New York, 1974.
32. Michael Polanyi, *Personal Knowledge: Toward a Post-Critical Philosophy,* Univ. of Chicago Press, Chicago 1968, p. 390.
33. Allen Newell and Herbert Simon, *Human Problem Solving,* Prentice-Hall, Englewood Cliffs, N.J., 1972, p 5.
34. *Ibid.*
35. Fritjof Capra, *The Turning Point* (Simon & Schuster Publications) p. 268.
36. Taube, 1978, p. 137.
37. Geoffrey Vickers "Rationality and Intuition," in *On Aesthetics in Science,* ed. by Wechsler p. 145.
38. *Ibid.,* p. 148.
39. *Ibid.,* p. 149.
40. *Ibid.*
41. C. Jung, *Man and His Symbols.*
42. Ibid.
43. G. Vickers, *On Aesthetics in Science,* p. 150.
44. G.H. Lewes, quoted by G. Vickers in *On Aesthetics in Science,* p. 151.
45. I. Kahn, quoted in "The Philadelphia Architect," *Philadelphia Sunday Bulletin* (August 25, 1968) p. 30.
46. Milton, quoted by G. Vickers in *On Aesthetics in Science,* pp. 151-152.
47. A.T. Minai, *Art, Science, Architecture.*
48. C. Jung, quoted by E. Newmann in *The Architectural World of Henry Moore,* p. 22.
49. C. Jung, *Man and His Symbols,* p. 309.
50. "Mechanistic synergy has been used to describe the natural as well as the organic world. Whenever a mechanism relating inputs to observed synergistic outputs is known, or can in principle be discovered, for a physico-chemico-biological interaction, then this interaction is an example of mechanistic synergy. In mechanistic synergy, then, it is possible (in theory, at least) to explain why the combination of inputs led to an output effect which was not equal to the sum of the effects of the inputs singly. This is in contrast to phenomenal synergy, for which such a statement cannot hold true." Radord, 1968, 162.
51. "Phenomenal synergy involves any action which takes place between two or more persons in a social context, the result of which is unpredictable. With mechanistic synergy, the agents involved in any interaction are physical, chemical, or biochemical compounds. In the case of phenomenal synergy, it is an event (as opposed to a substance as with mechanistic synergy) which is taking place since the actors are conscious beings. Thus the result is a social phenomena reflecting the social structure of a given institution." Brian William Thomas, "Synergy: Modelling, Values and Planning," p. 15.

3. Communication: Theories and Models

3.0. Introduction – Abstract

In this chapter a review of communication concepts and models is presented. The reader is introduced to some fundamental views of communication.

The relationship between man and his environment is viewed in terms of communication; that is, through the amount of information passed and thus communication performed. A message is meaningful to us if it is conveyed in an organized manner. The more obvious the organization the easier it is to understand the message, but the less information it contains.

All genuine metaphors arise from expressive shapes and actions in the physical world. A work of architecture, in whole and in part, acts as a symbolic statement which conveys messages.

First, major communication concepts are introduced, i.e., communication as consisting of *1.* issuance or exchange of messages, information, etc.; *2.* a message as a form of ink on paper, sound waves, impulses in an electric current; *3.* visual symbols in the form of meaningful environmental images or any other signal capable of being interpreted significantly; and finally, *4.* information channels as systems capable of conveying information.

Next, some examples of models developed in various areas of communication discipline are analyzed, acknowledging that there are as many forms of communication as there are communication models. These models, including the conceptual and physical, are interpersonal, visual, verbal, environmental, etc.

Finally, in this chapter the geometry of environmental communication field is introduced. In formulating such geometries both material "realities" and sensed "appearances" or the quantity and quality of environment are given equal importance and presence.

3.1 Communication Concepts

Communication is defined as a giving or exchange of messages information, etc. Wilbur Schramm[1] defines communication as follows: The word comes from the Latin *communis* "common." When we communicate we try to share a "commonness" with someone. That is, we attempt to show or share information, an idea or an attitude. Communication requires three elements— *source, message,* and *destination.*

The source could be an individual speaking, writing, drawing, dancing; a communication organization—publishing house, television station, motion picture studio; or the environment—events-patterns and objects. The message could be conveyed in various forms and shapes—sound waves, ink work, body movements and gestures, electric impulses, and visual symbols. Such symbols are reached via meaningful environmental images, or any other signal capable of being interpreted significantly. The destination could be an individual listening, reading, watching or a spectator experiencing environmental communication language.

Figure 3–1 shows the human communication system.

Information channels are systems capable of conveying information. If the channel is a typist, a measure of information would be made in words typed per minute. If the channel is a nerve fibre, the units of measurement would be in pulse per second. Within the communication theory system, the units are bit per second. For any channel, "the capacity C is defined as a maximum value of T (in, out) in bits per second." This value is determined by the structure and principles of the channel's functioning. In environmental communication terms, all genuine metaphors arise from expressive shapes and actions in the physical world. A work of architecture, in whole and in part, acts as a symbol system which conveys messages, through our senses, relevant qualities, and communication field situations. Symbolism in architecture could not be so effective, would not move us so strongly and profoundly and prevail over changes in cultural convention, if it were not rooted in a sociocultural mileau, in the strongest, most universal human experiences. The daily experiences of our lives endow architectural shape with very enriching, colorful, and dynamic symbol systems and their meanings.

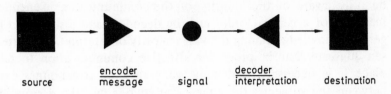

| source | encoder message | signal | decoder interpretation | destination |

Figure 3-1
Human Communication Systems

But when communication involves humans as information channels, problems arise; that is, it is not easy for scientists to measure inputs and outputs. One problem is the experimenter; he usually feels that the subject is to know the messages and how they are received. Another problem is that human subjects adjust themselves to probabilities as time passes and they receive information. Another problem is that when communication engineers study human channels they realize that human beings usually get bored and tired. Also, as humans age, channel characteristics also change.

Given: a message in a person's mind (source) travels to the receiver (destination). When this process interacts with environmental fields of physical interaction, psychological interaction, and sociocultural interaction, architectural communication occurs. Architects communicate through tangible and intangible properties. Tangible properties are presented to us in the form of buildings or natural and man-made places and objects. Intangible properties are represented in activity patterns formed within tangible properties.

Communication is the act of conveying a message, the transference of information. In order for the act of communication to take place, there must be a minimum of three integral elements—communicator (encoder), interpreter (decoder), and message. The job of the encoder is to produce and transmit clear, precise messages. It is often the responsibility of the encoder to fill a need or requirement that the interpreter may have or develop. The job of the decoder is to interpret and decipher information and messages transferred to him by the encoder. If the decoder is not careful, the message transmitted by the encoder may be misinterpreted and rendered useless. Even though the interpreter may not be fully aware of the identity of the communicator or encoder, messages of a general order may be decoded, and assumed to be general knowledge among the vast majority of interpreters. Mortensen suggests that in order for affective communication to take place it is necessary that some generality or commonnes exist between the subjects; the source can encode and the destination decode only in terms of the experiences each has had. If both have a lot in common, then communication is easy. If there is no commonality, i.e., if the experiences of the source and destination have been strikingly dissimilar, then it is going to be very difficult for communication to take place. The fact is that the sender, or source, and the receiver, or destination, must be in "tune"[2] with each other. The source, then, tries to encode in such a way as to make it easy for the destination to tune in the message—to relate it to parts of his experience which are much like those of the source.

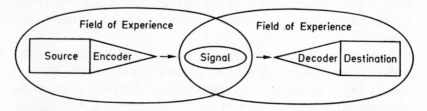

Figure 3–2
Communication as Intersection of Fields of Experiences

The communicator may take the form of an almost infinite number of words, signs, ideas, gestures, or sounds that, when presented to the interpreter, will make him act in some expected and predetermined form of behavior. An example of this is the angry shout of a mother when she wishes to school a child, or the puzzled look on a student's fact when he has failed to grasp the words of the instructor. In either case, the verbal shout of the mother or the nonverbal "look" of the student has effectively relayed a message to the intended interpreter. Thus the intent of the communicator is to produce specific content for an expected effect on interpreters, and to fill certain perceptual needs that the interpreter might have, causing the interpreter to conform to some alternate behavioral patterns.

Another characteristic of communications content is its utilization of signs and symbols. The definition given by Charles Morris is as follows: "a symbol as a sign produced by its interpreter that acts as a substitute for some other sign with which it is synonymous."[3] In human communication, symbols are not merely used to stimulate the senses, as are signs, words, and sounds. They may be used in conjunction with gestures to further communicate a message. Gestures are significant because the communicator who produces the gesture responds to it in the same way as the intended interpreter. Many everyday events and objects communicate predetermined messages to the general public. Objects such as photographs, portraits, maps, and architecture relay messages to us from communicators. These messages may be in the form of familiar symbolisms or abstract ideas. The manner in which certain words or symbols are presented to the interpreter may determine how the interpreter responds to this message. A shout may extract a greater response than a whisper. Colors that signify danger, such as red, will cause one to become alert and respond more readily than softer colors.

All communication that takes place between man and his peers, or from encoder to decoder, takes place via man's five senses. These senses are broken down into two main categories—long distance recepters (eyes, ears, and nose) and a short distance recepter, which is the skin itself.[4] For without the ability to perceive heat and cold, organisms including man would soon perish. People would freeze in winter and over heat in summer, simply because of the body's inability to communicate temperature changes to the brain. Because of the presence of "thermal communication," the body can often determine and communicate certain conditions to the brain.[5]

Communication should not be conceived only as a linear one-way action; rather it is a complex activity which through feedback processes generates new information. In the simplest communicative act, participants send and receive information simultaneously. Man continuously communicates, even when he is silent. It is impossible to conceive of man as one who does not behave. All face-to-face communication requires some sort of personal involvement and commitment which in turn creates and defines the relationship between respective parties. Communication not only channels information from one source to another, but also channels behavior.

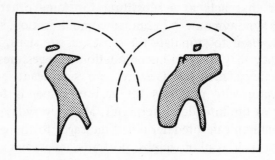

Figure 3–3
Field of Human Interaction

It is common to put a specific interaction into an organizational framework. This endeavor follows well-known, well-forseen lines. On an external level, this interaction—a series of mutually accepted statements—appears to unfold naturally without interruption. However each of those actually involved in the communication instinctively views or interprets this given interaction on a different level in keeping with his own perception of the initial point of communication commencement. It is imperative to note that disagreements as to punctuation points in such a sequence can easily result in disruptive feelings between relevant parties.

"Relationships are never static. They change over time, either in the direction of maximizing similarities between people or in accentuating individual differences. A symmetrical relationship evolves in the direction of heightening similarities; a complimentary relationship hinges increasingly on individual differences. The word *symmetrical* suggests a relationship in which the respective parties mirror the behavior of the other."[6] As noted by Wabzlawick, contrary to initial encounters, communication in lengthy relationships results in a distinct lowering of content. As stated, such a situation is contingent upon both parties being subconsciously in tune with the "rules" of the relationship. If each is not, the situation will, undoubtedly, become unstable. Mutual cooperation is essential. Each must immediately, without conscious thought, respond to the other.

Before discussing communication models, some major components of communication system are introduced.

Entropy

The method of measuring how much information a source conveys to a destination is called entropy. "The exact amount of transmitted information depends on how much the designation knows beforehand, and on the number of choices the source has in deciding what message to select from a number of alternatives."[7]

The degree of similarity of function or organization of any system in terms of probability can be considered entropy. The idea of entropy was first introduced in physics. In thermodynamics the tendency for a closed system to run down from an organized and improbable state to a disorganized, more probable and chaotic state is considered an increase in entropy.

In open systems, when entropy increases there is a tendency for higher order because of the fact that to increase entropy the system takes in energy from outside the system. This source of energy is also known as information. In other words, to exchange information is to give more order and organization to a system and to reverse the direction of change of entropy. In final words, information is the reduction of uncertainty which is the freedom of choice available in a system. Among the patterns of form or behavior of a system, lack of originality, uniqueness, and distinction indicates high probability and thus low information. Information theory then provides measurement criteria depending on the amount of information a message contains. The less the probability of occurrence of a message the more information it can carry. The concept is like the measurement of electricity as the potential difference at two points of a wire. It measures the uncertainty before and after an event.

REDUNDANCY

Any item in a message system that adds no new information is called redundant. Total repetition of a message system provides us with complete predictability of that system. Zero redundancy creates unpredictability because "there is no way of knowing what items in a sequence will come next"—there is no base for prediction. As a general rule, "no message can reach maximum efficiency unless it contains a balance between the unexpected and the predictable, between what the receiver must have understood to acquire understanding and what can be deleted as extraneous."[8]

NOISE

Any material or signal that may interfere with the perception of information is called noise.

CHANNEL CAPACITY

The most amount of information that a communication system could take in at a given time is called channel capacity.

3.2 Communication Models

A model is simply a representation of a system and as such its function is to integrate data about the system's behavior in such a way that it provides information concerning characteristics of that behavior. Usually such information is a simulation of the past behavior of the system, thus a form of prediction. Therefore there are two ways to analyze the characteristics of a model: one is in terms of the kinds of information which the model produced, and the other is in terms of the kinds of data which go into producing that information. There are two essential kinds of information a model can produce—knowledge and/or understanding.

There are as many forms of communication as there are communication models. There has been a movement from static classification systems to forms of representation that more fully account for the exceedingly complex makeup of communication. Early preoccupation with structural aspects of communication—

source, message channels, and receiver—has now been eclipsed by concern with communicative functions and a search for constituent processes.

When designing models, the "objective is to construct a model that most accurately and usefully shows what is fundamental to an act of communication,"[9] and behavior of the reality it represents. Models may be visual, pictorial, verbal, mathematical, or statistical. They provide simpler and more coherent frames of reference of reality or phenomena in question for scientific inquiry. They also justify the structure of complex events by reducing complexity to simpler and more familiar terms. Probably the most important function of a model is that it provides new ways of conceiving hypothetical ideas and relationships. Models can combine replicative and symbolic features, such as conceptual models dealing with the symbolic and intangible, in the sense that they rely on abstract ideas and concepts to represent the unit of behavior under study. The closer the likeness of a model or, in other words, the closer the attributes of the model to the idea that is being conveyed, the greater the potential payoff to the designer. A good model provides general perspective and particular points of reference from which to question phenomena under investigation and interpret the raw material of observation.

Models can guide us as to what to look for, how to identify and classify levels of analysis, how to distinguish and segregate among various typologies of elements ranging from the common to specifics, and how to focus on the major contingencies of what is said and done. "The aim of a model is not to ignore complexity or to explain it away, but rather to give it order and coherence. . . . A useful model is a touchstone for moving from description to explanation and prediction."[10]

In developing environmental communication models, it is essential to:

1. discuss some conceptual models developed by the social sciences,
2. illustrate a physical model from the physical sciences,
3. review communication models, and finally,
4. try to use some ideas involved in the above three types of models in developing comprehensive environmental communication models.

A. CONCEPTUAL MODELS

In chapter 2 we concluded that in dealing with environmental planning and design and architecture, the essential issue is the problem of the diversity and complexity of ordered-disordered patterns of varying nature and behavior. And owing to the unpredictability of various behavioral patterns of very complex information systems, one is apt to deal with the structural properties of material, conscious and subconscious, objective and subjective, organic and inorganic, etc., phenomena. Products capable of representing such complex phenomena are also too dynamic and adaptable to change and capable of predicting random behavior of multicomplex channels.

One side of this complex dilemma deals with issues related to those of concepts, meanings, and value systems, which are only shaped and reshaped in the human mind. To describe and analyze this aspect of our environment, conceptual model have been developed. To explain the nature of conceptual models and describe the function and characteristics of this type of model we shall introduce a case study of conceptual modes developed by the structural anthropologist, Lévi-Strauss.[11] This will be given along with three areas of discussion on linguistics, semiology and structural anthropology, and semiotics.

a. Linguistic

While Lévi-Strauss uses language as a key to the structure of the mind and an understanding of a given culture, Chomsky on the other hand thinks "linguistics is simply a part of human psychology: the field that seeks to determine the nature of human mental capacities and to study how these capacities are put to work."[12]

Chomsky suggests, "Each of us has mastered and internally represented a system of grammar that assigns structural descriptions to these sentences; we use this knowledge, totally without awareness or even the possibility of awareness, in producing these sentences or understanding them when they are produced by others."[13]

In environmental communication, the designer organizes the space and the masses (forms) so that they relate to the world of events-patterns (functions), as well as to the world of ideas (associations), and vice versa. In linguistics, a theory of grammar plays a role where "The specific concern of a grammarian is to determine the nature of the abstract connecting link between the world of sounds and the world of ideas, . . ."[14]

Chomsky gives the following description of the theory of grammar which could be similarly used for architectural expression when sound and meaning is substituted for form and symbols. "A person who knows a language has mastered a system of rules that assigns sound and meaning in a definite way for an infinite class of possible sentences."[15]

Again, like architecture, we do not know what makes the human intelligence use language "as an instrument for the free expression of thought and feeling; or, for that matter what qualities of mind are involved in the creative acts of intelligence that are characteristic not unique and exceptional, in a truly human existence."[16]

In this respect, linguistic models are one of the closest models to architectural models in the following ways:

1. Like architecture, they are tied to the subconscious, as well as conscious structure of the mind.
2. Like architecture, they represent that unpredictable semi-random behavior of subconscious mind through the nonrational behavior of subconscious mind through the nonrational hidden dimensions of sociocultural values and systems.
3. Like architecture, they "may be regarded. . .either from the outward form or from the inner meaning." The "phonetic" like the material aspect of architecture (objects), describes the "outward form." "Sound psychology," like sociocultural psychology of form in architecture, describes the "inner meaning."
4. And, finally, both "should assist us in undertaking what is going on in the mind. . ."[17]

In designing an object one uses a similar process to that involved in speaking a language. In architecture, one chooses a material component and by matching this against the symbol system in his memory, one tries to communicate. In language, one selects sounds and meanings, and then uses them in certain structural contexts which reflect one's conscious-subconscious thought patterns which are affected by sociocultural, psychological, and biological determinant factors.

b. Semiology and Structural Anthropology

To describe the area of sign communication, Peirce and Margaret Mead use the word *semiotics,* whereas Saussure and Lévi-Strauss have used semiology. Others have used both without any restriction or limitation. Singer has tried to compare these similarities and differences in order to put some light on the general issue which I think is useful to mention here. Singer points out that although these disciplines might have common objectives, they vary in subject matter, methodology, practical issues, and epistemology. He argues that the subject of semiology is geared to the area of linguistics, whereas semiotics is geared to the area of the "formalized language of mathematics, logic and the natural sciences,. . .and nonverbal communication, . . ."[18] Semiology is "language centered," whereas semiotics emphasizes the "logic-centered process of communication by signs of all kinds."

"A Sign or Representamen, is a First which stands in such a genuine triadic relation to a Second, called its Object, as to be capable of determining a Third, called its *interpretant* to assume the same triadic relation to its Object in which it stands itself to the same Object."[19]

Singer further argues that "All knowledge of the internal world is derived from hypothetic inferences from knowledge of external facts."[20] Or in Peirce's words, "what passes within we only know as it is mirrored in external objects."

Becoming aware of an inner world is a developmental process derived from observation and experience of the external world and other people. "We first see blue and red things. It is quite a discovery when we find the eye has anything to do with them and a discovery still more recondite when we learn that there is an *ego* behind the eye, to which these qualities belong."[21]

To describe a general theory of signs and symbols, linguists try to go beyond the formalistic appearances of linguistic presentation to find the underlying structural properties of such symbolism in sociocultural communication systems. Lévi-Strauss, the founder of structural anthropology, and some other cultural anthropologists have tried to define culture as "systems of symbols and meanings." Lévi-Strauss uses the term semiology for such a discipline. He argues that structural anthropology seeks to analyze the structure of the mind. To analyze a given culture, a structural anthropologist such as Lévi-Strauss chooses to analyze the structure of the language; this language structure, he believes, is tied to the behavior of the subconscious mind. Thus knowing the structure of the language through the analysis of conceptual models is a key toward understanding the structure of that culture.

The aim of structural anthropology is an isolation and description of the conceptual models upon which members of a given culture operate. Observed material phenomena do not necessarily represent the culture of a given people for such phenomena are, in reality, merely the illusory reflections of the conceptual models through which experiences are perceived and interpreted. If such a conceptual model can be established for any given people, it should then be possible to predict actual behavorial responses by individuals of a community in response to events which occur. The establishment of this type of model is complicated by several factors. There must be a method for accurately perceiving and describing these models, as well as translating them without misrepresentation, into a language which can be analyzed by researchers. The primary obstacle to be overcome is the isolation of such models because they are "unconsciously structured" and, in most cases, unknown to the very people whose thoughts and actions are based upon them. Once models are isolated and described, Levi-Strauss attempts to compare the cultural systems of various societies on the basis of the content and organization of the models.

The basic assertion upon which structural anthropology operates is that conceptual schemes or models are established and maintained subject to modification, as a direct consequence of the workings of the intellect and the communication of ordered linguistic elements and their corresponding meanings among members of a community. These linguistic systems mediate, as well as place limits on, social phenomena. Observed behavior, events, and arrangements are indicative of usually unconscious models. This is analogous to an utterance which is an outward manifestation of an underlying grammar. Of course, just as a single utterance does not illuminate the total grammar from which it originates, a single behavioral response does not fully express the underlying cultural scheme. One methodological problem which must be accounted for is the possibility of a misrepresentation of a linguistic or cultural model brought about by an altered communication of a linguistic or social element. To isolate a community's conceptual model with validity, an anthropologist must learn through observing behavior (linguistic and social) what it is that the members of the group in question have learned in order to participate fully in their culture. Since it is the human mind which creates and projects these models, a perceptive observer with his mental processes can master another community's model. Actually it is the structure of the mind itself which is being sought. However, since the structure of the mind cannot be observed directly, recourse is taken to the outward manifestations of its structure. Linguistic behavior is chosen as the prime target of structural studies because, *like* all behavior, it is unconscious and, *unlike* all forms of behavior, in most societies it is completely unconscious. That is, there are fewer cases of folk explanations for, or contrived models of, linguistic behavior than there are for other types of social behavior.

The purpose of conceptual models—the structural method—is not only the discovery of structures. It aims at differentiating and relating levels of phenomena and comparing societies' models which are expressed in social interactions. In building environmental models, one could use the same method; that is, deal with the subconscious properties of human experience in environmental communication. Thus the idea of such models would be to explain the underlying structure of visual perception and communication through the subconscious mind.

Lévi-Strauss noted that several distinctions should be made in setting up a model of the type described above. First of all, relationships should be viewed in operational terms with a distinction made between observation and experimental levels. The reality of a model depends on more than the observation and construction of methodological procedures. Models should be experimented with in such a way that it can be ascertained how a model will be affected by changes and comparisons with other similar or dissimilar models.

The second distinction is that between consciousness and un-consciousness. Those social structures which are most deeply embedded in a cultural pattern are, more frequently, totally unconscious and therefore easier to get at, since folk theories or conceptual categories have not evolved to explain their existence. On the other hand, those patterns which are closer to the surface are usually found to be more difficult to ascertain because in most cases inaccurate explanations or rationalizations for them exist in the collective consciousness. Such conscious reasoning does not of course affect the nature of the model in question. It simply makes the discovery of them a more arduous task since folk explanations "are not intended to explain the phenomena but to perpetuate them. Therefore. . .the more difficult it becomes to reach it (the structural organization) because of the inaccurate conscious models lying across the path which leads to it."[22]

The last two distinctions have to do with mathematical tools. A relation between structure and measure cannot be presupposed. This is due to the fact that structural studies are a direct result of more recent mathematical developments which emphasize a qualitative, rather than quantitative approach, and thus these studies are not necessarily dependent on metrical instruments and techniques. These models are divided into two types, mechanical and statistical.

c. Semiotics

This area of study, whether it be called a discipline or approach, is widely varied in scope and orientation in various areas and thus one could place it anywhere in Morris's spectrum of communication types (from specific to general); i.e., linguistics, signs, and general communication.

Thomas Sebeok defines semiotics as "a science that studies all possible varieties of signs, the rules governing their generation and production, transmission and exchange, reception and interpretation."[23] He further outlines the two major aspects of semiotics as "communication and signification."

Of course signification could be both a conscious and sub-conscious act—conscious being, e.g., the design of traffic signs, subconscious being the employment of gestures in human communication when such signals are coded relative to a particular cultural pattern. In defining semiotics Umberto Eco states that signs which "have a process of communication between two human beings (or, perhaps, between two living beings in general) require the material presence of a certain object, be it an artifact or a natural event, which refers back to something that is not itself."[24]

Peirce defines signs as ". . .anything which is on the one hand so determined (or specialized) by an object and on the other hand so determines the mind of an interpreter of it that the later is thereby determined mediately, or indirectly, by that real object that determines the sign."[25]

In his theory of signs Charles Morris describes semiotics in behavioral terms where "something takes account of something else mediately." In this process the first thing is called the "interpretant," the second the "designatum," and the mediator the "sign vehicle."[26]

The questions as to whether semiology is a branch of linguistics; linguistics, a branch of semiotics; or semiology and communication, aspects of semiotics; or vice versa does not interest me. Furthermore, whether or not linguistics or semiotics is an aspect of "general psychology," logic, or "social anthropology" does not concern me.

History shows a constant birth and rebirth and disappearance or shift of emphasis on the focus of attention in areas of human knowledge and thus the formation of disciplines. To me the utmost important concern does not lie on the notion of where the boundaries of these disciplined are, but rather on where their focus is and on the nature and angles of their orientation on major issues, such as the qualitative aspect of aesthetic environment and its communication. The domain of the above-mentioned disciplines and their activities, as well as how each of their specific communication styles is defined, is no exception in historical courses of action.

The following differences could be used as criteria for such redefinition:

1. Differences in scope and domain—differences in adoption of more specialized or comprehensive concepts of communication. As an example, Alain Rey suggests "The idea of semiotics of expression might prove more fruitful, since 'expression' as a

pragmatic concept could divide the discipline with regard to the level of exchange (i.e., communication vs. expression)."[27]

2. Differences of discipline vs. approach. Linguistics or semiology—"the study of the communication of verbal messages"[28]—is a discipline which views man as a rational animal and deals with his language in logical terms. Semiotics—"the study of the communication of any messages"—encompassing linguistics, seems to have started as either a comprehensive discipline following linguistic principles dealing with the totality of sign systems or an approach leaning toward an interdisciplinary analysis of man's signified communication system. Discipline areas vary, including linguistics, logic, social anthropology, biology, genetics, psychology, and even zoo semiotics. Both Communication and Information theory—"the central position of communication rather than the sign"—were started by the physical sciences with a materialistic and mechanistic orientation. These principles have been used by quite a variety of disciplines, thus demonstrating the potential of becoming an interdisciplinary approach as well as remaining a material discipline. There is a considerably distance between communication as a discipline and potential comprehensive interdisciplinary general communication theory. Whereas a mechanistic discipline deals with *a priori* mathematical and material signal-message systems, this discipline, combined with Information theory as an interdisciplinary approach, could be seen as an objective system of the observation of similarities and differences in various subcomponents of the total cosmic system.

3. Differences of attitude and philosophical orientation, i.e., which of these views is geared to logical, rational processes and which tends to deal with the emotional, instinctive, nonrational feelings of man? This notion is critical because it is not known where a boundary between the two can be defined, both completely overlap, or both stay in separate parts in the activities of the human brain.

Based on whether we still consider the relatively unknown emotional feelings of man a mysterious part of his functions or consider them performing the same as the material part of man, though random and unexpected in behavioral patterns, we would have two distinct approaches similar to "functional linguistics vs.

Information theory" with which to deal. If symbolic meanings are nothing more than that which is added to the material world in order to make them more communicative and expressive, "semiosis" or "signification" is the means through which they can be understood. If meanings are inherent virtues instinctively carried by matter, irrelevant of by whom and how they are understood, communication is the way we should study them.

If the logic and rational behavior of man is the predominant activity, signification by set rules and conventions, and even the adaption of norms, is the way to make the world more meaningful. But if emotions, feelings, and instinctive mind are considered important, unknown irregularities of nonnormative potentialities of dispositional information carried by individualistic behavior of random pattern could be more sensitive to an unpreconceived world of meanings.

To these spectrums of dialectic paradigms let me add Peirce's view. "I doubt very much whether the Instinctive Mind could ever develop into a Rational Mind. I should expect the reverse process sooner. The Rational Mind is the Progressive Mind, and as such, by its very capacity for growth, seems more infantile than Instinctive Mind."[29]

Alain Rey takes no side in this argument by saying "It seems in fact impossible to accept a dichotomy in which 'the science of communication' and the 'science of signification'—whether called semiotics or something else—are two different intellectual activities, or even two separate methodological trends. If signification (or semiosis) has been the object of centuries of philosophical though and discourse, communication as a delimited concept is a new epistomological problem."[30]

In using any one of the above three classes of criteria for a subdivision of disciplines, I would personally lean toward use of the third category. This is because I do not think either the problem of scope or discipline vs. approach is as important as the problem of the focus of attention. What does matter is throwing light on the darkest part of human knowledge, and that is where the logical or rational and feelings or emotions come together; where the duality of human desires lies; and where the arts and sciences in the traditional sense come together. What I am actually advocating here is underlining the understanding of this duality of human nature by redrawing a line under the historical subdivision.

To finalize the discussion I would say semiotics has greater pragmatic advantages to a broad view of communication, whereas communication has the advantage of being a unifying comprehensive framework. This is in tune with Morris's idea of both when he defines scopes of communication (linguistics, semiotics and communication) and their relative practicality. Relative to the former, Morris calls Peirce's semiotics "pragmatic semiotics." He specifies how this pragmatism "has embedded semiotics in a theory of action or behavior. The relation of a sign to what is signified always involves the mediation of an interpretant, and an interpretant is an action or tendency to action of an organism."[31] Semiotics definitely is a subset of general communication, but due to its narrower scope semiotics has many more pragmatic and practical implications.

B. PHYSICAL MODELS

Physical modes (masses and voids) deal with potentialities of environmental physical forms due to their organizational structure—form—and material characteristics. These models only deal with the material environment surrounding man and not man himself. The total spatial experience of man is a twofold interaction between man and his surrounding environment which can be seen in comprehensive environmental communication models which also deal with the nonphysical aspects of man's experiences—a highly unpredictable pattern which is partly ordered subconsciously.

This model is not intended to demonstrate the architectural characteristics of either masses or space. It is merely supposed to help point out the *a priori* attributes of physical entities in forming a shape, and to illustrate the potential of a point (or points) due to its relation to the whole. In other words, this model is intended to help us recognize, the *potential* of *physical forms*, not that potential which we think they possess or want them to possess, but rather the potential they themselves have or ought to have due to the nature of physical substances and their structure. Thus what we are dealing with is what a physical set of matter actually "wants to be."

Physical modes are classified into the two following groups:

a. tangible (masses)
b. intangible (voids)

Both types are closely integrated to the extent that each makes the other: space is created and defined by masses, and masses are what they are and how they are because of the voids.

a. Models of Tangible Entities (Masses as a Special Case). A tank is set up (Figs. 3–4.a and 3–4.b) with *ABC* and *DEF* representing two walls enclosing space *S*. The physical character of space *S* can now be analyzed due to the nature of the equipotential and field lines within space *S*.

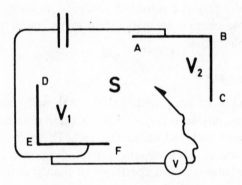

Figure 3–4a
Electromagnetic Tank

The model reflects the most general case when each point of ABC and DEF (thus space *S*) has a specific potential which is due to the two factors of atomism and structuralism (elements and the structure-linkage systems between the elements). This is due first to the nature of each point, and secondly to its relation to the structure and order of the total points involved in the set. A visual example of the first case is a room covered with a set (*N*) of squares of colored ceramic tiles (blue, black, red, and yellow). The ceramic tile *X* at point *A* of the set has a potential *K* depending first on the nature of *n* (the number of blue ceramic tiles in the set), as well as *N*, since *A* is the only blue tile in the room. (The rest are accounted for by 20 red, 5 black and 3 yellow tiles, all

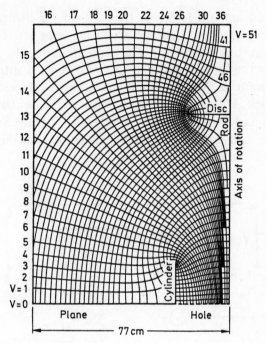

Figure 3–4b
Electrostatic Field in a Transformer Tank

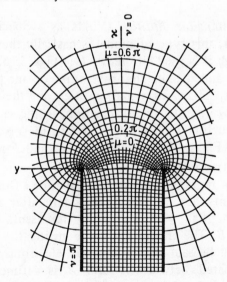

Figure 3–4c
Fields Between Transmission Line Conductors

equal to 100 and randomly distributed on the assumption that other variables such as light and so on are kept at a constant for all points in this example.) The potential of tile X depends secondly on the location of A in the set (which is different from any other point in the set). A visual example of the second case is that in which ABC and DEF each have one potential for all of their points and the potential of each point of space S is only due to the form, and not to each individual point. (All the points are colorless and undifferentiated.)

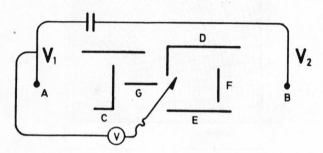

Figure 3–5a

Electromagnetic Tank

b. Models of Intangible Entities (Voids as a Special Case). As explained earlier, this type of model is basically the same as the first type, though it is used differently (see Figs. 3–5. a & b). The conductors V_1 and V_2 in the first type of model represent tangible (or, in special cases, visual) entities, and their potential is intended to show its order or organization. In the second type of model the conductors V_1 and V_2 illustrate the observer at two different times (Fig. 3–5.b) when C, D, E, and F represent the tangible entities (masses).

Conductor V_1 represents observer X at time t (his state now) and V_2 represents him at $t + n$ this state after reaching his destination), Potential, $V = V_1 - V_2$ represents the tension between A and B. The greater the V the greater the tension and vice versa. It can be said that whereas in electromagnetics ($V = IR$) tension created between A and B is a function of the resistivity of the path AB and the velocity of X going from A to B, resistivity can be thought of as the degree of X's involvement in

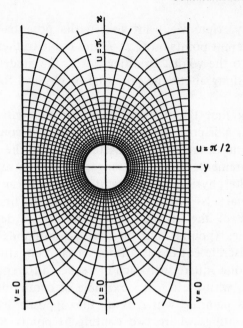

Figure 3–5b

Field Waves Between Parallel Conductors

his surroundings on path AB; or in other words, the degree of attraction power of X's surroundings while moving from A to B. The greater the degree of rigidity of the path and observer X, or in other words, the less the degree of their fluidity and resistance, the easier it is for X to go from A to B and vice versa.

We set up the model with an arbitrary potential between A and B depending on how we want the nature of movement from A to B to be. For example, if the path is meant to be a "connector" I should be greater and R should be smaller than when it is meant to be "shelter," because in the first case AB's function is only to transfer X from A to B, whereas the task of shelter is to transfer A to B, as well as additional activities which should take place along AB. The character of equipotential and field lines is a function of V or I and R.

Again, we do not expect the model to show *how* the observer is moving from A to B (his complete experience). This will be seen in comprehensive environmental communication models which also deal with a highly unpredictable pattern which is partly ordered subconsciously. Here we want to see the potential of physical form and different points on C, D, E and F due to their disposition and relation to the whole. In other words, the model is supposed to state something about the potential of physical forms and not man.

Considering that the physical environment consists of space-time events or a disposition of sets of matter, and considering that the fluidity and discreteness of matter is due to the criteria used for its measurement, there is a range of possible sets of matter which form the physical environment. These sets can be classified into two general sets—discrete and continuous; the first of which is a special case of the second. In this model we deal first with discrete entities (points) and then with continuous entities. An example of discrete entities is a floor mosaic consisting of a set of n squares of one square inch each in a set of different colors (red, yellow, black, white, etc.). An example of continuous entities is the case of a painting which is at the opposite extreme from pointilistic paintings where two contingent points can hardly be distinguished. In our studies, especially in the case of experimental studies, we treat our models as if they were sets of discrete points.

Although architectural space as a physical manifestation of human behavior, psychological context, and socionatural interactions is an end in the creation of the physical environment, in concrete terms, it is produced as a by-product of its tangible boundaries; i.e., walls, floors, ceilings, and objects. In order for such spatial forms and patterns to follow their above—mentioned content performance, they ought to be fluid, continuous, containing the same structural characteristics. If we look at most of today's architecture, we see that this is not the case. Most architectural spaces are produced in the manner of box shapes and with angles. Do any of the above-mentioned intangible elements withhold such angular properties? In corridors, rooms, and square and rectangular shapes do we use the corners? The answer to these questions is, No. The way we functionally use these shapes is as drawn in fig. 3–5.c. If we are walking along the walls of a corridor, as in the case of ADC, we eliminate the corner, and in the case of DEF we make a smooth curve eliminating part of the space between the curve and the corner.

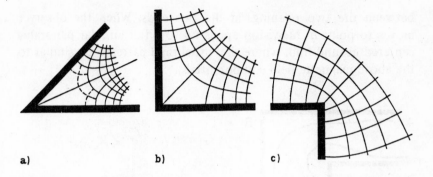

Figure 3–5c
Field Near Conducting Corners

The question then is, Do we go back in history and look for the origin of such angular architecture to see whether it was imposed on man because of his incapability of making the needed form? I would claim that this is true. The structural notion of post and beam and also its past evolutionary process since the stone age manual habitats resulted from man's technological handicaps in building the forms and shapes needed to manifest human behavior and sociopsychological patterns.

Today when the capabilities of construction technology has tremendously improved since the stone or post and beam construction methods, we can ask this fundamental question regarding conventional grid box shape architecture.

The notions of field concept developed by the physical sciences in the early 20th century have been widely used by various disciplines, including psychology, political science, anthropology, economics, ecology, etc. In architecture, a few people have mentioned this notion, however it has not been fully utilized.

Comparing some pattern representations of magnetic fields with those of man's sociopsychological behavior, we find quite a lot of similarities (fig. 3–5.d).

The magnetic field having resulted between two parallel slabs (fig. 3–5.d) and a visual field experience having resulted in a similar corridor shape seem to be basically the same. For an observer at point *A*, within the confined corridor, visual fields result from the interaction between rays of light bouncing between the textural patterns of the two surface walls, as well as between the two openings at the two ends. When the observer moves to point *B*, his vision opens up to a full circular panorama centered around him, where the visual field patterns are similar to the above magnetic field equipotentials.

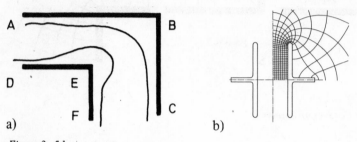

Figure 3—5d
Concentration and Expansion of Fields

It seems to me that animals, in responding to their instincts, have created many more meaningful shapes for their habitations. Man has used linear pieces of wood and created angular shapes irrespective of his needs, whereas a bird uses the same linear pieces of wood but puts them together in a manner which gives him a curvalinear, round form relevant to his body form.

Is it that we have lost our end during this process because of either the incapabilities of our means or because our intellect has been trapped by triggering problems created by such incapabilities, i.e, we still spend all of our energy trying to solve structural problems related to the post and beam system and try to increase the magnitudes of such spans rather than, once in a while, questioning the whole thing and its alternative substitutions.

When you look at Gandi's work you can see that he is definitely not caught in such a trap. Although he is not looking for new structural means to develop new architectural spaces, he is responding to his inspirations, human instinct, and feelings. He creates spaces that are definitely not victims of the means of structural and material circumstances. His spaces are angleless, fluid, continuous, dynamic, and organic. Structural and mechanical components as a means of providing this envelope for human spatial experience are hidden behind the envelope.

Although I very much admire what Gandi has done, it is nevertheless not exactly what I am advocating. He used construction technologies of the past. Thus in most cases, the pattern of the structural system and the envelope do not quite correspond to each other. Hence he sacrifices the means for the end, whereas the means and the end should be totally one. However I am looking for a new structural system capable of folding, curving, and undulating to whatever form we want it to, to give all the freedom needed to create Gandi's spatial envelope, within the envelope itself, rather than hide the structural system behind the envelope. If the laws of the universe are constant, irrespective of material changes, the structure or order of mass and void or tangible and intangible properties of the environment should follow the same order; i.e., the geometry of intangible fluid space and tangible hard masses should follow the same order.

Although man at this time has not yet been able to create methods and techniques, as well as necessary materials, to enable him to make "fluid mass," he has gone far ahead in that direction.

Louis Kahn's observations when he talks about the significance of the angles in a square space are to be noted here. He says that corners of a square carry powerful attributes. I agree with him, but actually I think it is the power of the taio or the power of "not to be" equal to the power of "to be," i.e., what Kahn is actually doing in his design is eliminating them by making them so important. He locates the entries to these square spaces at the corners and thus eliminates them in eliminating the corners. Since the two lines of a cornerless angle lead to an imaginable point and angle, the absent corner carries the power of the point of the angle as if it were there.

C. COMMUNICATION MODELS

We illustrated two types of models which represent two types of situations; namely, conceptual and physical models. Whereas *conceptual* models deal with normative social theory and with "appearances" (in Locke's theory) or with attitudinal characteristics (in Parson's theory), *physical* models deal with theories of the natural and physical sciences and with "real" things (in Locke's theory) or with biophysical objects (in Parson's theory).

Communication models, on the other hand, are both physical and conceptual; they deal both with man and his world. The concept of communication was first developed in the physical sciences and its channels were solely mechanistic. Soon the same concepts were widely used for human communication as well. Although communication models deal with both man and his environment, they are not yet comprehensive enough to be used as environmental communication models.

Before we deal with environmental communication models, we shall review some of these models.

To review schematically some basic attitudes of a few major communication models, we follow C. D. Mortensen's description. He defines communication models and their place in human activities as follows: "Man's need to create images of his experiences is ineradicable; and, after defining in personal terms, he wants to share them with others." Some of these images are "idealized models designed to make abstract experience concrete and meaningful to others." He further states that, generally speaking, "A model is a systematic representation of an object or events in idealized and abstract form."[32] When one abstracts in using models, nonessential substances are subtracted or eliminated so that attention can be focused on important elements that are needed to get a point across. Models are one way of gaining general perspective, specific insight into a particular subject matter. Models provide an opportunity to make practical application, to serve as a "tooling-up" exercise for more advanced topics, to grasp the complexity of forces at work in even the simplest act of communication and to gain an appreciation for the theoretical organization which governs the conduct of communicative research.

Claude Shannon conceived of a communication model as a system made up of five necessary functions for the transmission of information: "(1) A *source* generates one signal from a number of alternative possibilities. The signal is then traced from a (2) transmitter through a (3) *channel* to some (4) *receiver*, where the transmitted signal was reconnected into its original form for its (5) destination."[33]

Shannon further defines the concept of *message* as any "input" to the transmitter and *noise* as any "distracting disturbances" which occur in the channel during the process. As an example, the words of one speaker are picked and encoded by the transmitter into a channel, received from the channel, and then decoded by the receiver into words to the listener. Later Shannon added a mechanism in the receiver which checked the signals from the transmitter against the received signal; this monitoring or correcting mechanism was the beginning of what later was defined as the concept of feedback, or information, which a communicator receives from others in reference to his own signals. Many behavioralists adapted this mathematical communications signal to countless interpersonal situations.

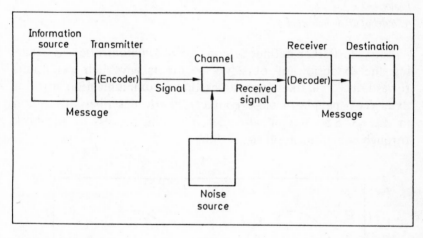

Figure 3–6
Information Processing Model

Wilber Schramm altered Shannon and Weaver's mathematical model. "He conceived of *decoding* and *encoding* as activities maintained simultaneously by sender and receiver; he also made provisions for a two-way interchange of messages"[34] (figure 3–7).

There are strong logical grounds for examining an alternative design. One is the immediate need to guard against oversimplification, a confusion of models with reality, and premature boundaries.

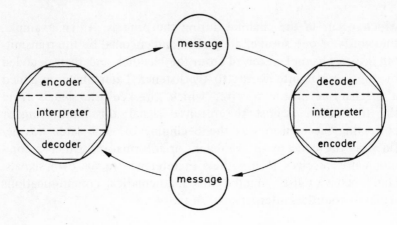

Figure 3–7
A Model of Communication

Larry L. Barker defines *interpersonal communication* as "snaring the extension of ourselves to others and their extensions toward us."[35] Barker also states that "Communication involves dyad (two people in close contact)."[36] He describes this action in fig. 3–8.a. Barker also describes the process of feedback through communication fig. 3–8.b.

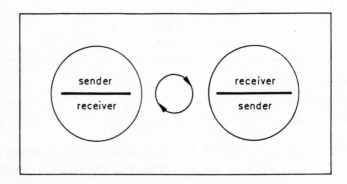

Figure 3–8a

Self-Feedback and Listener Feedback Models

In this model Barker shows the relationship of self-feedback and listener feedback, where self-feedback applies to the words and actions that are fed back into your nervous system as you

perceive your own muscular movements and hear yourself speak.
Listener feedback involves verbal and nonverbal responses.

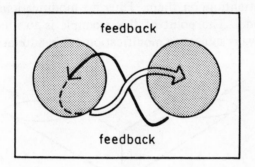

Figure 3–8b

Self-Feedback and Listener Feedback Models

T. M. Newcomb developed a conceptual model of communication between two individuals (*A* and *B*) with regards to some
object or situation (*X*).
"He asserted that the affect on B of receiving messages from A
about X could be explained by four types of variables.
1. B's attitude toward A: (BaA)
2. B's attitude toward X: (BaX)
3. B's belief about A: (BbA)
4. B's belief about X: (BbX)"[37]
Newcomb's model was used in two ways. First of all, the
model includes all participation interaction, i.e., the "conflict"
behavior of each participant. Secondly, the model uses *X* as the
environmental in which *A* and *B* interact—"a conflict-cooperation
game."
James R. Emshoff used this model as the basis for an initial
assumption: "In an interactive situation (involving either cooperation or conflict), the behavior of each participant could
be explained by analyzing his attitudes toward, and beliefs about,
the other participant and the conflict situation."[38]
If a given model does not effectively communicate what it
was intended to, it can be altered or abandoned, or useful features
can be incorporated into another model. An example would be
Broadbent's elegantly simple model of human attention. Con-

sequently investigations of this model uncovered evidence that under certain circumstances people seemed to recognize items that had been ignored, even when they were not directly placing their attention on them. Thus no modifications were made on the model. The point of this example is to illustrate that a model is always subject to modification or abandonment.

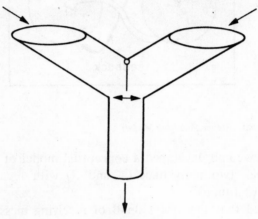

Figure 3–9
A Model of Human Attention

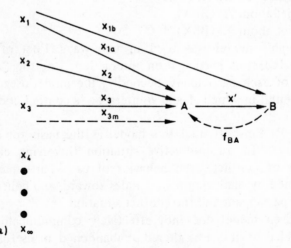

Figure 3–10a
A Verbal Communication Model

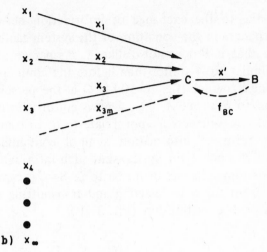

Figure 3—10b
A Verbal Communication Model

Broadbent used his Y-shaped tube to represent *human attention*. The design of the tube is such that when two balls were placed in two branches at the top, only one ball at a time could pass downward through the main passageway. If the two reached the main passage at the same time they would jam, and neither would pass through. Broadbent likened "this jamming process to what happened when two bits of information reached the human sensory system simultaneously."[39] This model brought on a great deal of controversy. (Fig. 3—9)

Verbal communication between two persons is a process in which the return or feedback plays an important role because it tells us how our messages are interpreted. (See fig. 3—10.a and fig. 3—10.b and 3—10.c)

In the following models, Westley and MacLean[40] presented interpersonal communication ranging from simple face-to-face to indirect communication in which all the communicative parties are not present, to complicated mass media communication. Their models deal with communicative behaviors in idealized form and differentiate between mass and face-to-face communication.

In the first version of the model (fig. 3—10.a), *A* communicates to *B* about *X*, as, for example, in a gossip situation. In such a situation, due to the exchange of information between parties involved, changes in the condition of the system can be expected. Let us say that if B does not dislike A, B's perception of X will be more similar to A's after than before the communicative act.

In the next model (fig. 3–10.b), C is the person who gives information to B about A, e.g., a news editor who can a) select the news of issues-objects X appropriate to B, b) transform them into some form of information symbol containing meanings shared with B, and c) finally transmit such information symbols by means of some channel or media to B. So C is capable of serving as an agent for B in selecting and transmitting information about an X or A-X relationship. (Fig. 3–10.c)

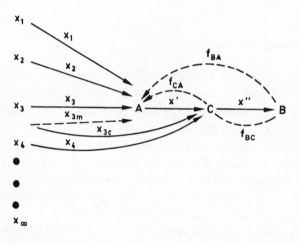

Figure 3–10c

A Verbal Communication Model

The concept of communication–adapted to any situation–implies active participation on the part of all entities involved; i.e., even the indifferent listener gives signals as his reaction to the communication situation. Since in human interactions the sender and receiver get involved, they designate particular communicative *functions* which are different from stated *entities.* In this regard then our models must account for the reciprocal aspects of communication. They are best represented by nonlinear models discussed by F.E. Dance who proposes an alternative to linear models. He suggests that communication is a dynamic process in the form of a *helix* (fig. 3—11). The helix shows how communication evolves in a person from his birth to the existing moment. In other words, "the helix implies that communication is continuous, unrepeatable, addictive and accumulative; that is, each phase of activity depends upon present forces at work as they are defined by all that has occurred before."[41]

Everything in past experience contributes to the formation of the unfolding moment. There cannot be found any break in the continuity of any action, nor can any fixed beginning or end or redundancy be found.

The helix underscores the integrated continuity and unity of aspects of all human communication as an evolving process permitting growth, changes, and discovery.

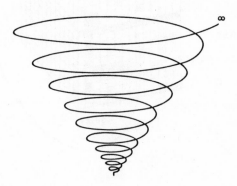

Figure 3—11

Helical Spiral, Nonlinear Models of Human Communication

A *mosaic model* takes into consideration all the composite sets of messages as they interact over time and across various situations. Becker (fig. 3—12) has developed a fascinating analogy called the "communication mosaic." He assumes that "most communicative acts link message elements from more than one situation."[42] Becker likens complex communicative events to the activity of a receiver who moves through constant changing cubes or mosaics of information.

A risk of regarding communication in abstract and idealized terms is that we somehow come to think of it as a singular or "pure" process; a "thing" devoid of particular context and background. Though much is to be gained by a scrupulous use of abstractions, we must always relate the tools of the abstracting process —symbols, arrows, cubes and the like—to particular types of social situations and to concrete classes of behavior. Furthermore, a communicative act functions always in the particular and the concrete.

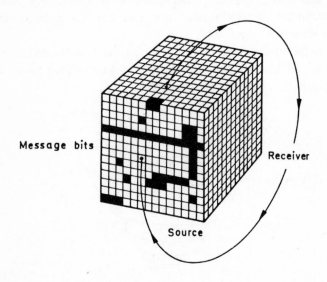

Figure 3–12

Mosaic Model of Communication

A *functional model*[43] conceived by Ruesch and Bateson expresses communication as a simultaneous function at four levels of analysis: (1) intrapersonal, (2) interpersonal, (3) group interaction, and (4) cultural level. Moreover each level consists of activities divided into four functions: (1) evaluating, (2) sending, (3) receiving, and (4) channeling (fig. 3–13).

Transactional models are the most systematic functional models developed by D. C. Barnlund (fig. 3–14). In this model he viewed communication as "transactions in which communicators attribute meaning to events in ways that are dynamic, continuous, circular,

unrepeatable, irreversible, and complex."[44] Barnlund translated his
assumptions into two models. The first model deals with intrapersonal communication, and the second model with interpersonal
communication. Because of similarities in the two models, we shall
just explain the first one. In this model the use of curved lines
particularly underscores the "unrepeatable," "irreversible" relation between encoding and decoding or, in other words, the
absence of any direct linear relationship between the person and
his physical environment.

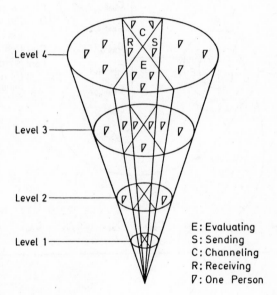

Level 4

Level 3

Level 2

Level 1

E: Evaluating
S: Sending
C: Channeling
R: Receiving
Ⅴ: One Person

Figure 3–13

Functional Model of Communication

D. COMPOSED MODELS (PHYSICAL, NONPHYSICAL)

The models involve two aspects of reality; one is the objective
reality (ordered and seen through the conscious mind) studied
from the outside; and the other is the "supernatural" reality
(ordered-disordered pattern seen through conscious-subconscious
mind) with which man and his society order themselves. Moreover,
each society is composed of a network of interdependent "orders"
of relationships between persons, objects, and persons and objects.

However, in analyzing these orders, the observer must be careful to see how much correlation exists between the way a society consciously and subconsciously perceives its orders and the way these orders do indeed conform to reality.

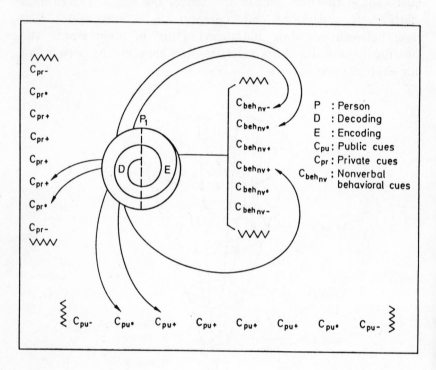

Figure 3–14

Transactional Model of Communication

Having the results of the two types of models (conceptual and physical), the next step in the development of environmental modes is to combine and alter, if necessary, these various results represented in different models. To do so, we use a rationale opposite to Northrop's theory; i.e., we work with physical models representing the natural and physical world, dealing with "real things," "appearances" or biophysical objects. Then we bring in the results of conceptual studies represented in normative social theories.

In other words, we are adapting the combined physical models to the outputs of the sociopsychological data by assigning potentials to their entities; or as Parsons might say, we have the biological objects, the cause of action and behavior of which is attitudinal. That is, in this theory biological objects are treated as physical and the attitudinal are treated as nonphysical. So first we shall see what a combined physical model is and then bring into it the nonphysical (sociocultural) elements. In doing so we can say we have come close to Northrop's point of view of regarding normative social theory: we have defined our social theories and tested them against physical and natural principles for verification. Hence the first step is to combine the two physical models and see the pattern obtained due to the tangible field created by the masses (first model). As well as the intangible fields created by spatial cavities (second model). This will then be added to the third pattern obtained through conceptual models. Thus we draw the field pattern obtained in both bases (1 and 2) in a single plan. These patterns can be analyzed as representing a dynamic field obtained due to the physical forms of environment. Now, the result of conceptual models or the contributions by psychologists, anthropologists, and sociologists on the nature of man (P) can be added to the model resulting from the combination of one and two to more fully complete our search for understanding the nature of environmental communication fields of "pattern of stimuli" or behavior (B) as a function of a person (P) and his environment (E).

Kurt Lewin[43] has explained man's behavior as a function of $P + E$ in the equation:

$$B = F(P, E)$$

3.3 Geometry of Communications Field-Space

At this point it would be worthwhile to consider Reichenbach's analogy of the relativity of geometry and the influence of causality in order to see the extent to which we have control over the environment or, in other words, the degree of our uncertainty in regard to our conception of nature. Before we look at Reichenbach's view on this point, let us elaborate on a comparison of the physical and nonphysical models. A clearer way to explain what we have already discussed is to say that we are following Locke and Descarte's philosophy of "material substances" which are "located in public mathematical space and which act upon observers who project back colors and sounds in sensed space and time as appearances where "both nature and man is to be understood as an aggregate of physical objects. . . ."[46] The point at which we diverge from Locke and Descartes is when we treat both the primary and secondary ("reality" and "appearances") qualities of nature as equally important. This is where Whitehead departs when he rejects the theory of the bifurcation of nature: "There is but one nature, namely apparent nature, and atoms and others are merely names for logical terms in conceptual formulae of calculation."[47] In addition, instead of having a double standard, we substitute "secondary" qualities (investigated through conceptual models) for their equivalent (artificially reached by experiment) potential energies.

Going back to our discussion of the formula $B = F(P,E)$ we note that Reichenbach says that experience in space can be explained as $G_o + F + A$ where G_o is Euclidean geometry, F is universal force and A is causal anomaly. In reference to causality he says that "The interdependence of all events at corresponding points cannot be interpreted as ordinary causality, because it does not require time or transference and does not spread as a continuous effect that must pass consecutively through the intermediate points."[48] Reichenbach says that it does not matter which geometry one perceives as nature, as long as one is aware of the artificial nature of G in regard to F and A. Now putting aside the notion of causality and only dealing with G and F, he says. "It is a mistake to say that Euclidean geometry is 'more true' than Einstein's geometry or vice versa, because it leads to simpler material relations."[49] It is simpler only because in the above formula $F = C$, "we deal with a less complex relationship. However, simplicity is not a criterion for truth."[50] Thus "it is meaningless to speak about any geometry as the *true* geometry."[51] We can only speak about any geometry G wherein we know the nature of the universal field of force F. Now if the nature of things is equal to $G + F$, when universal force $F = O$, then G is physical reality. Suppose F is defined through experimental measurement. Then "the visual *a priori*" $G = G_o$. In regard to the notion expressed earlier that geometry is simpler and the question of what the simplest form of $F = G$ is, Reichenbach states that "physics is not concerned with the question which *geometry* is simpler, but with the question which *coordinative definition* is simpler."[52] They chose the case where $F = O$ so that they only have to deal with G, i.e. $G + F$, $G + O$. Of course they cannot do away with F. They use it in choosing their hypothesis.

On the basis of this theory, Professor McCleary defines the problem of architecture as dealing, on the one hand, with the *a priori* and intuition ($G = G_o$) and, on the other hand, with "appropriate" coordinative definitions ($F =$ "some value") where $G_o =$ intuition and $F =$ visualization.[53] He mentions Corbusier's modular theory as such visualization F and states that this visualization has a subjective ground; i.e., the choice of coordinative definitions is due to the individual creator.

Consequently, in keeping with the above discussion, we can compose the physical and nonphysical aspects of the environment into one system by taking into consideration Locke's and Descartes' theories of material substances, Northrop's normative social theory, Parson's theory of action, Lévi-Strauss' structuralism, and Edward Hall's theory of man's patterns of behavior in relation to spatial factors. It is clear that the scope of entities with which normative social theory deals (before they are verified by the natural and physical sciences) is larger than Locke's materialistic scope. This means that if $N =$ the scope of the set of normative social theory before its verification by the natural and physical sciences, and M equals the set of theory of material substances, then MN.

To find a methodology for the composition of the material and nonmaterial aspects of the environment, we consider Northrop's theory and note "the role of the deductive method in deductively formulated scientific theory, which exhibits itself both in the verified theory of natural science and in the normative theory of social science. Any deductive theory analyzes into its primitive concepts and basic postulates or assumptions. By making these

primitive conceptions and postulates identical in both the normative theory of social science and the factual which is different
from factual social theory. . ."[54]

Suppose N^1 *is the set of normative social theory* after its
verification by the natural and physical sciences. Considering levels
of cognition and abstraction in the two theories, here $(M = N^1)$ is
where the boundary between the theories of the two are identical-
ly defined. We stated that it is logical to follow Northrop's theory
and check N against M and get N^1. This is our answer—the
normative social theory. But such a process is too complicated for
our purpose. What we may do as architects is go the other way
around. That is, instead of spending a long time working with N
and checking it against M we can start with M always being sure to
keep in touch with N. That is, we can work with natural and
physical theories (which are more capable of direct measurement)
all the way through the process and bring sociopsychological
theories into it.

An environmental communication field representing such an
approach can be analyzed in two ways: in "atomism" where the
emphasis is on the reduction of complexity to finite units, and in
"structuralism" where the emphasis is on the structure and
interrelation of the elements and the process. Lancelot Whyte sees
the natural philosophy of form through the "anthesis of atomism
and form." The term atomism implies "analysis, logical precision,
and quantitative accuracy. *Reduce everything to discrete unit
factors, and investigate their properties*! This is the only systematic procedure for advance yet invented, though it often leads to the
neglect of order and it does not always work." Form or structuralism "honors the integral object, the entire character of anything,
either seen from outside or still forming in our own minds.
Respond to form, and neglect analysis!"[55]

3.4 Advantages and Disadvantages of Models

One advantage of a model is the ease with which it handles a
multitude of variables, and relates their effects upon each other in

highly complicated ways that preserve the integrity of events under study. To this must be added the heuristic or classifying advantage of the model.

The design of a model is forced to identify variables and relate them with a precision that is impossible for the writer to achieve because of the stylistic demands of effective writing. Also, one of the considerations that must be taken involves the advantages of the compact nature of the model. Short of a mathematical equation, it is the most cryptic form in which a theoretical position can be communicated.

Many critics charge that models tend to invite oversimplified ways of conceiving problems. Critics also charge that model builders see human beings mechanically. However the act of over simplification can be avoided by recognizing the fundamental distinction between simplification and over simplification; models do simplify. If the essential attributes or particulars of an event are included, then the simpler of two interpretations is superior. Simplification is inherent in the act of abstraction. Most criticism could be the result of the tendency to read more into a model than what is there, and tacitly to associate the form of representation with the totality of the event being modeled.

In relation to simplification and/or over simplification of models, Kaplan noted, "Science always simplifies; its aim is not to reproduce the reality in all its complexity, but only to formulate what is essential for understanding, prediction or control. That a model is simpler than the subject-matter being inquied into is as much a virtue as a fault, and is, in any case, inevitable."[56] The main objective of a model is to simplify. The model designer may escape the risks of oversimplification and map reading and still fall prey to dangers inherent in abstraction. To press for closure is to strive for a sense of completion in a system. The very nature of a model imposes a definition of boundaries because of the way it includes some factors while ruling out others as extraneous. So while the process of abstraction may bring a complex event into manageable propositions, this may be a liability. Since the danger of premature boundaries is not generally due to the fallibilities of thought, there are no hard and fast rules for minimizing the problem. One can reduce the hazards by recognizing that physical reality can be represented in a number of ways.

Another factor that can propose problems is that models are sophisticated versions of scientific analogies (they compare two things in principle only). A model must eliminate the aspects that are noncomparable and possibly distracting, so that one can relate to the essence of the behavior under study. In essence, a model simply posits that in certain ways, not totally, the object or concept being modeled acts "like this."

Another criticism of models is that they tend to be readily confused with reality. A model represents a process of reality, but it does not *constitute* the process; a model is not a literal description of reality. The model-reality problem is largely due to faulty interpretation and not to any inherent liabilities of models.

ADVANTAGES OF ENVIRONMENTAL COMMUNICATION MODELS

The reason for taking this approach—namely, architecture as environmental communication—is to come up with some theories regarding the totality of man's environment; that is to say, to study environmental communication as man's relation to man, his society, and the environment. In using "communication approach," theories developed in that field are not used, but rather an attitude is initiated that seeks to understand man not as an outsider in the midst of the physical environment, but as an integral, inseparable part of the environment. The field communication or system's approach to architecture is applied here in order to see architecture as an integrated set of interrelationships of all interdependent components of a common field, whether physical or nonphysical components, tangible solids or intangible voids, or psychological or social entities. Field communication's approach to environmental design and planning also necessitates that the environment be dealt with in a dynamic and constantly-evolving fashion rather than a static closed system. Man and his activities are part of architectural environment, both influencing it and being influenced by its properties. The flow of various types of energy-information between man and his environment constantly reshapes and regenerates new energy-information.

Notes to chapter three

1. Wilbur Schramm, "How Communication Works," in *Basic Reading in Communication Theory*, by C. David Mortensen, Harper & Row, Publishers, New York, 1973, p. 28.
2. C.D. Mortensen, *Basic Reading in Communication Theory*, p. 31.
3. Quoted by W. Schramm in "How Communication Works," pp. 28-36.
4. Edward T. Hall, *The Hidden Dimension* (Garden City, N.Y.: Doubleday and Co., 1969).
5. *Ibid.*
6. C.D. Mortensen, *Communication: the Study of Human Interaction*, McGraw Hill Book Co., 1972, p. 58.
7. *Ibid.*, p. 38.
8. *Ibid.*
9. *Ibid.*, p. 30.
10. *Ibid.*, p. 31.
11. C. Lévi-Strauss, *Structural Anthropology*, Doubleday & Co., New York 1963.
12. Noam Chomsky, "Form and Meaning in Natural Languages," in *Language and Mind*, Harcourt, Brace & World, New York, 1968, p. 103.
13. *Ibid.*, p. 104.
14. Otto Jespersen, quoted by Chomsky in *Essays on Form and Interpretation*, Elsevier North-Holland, Inc., New York, 1977, p. 28.
15. N. Chomsky, "Form and Meaning in Natural Languages." p. 103.
16. *Ibid.*, p. 101.
17. O. Jespersen, quoted by Chomsky in *Essays on Form and Interpretation*, p. 25.
18. Milton Singer, "For a Semiotic Anthropology," in *Sight, Sound, and Sense*, ed. by Thomas Sebeok, Indiana Univ. Press, Bloomington & London, 1978, p. 214.
19. C.S. Peirce, quoted by M. Singer in *Sight, Sound, and Sense*, p. 217.
20. M. Singer, "For a Semiotic Anthropology," p. 220.
21. C. Peirce, quoted by Singer in "For a Semiotic Anthropology," p. 220.
22. C. Lévi-Strauss, "Social Structure," in *Structural Anthropology*, Doubleday & Co., Garden City, New York, 1963, pp. 273-274.
23. T. Sebeok, *Sight, Sound, and Sense*, p. viii.
24. Umberto Eco, "Semiotics: A discipline or an Interdisciplinary Method," in *Sight, Sound, and Sense*, p. 74.
25. C. Peirce, quoted by Max Fisch in "Peirce's General Theory of Signs," in *Sight, Sound, and Sense*, p. 55.
26. Charles Morris, quoted by Alain Rey in "Communication vs. Semiotics: Two Conceptions of Semiotics" in *Sight, Sound, and Sense*, p. 102.
27. A. Rey, "Communication vs. Semiotics: Two Conceptions of Semiotics" in *Sight, Sound, and Sense.* p. 101.
28. *Ibid.*, p. 99.
29. C. Peirce, quoted by Décio Pignatari in "The Contiguity Illusion" in *Sight, Sound, and Sense*, p. 86.
30. A. Rey, "Communication vs. Semiotics: Two Conceptions of Semiotics" in *Sight, Sound, and Sense*, p. 100.
31. C. Morris, quoted by M. Singer in "For a Semiotic Anthropology," p. 224.
32. C.D. Mortensen, *Basic Reading in Communication Theory*, p. 29.

33. C. Shannon & W. Weaver, *The Mathematical Theory of Communication,* University of Illinois Press, Urbana, Ill., 1964.
34. W. Schramm, "How Communication Works."
35. Larry L. Barker, *Communication,* pp. 138 & 61.
36. *Ibid.*
37. T. M. Newcomb, referred to by James R. Emshoff in *Analysis of Behavioral Systems,* Macmillan, New York, 1971, p. 86.
38. T.M. Newcomb, quoted by J. Emshoff in *Analysis of Behavioral Systems,* p. 80.
39. D.E. Broadbent, "A Mechanical Model for Human Attention and Immediate Memory," in *Psychological Review,* 1959, 64: 205-215.
40. B. Westley & M. MacLean, "A Conceptual Model for Communication Research," in *Journalism Quarterly,* 1957.
41. Frank E. Dance, "A Helical Model of Communication," in *Foundation of Communication Theory* ed. by Kenneth K. Sereno & C. David Mortensen Harper & Row, New York 1970, pp. 103-107.
42. S. Becker, referred to by C. Mortensen in *Basic Readings in Communication,* p. 47.
43. J. Ruesch and G. Bateson, *Communication: The Social Matrix of Psychiatry,* Norton, New York, 1951.
44. D. Barnlund, "A Transactional Model of Communication," *Foundations of Communication Theory,* pp. 83-102.
45. Kurt Lewin, *Field Theory in Social Science: Selected Theoretical Papers,* ed. Dorwin Cartwright, Harper & Row, New York 1951, p. 25. Hereafter cited as *Field Theory.*
46. F. Northrop, *The Logic of the Sciences and the Humanities,* World Publishing Co., Cleveland and New York, 1959, p. 350.
47. Alfred North Whitehead, *Concept of Nature,* Cambridge University Press, Cambridge, 1964, p. 45.
48. Hans Reichenbach, *The Philosophy of Space and Time,* Dover Publications, New York, 1958, p. 65.
49. *Ibid.,* p. 35.
50. *Ibid.,* p. 34.
51. *Ibid.,* p. 33.
52. *Ibid.,* p. 34.
53. Peter McCleary, unpublished notes.
54. F. Northrop, *The Logic of the Sciences and the Humanities,* p. 343.
55. L. Whyte, "Atomism, Structure and Form, a Report on the Natural Philosophy of Form," in *Structure in Art and in Science,* ed. by G. Kepes, p. 25.
56. Abraham Kaplan, *The Conduct of Inquiry,* Chandler Publishing Co., San Francisco, 1964.

4. Environment Field Information

4.0 Introduction–Abstract

In this chapter some reference material is produced. *Information theory* and *Field theory* and their application in the physical sciences and social sciences is introduced. Then the environment in its totality—physical and nonphysical—is viewed as a communication field. The designer's provision of a series of probabilistic patterns in his design is to help the observer resist and react to such patterns with curiosity. This can be interpreted as the designer's conformity with Information theory which postulates than the greater the probabilities resisted the more excitement to the experience.

The adaptation of concepts of Field theory to environmental communication in the second half of this chapter corresponds to a concern for the vitality, dynamics, and spontaneity of the environmental communication experience. The planning and design of any object-event is considered a change in some state of a field in a given unit of time. Any object or event within any environmental communication field is not considered an isolated element, but rather it is seen as tied to or reflecting total field structure and order. Furthermore, the designer's conformity with these ideas and his adaptation of Field theory to environmental communication enables him to search for harmony and unity through the fusion of environmental elements into a higher order of complexity by the reduction of space to field.

Finally in this chapter environmental field components—namely, psychological space and time, physical space and time, positive and negative, and qualitative and quantitative energies—are analyzed.

4.1 Information Theory

Information is defined as a measure of one's freedom of choice when selecting a message. It is based upon differences one sees in a given pattern. For example, as previously pointed out, if one has a pattern of black and white squares, and colors one square red, then the red square gives the most amount of information. It is the square that stands out. The higher the probability of occurrence, the lower the probability of information communicated. Thus if one has one hundred squares, ninety-nine black and one red, the probability of the occurrence of the red square is one/one hundred, which is less than the black squares. Therefore, the red square gives the most information.

A. CONCEPTS OF INFORMATION

Information in environmental communication consists of a series of alternating signals; rough and smooth, dark and light, large and small, etc.

In the broadest sense information can be defined as the context of any message sent from one source to another. It is from this definition that Information theory is developed. Information theory depends heavily on the use of the principles of probability. The basic content of measurement of information depends on the degree of uncertainty involved; the more uncertain the outcome of a message in a situation, the greater the amount of information carried. In other words, the greater accuracy with which the answer of a message can be predicted, the amount of information one receives is less and vice versa. Information is received where there is some doubt; doubt is accompanied by the existence of an alternative choice.[1] Information is a measure of the probabilistic occurrence of object-events. "Information is not just *any* combination of displaced mater, but those which are possible."[2]

The similarities and differences perceived in matter in the environment by man provide him with messages. The disposition of matter in space-time also creates changes which add new messages to the former ones. Such changes are the source to which the mind refers for its information.

Communication theory is specific in a sense because only the physical or material side of communication is consulted, concerning the nonmaterial side. For instance, in dealing with an act of speech, the words and their meanings are dismissed and only material aspects (movement of the lips, etc.) are considered.

Man's behavior is dealt with as one aspect of the environment and his behavior is conceived of materially by the receiver. In this theory everything is regarded as a change in states of matter.

To clarify the word *information,* we can first look at how it is used in Communication theory. As Weaver says, information "relates not so much to what you *do* say, as to what you *could* say. That is information is a measure of one's freedom of choice when one selects a message."[3] The question is not, "What sort of information?" but rather "How much information?"[4] As Weaver states, the most simplified situation is when one is to make a choice between two alternative messages, where one unit of information is involved. He also states that information, in contrast to meaning, is applied not to individual messages but rather to the whole situation. "The unit of information indicat(es) that in this situation one has an amount of freedom of choice, in selecting a message, which it is convenient to regard as a standard or unit amount."[5]

As stated previously, information is received where there is some doubt; doubt is accompanied by the existence of an alternative choice. "Discrimination is the simplest and most basic operation performable."[6] One's prediction of the location of specific matter and the occurrence of an event depends on the chaotic and orderly nature of the pattern. The higher the order of such patterns the higher the probability of prediction or understanding of the behavior of the matter. Thus both probability and the behavior of matter are essential. The amount of information from the source is equal to its probability.

If all notation in a pattern is the same, no information is gained. As soon as there is a difference, information is gained. Similarities create dullness and passiveness. No information is gained. The more frequently an object appears, less information is received. Repetition becomes monotonous.

A set of patterns in which sequences occur according to specific probabilities is termed a "stochastic process."[7] The special case in a stochastic process in which each situation depends on the previous situation is called *Markoff's chain*. Entropy is the key concept for meeting the requirements for setting up information. It is based on the degree of order of patterns and degree of their occurrence. It is expressed in terms of the various probabilities involved—those of getting to certain stages in the process of forming messages, and probabilities that, when in those stages, certain symbols are chosen next.

Information theory is so widely used by various fields that Tribus says "It is rather difficult to say where the field of information theory ends and other fields begin." He further argues that theory is used in the following three ways:

(a) as a criteria for the choice of probability distributions,

(b) to determine the degree of uncertainty about a proposition; and

(c) as a measure of the rate of information acquisition.[8]

It is obvious that Information theory covers all architectural subdisciplines.

B. INFORMATION PROCESSING SYSTEMS

Before I finish my discussion of Information theory, I also have to give a short description of information processing systems. This branch of science no doubt has greatly influenced the practicality and implementation of communication systems. The advances made in the development of computer sciences in recent years has been significantly influential in communication technology. They have gone so far as to challenge and duplicate a higher and higher percentage of human intelligence in what is called "artificial intelligence." No doubt such advances are first geared toward an understanding of how humans think. Toward this end, Allen Newell and Herbert Simon in their theory of human problem solving consider man to be an information processing system. They define a human being as "a system consisting of parts: sensory subsystems, memory, effectors, arousal subsystems, and so on."[9]

In considering human beings as processors of information, they assert that thinking can be explained by methods of information processing. To go toward the technical side it means that the computer and man could be metaphors for each other or man could be molded as a digital computer.

As is obvious the theory does away with generalities about human beings. However as a problem solving tool it gets into the practical matters of specific men doing specific "tasks." The early and best task-oriented works of the computer sciences have been generally centered around works such as chess and symbolic logic. Linguistic pattern recognition is part of the work building around artificial intelligence machines.

This is the way the theory is defined: "The theory posits a set of processes or mechanisms that produce the behavior of the thinking human. Thus, the theory is reductionistic; it does not simply provide a set of relations or laws about behavior from which one often concludes what behavior must be."[10]

An IPS is an information process system which has four components: (1) a memory containing symbol structures, (2) a processor, (3) effectors, and (4) receptors as shown in figure 4–1. To give a short description of information process system (IPS) it would probably be best to quote Newell and Simon as follows:

1. There is a set of elements, called "symbols."
2. A *"symbol structure"* consists of a set of *"tokens"* (equivalently, "instances," or "occurrences") of symbols connected by a set of *"relations."*
3. A *"memory"* is a component of an IPS capable of storing and retaining symbol structures.
4. An *"information process"* is a process that has symbol structures for (some of) its inputs or outputs.
5. A *"processor"* is a component of an IPS consisting of:
   (a) a (fixed) set of "elementary information processes" (eip's);
   (b) a "short-term memory" (STM) that holds the input and output symbol structures of the eip's;
   (c) an *"interpreter"* that determines the sequence of eip's to be executed by the IPS as a function of the symbol structures in STM.
6. A symbol structure "designates" (equivalently, "refers" or "points to") an object if there exist information processes that admit the symbol structure as input and either:
   (a) affect the object; or
   (b) produce, as output, symbol structures that depend on the object.

7. A symbol is a *"program"* if (a) the object it designates is an information process and (b) the interpreter, if given the program, can execute the designated process. (Literally this should read, "if given input that designates the program.")

8. A symbol is "primitive" if its designation (or its creation) is fixed by the elementary information processes or by the external environment of the IPS.[11]

In this system Newell and Simon assume that an "object" encompasses three things:

1. symbol structures stored in one or another of the IPS's memories, which are often usefully classified into (a) data structures, and (b) programs (see item 7 in the list above);

2. processes that the IPS is capable of executing;

3. an external environment of sensible (readable) stimuli. *"Reading"* consists of creating in memory internal symbol structures that designate external stimuli; "writing" is the inverse operation of creating responses in the external environment that are designated by internal symbol structures.

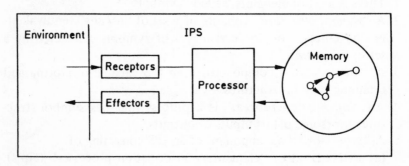

Figure 4–1
Information Processing System

C. INFORMATION AND ENVIRONMENTAL COMMUNICATION

An example of how information is used in architectural/environmental communication can be found in Jenck's analysis of Alvar Aalto's work.[12] Often with an architect there is a characteristic image—the result of his sketching technique—that summarizes his work. With Aalto that image is the place where one system blends into another. Aalto is obsessed with presenting a range of full visual elements and passing this obsession onto the viewer, so that he becomes sensitized to an aspect of the environment which has remained largely subconscious. Often Aalto singles out an aspect, uses it consistently and dramatically and thereby "recodes" a person's visual experience. From now on, undulation profiles will never be the same. It is commonplace that artists make us see the world differently by giving us a new conventional language of vision. Aalto has evolved an architectural language that has made full use of the gamut of expressive means.

Aalto's subtlety is of a multivalence of meanings where one part of the architecture interrelates with another and thus modifies it. Not only do the visual elements modify each other, but so do the functional: the requirements which determine the indulating principle were reinforced by the wood-joining technique of parallel slats and the need for an overall, spatial definer. Thus the mutual modification here appears in reinforcement, yet it can also work equally well through opposition.

Aalto has consciously set up a series of probabilities only to resist and distract them and, as Information theory postulates, the greater the probabilities which are resisted, the more exciting the experience.

Whereas signals do not convey information, signals have an information content by virtue of their potential for making selections. Signals operate upon alternatives forming the recipient's doubt. They give power to discriminate amongst these alternatives, or select from among them. The alternatives facing the recipient's doubt are *both* his past knowledge and immediate present schemata—his interest and purpose.

An individual and his environment form an interacting unit. This interaction is expressed in a finite set of messages composed of similarities and differences which characterize the external world. Such messages are not simplified, isolated entities. As explained previously, they are superimposed and constitute integrated levels. Points, lines, and surfaces are the elements, and a message is grasped by an observer on the basis of that scale at which a set of points or elements are meaningful to him. Owing to superimposition, one element might simultaneously participate in the formation of different messages on different levels. The repertoires are known to the "perceptor" (R_1, R_2,. . .R_n). Such a set of repertoires has two sources, one in the mind of the creator (i.e., it is intentional) and another in that of the receiver. The two sets do not have to possess the same properties. "Perception, therefore, is anything but a passive reception of impressions. We may change the phenomena by changing our attitude."[13] Or if we replace "intention" for attitude as Brunswik suggests, we see a dynamic two-way process of intentional activities involving the perception and creation of the message. "The creative intention usually starts with a general idea of the goal object, analogous to the experience we have when we *think* of a piece of music without being able to 'hit upon it'."[14] If the ideal goal is to bring the properties of two sets as close as possible (to enable the architect to foresee what the people's susceptibility to perceiving his intentions is), then, "a greater *'intentional depth'* is needed, or let us say, when we have to study the thing more closely and judge it more actively, our everyday classifications fail, and we do not fully 'grasp' the situation."[15]

4.2 Field theory

INTRODUCTION

All behavior is conceived of as a change of some state of a field in a given unit of time. Any behavior or any other change in a psychological field depends only upon the psychological field *at that time.*

In describing the concept of field theory, we begin, as Kurt Lewin does, with the relation of a specific notion of Field theory to that of field in general, and physical field in particular. He notes that history demonstrates that new ideas often appear at first to be nonsense. Then, as attention is focused on them, they are critically evaluated and often finally accepted. Clark Hull has said, "As I see it, the moment one expresses in any very general manner the various potentialities of behavior as dependent upon the simultaneous status of one or more variables, he has the substance of what is currently called field theory."[16] Lewin, in considering field, feels that "All behavior (including action, thinking, wishing, striving, valuing, achieving, etc.) is conceived of as a change of some state of a field in a given unit of time , $\frac{dt}{dx}$."

In explaining something, one might commence with general notions and gradually proceed to more specific ones or vice versa.

Field theory was first invented by the physical sciences, therefore we should start with the specifics (physical fields) which are now more familiar to the reader. We can proceed later to general concepts and finally examine how we can use Field theory in architecture. Some understanding of Physical Field theory is necessary as it is referred to when we consider architectural fields.

A. PHYSICAL FIELDS

"We can never be aware of the world as such but only of. . . the impingement of physical forces on the sensory receptors.[17] Thus in the physical world, $\frac{dx}{dt}$ is a change at the point x in time dt.[18] The principle of Field theory is that $\frac{dx}{dt}$ at t depends only on the situation St at t and not on the past or future. $\frac{dx}{dt} = F(St)$ (1) $\frac{dx}{dt}$ could be a function of (S^{t-1}) or (S^{t+1}) if in the case of "closed systems" one could define such a function, or in other words, if that function was known. In such a case we could write:

$$\frac{dx}{dt} = F(S^{t-n}) \qquad\qquad \frac{dx}{dt} = F(S^{t+n}) \qquad\qquad (2)$$

$$F(S^{t-n}) = St = F(S^{t+n}) \qquad\qquad (3)$$

In closed systems, the state of an entity is deterministically conditioned by its past through a known function. Thus one can predict its behavior in another state in the past or future.

No material entity is seen as it is in reality. Its image is colored by the perceptive apparatus of the mind. Nothing can be viewed as a physical reality. In regard to qualities such as color, a theory is suggested of "primary and secondary" qualities. There are some attributes of matter which we do not perceive. These are the primary colors, which are not attributes of matter, but are perceived by us as if they were such attributes. These are the secondary qualities of matter.

One should be aware that it is the mind through which nature becomes meaningful to us and whereby the nature of things becomes manifest to us, both as they are and the way we want them to be. Neither one should receive priority.

B. PHENOMENOLOGICAL FIELDS

In physics "phase space" is defined as representations of "multiple factors influencing an event." In architecture, "architectural space or architectural field" can be thought of as a representation of human experience. Such a field of architectural space should not be confused with either physical three-dimensional space or with the historical definition of architectural space. Its space-time demonstrations are psychological ones which were defined earlier. It has not only three dimensions but also n dimensions (including the four dimensions of physical space-time). Moreover, these dimensions are not merely quantitative continuums but rather qualitative properties capable of being translated into quantitative mathematical systems by means of predefined methods. Starting with the concept of "field" in physics as an introduction to the theory of architecture does not mean that such a theory should include all the properties of a physical field, even if Field theory, within which all the causal relationships of matter and energy operate, is accepted. This choice is only based on apparent similarities between this architectural theory, Field theory in physics, and psychology. So I believe we can more or less accept Lewin's definition of Field theory. In architecture, "Field theory is probably best characterized as a method: namely, a method of analyzing causal relations and of building specific constructs."[19]

If that is the case, there is no reason why in addition to physical fields (developed by physicists) and sociopsychological fields (developed by psychologists) we cannot use the notion of Field theory in the study of mental stimuli responses to physical patterns in the environment, where the composition of these fields gives us architectural fields.

In order to use Field theory in environmental studies for both matter and mind, we can divide environmental activities into two parts—one physical and the other nonphysical (this pertains to mental activity and is phenomenological). Or as Ushenko would say, there are two areas of meaning. "The one is essentially aesthetic, the other scientific." He distinguished them, in De-Quincey's words, "as the literature of power and the literature of knowledge."[20] The study of architecture as an aesthetic experience, as well as a sociopsychological interaction would be the combination of both. In such phenomenal activity patterns it is not a response to a specific element of field in a specific place and time which is important, but rather the total experience. In other words, holistic characteristics in phenomenological fields are much more important than they are in physical fields.

In phenomenological fields, as in field physics, it is expected that the parts, regardless of the subject matter, are integrated into a uniform whole by means of organized methods. An illustration given by Ushenko can clarify this point. Let us imagine a room furnished in such a way that one could hardly distinguish a chair from a table or any other piece of furniture. In such a situation the word "chair" or "table" would not be enough to locate any piece. Instead, an object could be called a chair by virtue of its location, e.g., at the corner of the room. This illustrates that in such fields we do not recognize the components through their isolation, but through their specific function within the whole. Ushenko further notes with regard to such contextual fields that "in disregard of the context of the room as a whole, we may identify the furniture, piece by piece, provided each piece is marked off from others by participation in some standard context."[21]

Furthermore, field theory creates unity "(1) by a fusion of distinct fields into one of a higher order of complexity, (2) by a reduction of particles to field, (3) by a reduction of matter to space, and (4) by a reduction of space to field."[24] He further argues in favor of Eddington's interpretation of Einstein's basic tensor equation as "reduction of matter to the curvature of structural space."[23] But such a reduction would be meaningless even to Einstein himself. "There is no such thing as an empty space unless we interpret the structure of a space not purely geometrically but in the sense of geometrical pattern in a field of tension. And such an interpretation would, in effect, reduce space to a field."[24]

Ushenko, like Eddington, uses the notion in arguing for the existence of visual data in a field of vision. He would say that without such data there would be no continuous field of vision. Thus "there would be nothing outside the self either to stimulate or to sustain his vision."[25] Vision by its very nature "does not exhibit visual appearances for their own sake, or for the sake of enjoyment, but as indications of forthcoming encounters and, therefore, in order to prompt the spectator's adjustment to the expected change of environment."[26] Thus vision can be thought of as a field of "action." In other words, vision has the acting power of pulling, pushing, and stopping human activities. Such powers are dependent on the degree of one's involvement and interaction with his surroundings. Ushenko has classified these forces into two sets, outwardly and inwardly directed vectors.

These forces can be classified into two groups involved in a dynamic balance. One represents the spectator's expectation of his external surroundings. The other is the force of the object's resistance against the above expected force. These forces are called "outward" and "inward" by Ushenko, and the field of dynamic duality between the forces is termed "geocentric" fields. Visual space is considered a function of such a field. The neighboring region under the self's control is called "here" and the elsewhere "there." Inward vectors converge onto the self's *here* and the outward vectors diverge form the self's *here* to *there*. The visual distance then depends on the intensity of inward vectors— the stronger their intensity, the closer they seem to the spectator and vice versa. "The features of the field of vision. . .are recognizably similar to the characteristic features of a physical vector field. The self and the visible others are reducible, with the aid of the pattern of inward and outward vectors, to field terms. Visual space is, likewise, reducible to field. And the power to change directions makes for the plasticity or pliability of vectors."[27]

We said that architectural fields consist of a dialectical process of interaction between physical fields with nonphysical (phenomenological) fields. Before man can see nature as energy without discriminating between matter and mind (if ever), he must alter his visual viewpoint. We are apt to deal with its two manifestations, physical and nonphysical, separately, although it has been proven that such a distinction is not valid and the causal relations of the two cannot be separated. Thus here we define the two above fields separately. After defining them, we define models as representative of those fields. In so doing, our emphasis is directed especially to physical fields and their models. Only some explanations of sociocultural fields and their related models by Lewin and Lévi-Strauss will be examined.

The organization and integration of all these fields is the job of the architect. This is why the responsibilities of the architect are among the most complicated of man's activities. They are dealing not only with physical or sociopsychological phenomena but with all phenomena. In light of such considerations, the approach of this section is twofold; nonphysical and physical fields will be considered throughout. In so doing, the outputs of other sociocultural conceptual research and models are integrated as an input into these physical fields. For example, an act of a man (e.g., speaking) is dealt with as a sequence of physical events, wherein cause and motivation are handled simultaneously with sociocultural forces.

C. COMMUNICATION FIELDS

Franklin Fearing in, "Toward a Psychological Theory of Human Communication"[28] presents a broad conceptual framework within which "the how and why of human loquacity" or talkativeness is explored. In this study, Fearing defines communication in field concepts. He infers that "all practical and theoretical problems of communications research lie in four major areas." They are "(a) the forces which determine the *effects* of communication, i.e. constructs regarding individuals' designated *interpreters;* (b) the forces which determine the *production* of communications, i.e., constructs about *communications;* (c) the nature of communications *content* considered as a stimulus field; and (d) the characteristics of the *situation* or *field* in which communication occurs." These four main topics are derived from a theory that communicative behavior is a specific form of discrete behaviors which occur in a situation or field possessing specific properties, the parts of which are in interdependent relationships with each other. Fearing states that a theory of such behavior is concerned with forces, psychological, social, and physical, "which determine the course of this behavior and its outcomes in relation to the culture in which it occurs." In other words, communication is influenced and altered by various factors that are interdependent on each other. These factors affect the initial communication and interpretation of the communication.

Fearing goes on to define some terms referring to the regions of the communication field. He defines the *communicator* to be the person or persons who produce or control the production of a body of sign-symbol material with the intent of cognitively (knowingly) structuring the field of specific needs and demands. The interpreters may not be physically present, but are always part of the psychological field of the communicator. The communicator reacts or is capable of reacting in the same manner in which he anticipates the interpreters will react.

"The *interpreter* perceives a specific body of sign-symbol material produced by specific communicators as a stimulus field in terms of his existing patterns of needs, expectancies and demands."

"The *communication content* is an organized stimulus field consisting primarily of signs and symbols produced by a communicator and perceived through single or multisensory channels. It must be susceptible to similar structuralizations by both the communicator and the interpreter."

"The dynamics of the interrelated parts of the *communication situation* may be summarized as follows: "(a) the existence of specific tensional states related to perceived instabilities, disturbances or needs in the psychological fields of the individuals involved; (b) the production of structured stimulus field (communications content) consisting of signs and symbols and (c) the achievement of a more stable organization through cognitive restructuring of the fields induced by such content. The relationships in the communication situation have a strategic character in that they involve a variety of manipulatory activities through which individuals strive to achieve an understanding of each other and their environments."[29]

When Fearing goes on to explain the distinction between interactions among individuals in the communication situation and other forms of social interaction, he refers to studies by Maslow who differentiates between "instrumental" or "coping behavior" and "expressive behavior." The former refers to postural, gestural, and other body changes which are perceived and cognized by others and "is essentially an epiphenomenon of the nature of character structure." The latter "is essentially an interaction of the character with the world, adjusting each to the other with mutual effect."

Fearing further states that "the special, almost uniqe, characteristic of the communication situation is the production of a stimulus field processing special characteristics which differentiates it from other stimuli to which organisms respond. These are: (a) it is *produced* by one or more individuals in the communication situation with the *intent* of structuring the fields of both its producers and interpreters; (b) it utilizes sign-symbol materials which have common significations for both the producer and interpreters; and (c) it implicates specific interpreters and communicators who are assumed to possess certain need patterns and perceptual capacities for which the produced content is relevant."[30] In the act of producing content, the interpreters are always in the psychological field of the communicator. The communicator's perception of the interpreter may determine the character of the content he produces.

Stimulus material produced by the communicator under the organizing forces is defined operationally as an organization of sign-symbols which may be subject to content analysis. Content analysis refers to a specific set of procedures, the object of which is to make available quantitative and qualitative statements regarding communications content. One effect of this requirement is that communications content must be capable of being reproduced in permanent form.

A second characteristic of communication content is its utilization of signs and symbols. Fearing adopted Morris' definition of a symbol as a sign with which it is synonymous. Morris notes that although language plays a central role in the life of man, this is not the only type of symbolic material. An important type of nonlinguistic symbolic material is that which Morris terms "iconic." "An iconic sign is any sign which is similar in some respect to that which it denotes."

Highly specified or "planned" communications are usually interpreter-centered. The communicators are (a) explicit regarding the effects to be achieved on particular interpreters and (b) consciously manipulating content in the light of these assumptions. Communications which are relatively unspecific, on the other hand, are to a greater degree communicator-centered. That is, in general, the communicator is more concerned with expressing himself than with possible effects on others.

The reality dimension refers to the degree to which a communications content reflects or is identifiable with psychological or physical reality. Operationally, the degree of reality as here defined is a function of the manipulatory activities of the communicator in producing content. These include selecting, isolating, or otherwise ordering content and contextual variables.

The authenticity dimension refers to the degree to which communicator's content contains cues which the interpreter accepts as congruent with "reality" as he knows it. Such cues are in the content or provided by its context, and they are perceived by the interpreter as an indication that the content has been manipulated by the communicator.

The ambiguity dimension is concerned with properties of communication content which make it susceptible to variant structuralizations by interpreters. A content may be said to be relatively unambiguous when it is maximally resistant to such variant structuralizations.

The congruency dimension refers to the degree to which the presented content is relevant to the need-value-demand systems of the interpreter. The relevant variables are those in his need-value, structure, and symbol-manipulating habits, conceived as acting on the content of specific structures.

Specific dynamic relationships between communicators and interpreters are hypothesized. These are distinguished forms of social interaction by: (a) their instrumental creative characteristics and (b) the production of a stimulus field possessing particular properties. In responding, both communicators and interpreters cognitively restructure the situation in the direction of a greater understanding of each other and their environments. Some of the organized processes in the communicator's situation are expressed genotypically in the form of hypothetical dimensions.

4.3 Environmental Architectural Field

Since the beginning of the century, there have been great advances made from the idea of matter in the traditional sense of the word, in the physical sciences (relativity, quantum theory), and in the social sciences and psychology, which have followed the physical sciences (Field theory in psychology). As Stephen Pepper says, "The problem of potentiality—or, as some call it, of 'dispositional properties'—is probably the central philosophical problem of this and the next few decades. It is instanced in logic, in the problem of the 'conditional contrary to fact'; in scientific method, in the operational theory of truth; in ethics, in the emphasis on attitudes; in the general theory of perception, and here in the theory of aesthetic perception."[31]

Thus energy seems, at least for the time being, to be the clue. It solves some problems (causality, duality between two units of measurement, etc.) and creates new ones (e.g., there is no exact unit with which to work, no perceivable order).

In architecture as well we could use energy as a unifying element. In this way all the disciplines could work with one another and be one common unit (the physical, social, or psychological sciences). The problem of qualitative and quantitative, subjective and objective could thus approach a solution. One could assign quantitative values to relatively qualitative ones, not as an absolute answer but rather of necessity and in an effort to solve today's problems.

It would be helpful to touch on some of the studies of the social sciences and psychology in regard to Field theory.

The question of aesthetics or any phenomenological theory like that which has been discussed previously, should be divided into two levels:

Abstraction (phenomena) and concreteness (pragmatism). The concrete theories should consist of the "collection of perceptions of the physical stimulus progressively accumulated by a spectator."[32] And also, "an ideal terminus of a spectator's progressively enriched perception of the physical stimulus."[33]

Whereas in the first case we would deal with preconceived elements as part of a total system, in the second we would delve further into the question of the nature of such defined subsystems. In other words, in the second type of theory the form of such institutional functions as "schools" or "streets" would be questioned. (What is a school meant to be?) For practical purposes we take it for granted that the concept of the institution "school" has been defined, and thus the task is to organize predefined elements into a whole.

Such categorization is clearly demonstrated in the behavioral sciences. For example, psychologists in dealing with the "stimulus-response" theory, treat "frustration" as a "concept" or "element of construction."[34] However, in Field theory such elements are under question. "In fact, field theory considers it impossible to investigate the laws of frustration, hope, friendship or autocracy without investigating at the same time what frustration, hope, friendship or autocracy 'is' psychologically."[35]

In order to use Field theory in environmental studies for both matter and mind, we can divide environmental activities into two parts—one physical and the other nonphysical. The study of architecture as an aesthetic experience would be a combination of both. In such phenomenal activities it is not a response to a specific element of field in a specific place and time which is important, but rather the total experience. The holistic characteristics of phenomenological fields are much more important than they are in physical fields. But this is exactly what expressionists deny. They assert that there are some meanings intrinsic within a form which convey themselves directly, regardless of the context.

In effect, the combination of information and expression allows the architect to play a richer symphony in which most meanings are working in a cluster while other ones are working negatively. Meanings are multivalent. They are meant to be interpreted as ambiguous.

One of the major constituent components of architecture is visual perception and its relevant field of visual interactions. Visual communication by its very nature does not exhibit visual appearances for their own sake, but rather as indications of forthcoming encounters and, therefore, in order to prompt the spectator's adjustment to the expected change of the environment. So vision can be thought of as a field of "activity." Vision has the acting power of pulling, pushing, and stopping human activities. Such powers are dependent on the degree of one's involvement and interaction with his surroundings. These faces have been classified into two sets, outwardly and inwardly directed subjects. These faces can be classified into two groups involved in a dynamic balance. One represents the spectator's expectation of his external surroundings. The other is the face of the object's resistance against the above expected force.

Architects, like scientists, should endeavor to transform phenomena into "concept" in order to work with them. We will not get anywhere by saying that art cannot be measured because it involves qualitative values. Granted, art is subjective and qualitative but we need theories which will enable us (1) to deal with phenomena both qualitatively and quantitatively in a single system, and (2) to perceive the basic, inherent universal laws of the phenomena. An example of such "elements of construction" can be seen in points of movement, the basic producers of a line, surface, etc. These elements, "genetic definition,"[36] have been recommended by Cassirer as a means of coordinating qualitative and quantitative approaches to phenomena. He asserts that this method "is able, at the same time, to link and separate; it does not minimize qualitative differences and still lays open their relation to general quantitative variables."[37] In addition, theories are needed (3) to break phenomena down into smaller elements so that they can be dealt with and also be put back together again, and (4) to develop means of evaluating and measuring both qualitative and quantitative values.

Suppose the equivalent to $\frac{dx}{dt}$ in physics is the concept of "architectural experience" in architecture. The theory will then express architectural experience (A), while, at the same time t as a function and situation S:

$$A^t = F(S^t) \quad (2)$$

S is also a function of a person and his environment:

$$S = G(P \text{ and } E) \quad (3)$$

I would like to stress that the principle of Field theory implies that "any behavior or any other change in a psychological field depends only upon the psychological field at that time."[38]

At first glance, the principle of Field theory in architecture (as in physics and psychology) seems to have nothing to do with the past or future. We also know that such experience is a function of heredity, history, and environment. When we talk about one's state of experience at t as a part of one's state of personality (P) at t, we have already considered heredity and history. The difference between the concept of Field theory and other concepts of "closed systems" is that in a closed system, it is taken for granted that we know how the change from a state t to $t + 1$ is made. In reality, however, this is not known. Let us present the time as past $tm \ldots tg \ldots t - 1 \ldots t \ldots t + 1 \ldots ti \ldots tn$.

In closed systems, the state of an entity is deterministically conditioned by its past through a known function. Thus one can predict its behavior in another state in the past or future. But we know each state is dynamic, not static. This means that the interconnection between past ti to future tg is not a direct one but rather an indirect one. Thus we do not know whether it is a state of tg in the past pushing the entity into the future or whether it is state ti in the future pulling the entity toward the future. Moreover, we do not know how this is being accomplished. Thus according to *Field* theory, in determining the state of an entity at t, all the data of its behavior in the past is necessary but not sufficient. Thies seems to be half way true; what remains would be the future.

Let us now go back to the formula $S = G (P + E)$. Not only do we have difficulties in differentiating the physical and sociopsychological forces of the environment, but we also have difficulties differentiating between perception and an *a priori* knowledge of the nature of things.

Consequently we should now say a word about the nature of things in relation to how they are perceived. No material entity is seen as it is in reality. Rather its image is colored by the perceptive apparatus of the mind. Hence nothing can be viewed as a physical reality. Thus in regard to qualities such as color, Locke suggests a theory of "primary and secondary qualities. Namely, there are some attributes of matter which we do perceive. These are the primary qualities, and there are other things which we perceive, such as colours, which are not attributes of matter, but are perceived by us as if they were such attributes. These are the secondary qualities of matter."[39] So there is no doubt that man has inherent difficulty in perceiving the real nature of things. But the question, as Alfred North Whitehead points out, is "Why should we perceive secondary qualities? It seems an extremely unfortunate arrangement that we should perceive a lot of things that are not there. . . . The modern account of nature is not, as it should be, merely an account of what the mind knows of nature; but it is also confused with an account of what nature does to the mind."[40] Hence Whitehead protests against the concept of the bifuracation of

> . . . The nature apprehended in awareness and the nature which is the cause of awareness. The nature which is the fact apprehended in awareness holds within it the greenness of the trees, the song of the birds, the warmth of the sun, the hardness of the chairs, and the feel of the velvet. The nature which is the cause of the awareness is the conjectured system of molecules and electrons which so affects the mind as to produce the awareness of apparent nature. The meeting point of these two natures is the mind, the causal nature being influent and the apparent nature being effluent.[41]

Whitehead calls this theory "psychic additions" to nature which are in no proper sense part of nature. For example, we perceive a red billiard ball at a specific time, space, motion, hardness, and inertia. Its secondary characteristics such as warmth and sound when hitting other balls are psychic additions, which are the mind's way of perceiving nature. To Whitehead this theory of psychic additions is sound theory which "lays immense stress on the obvious reality of time, space, solidity, and inertia, but distrusts the minor artistic additions of colour, warmth, and sound."[42] Whitehead is against any division in a search for an understanding of nature and suggests that we should produce "the all-embracing relations. . .namely, warmth and redness on one side, and molecules, electrons and other on the other side. Then the two factors are explained as being respectively the cause and the mind's reaction to the cause."[43] He further states that "so far as reality is concerned all our sense perceptions are in the same boat, and must be treated on the same principle."[44] This is what we architects should be concerned with; i.e., we should be aware that it is the mind through which nature becomes meaningful to us and whereby the nature of things becomes manifest to us as they are and as we want them to be. Neither one should receive priority. In the words of Inge,

The Platonic doctrine of immortality rests on the independence of the spiritual world. The spiritual world is not a world of unrealized ideals, over against a real world of unspiritual fact. It is, on the contrary, the real world, of which we have a true though very incomplete knowledge, over against a world of common experience which, as a complete whole, is not real, since it is compacted out of miscellaneous data, not all on the same level, by the help of the imagination. There is no world corresponding to the world of our common experience. Nature makes abstractions for us, deciding what range of vibrations we are to see and hear, what things we are to notice and remember.[45]

4.4 Environmental Field Components

> Remember that a picture, before it is a battle horse, a nude, or some anecdote, is essentially a plane surface covered with colors assembled in a certain order.
>
> Maurice Denis

To define environment, environmental form, and finally, environmental field communication, we must begin with a very broad concept of that set of space-time events within which environment is contained. "Events, infinite and finite, are the primary type of physical facts."[46] "To think of nature as a mere passage of events without objects, or as a mere collection of objects unrelated to events, is an abstraction."[47] In physics, such a set of events is presently conceived of as the activity pattern of matter and energy in space-time field physics. Man also, as a set of those events, is subject to scientific research, or, as Teilhard de Chardin states, "mankind in its totality is a phenomenon to be described and analysed like any other phenomenon: it and all its manifestations, including human history and human values, are proper objects for scientific study."[48]

For those who consider mental activity patterns to be something other than mere physical laws, another space-time activity would be added to the previous physical one, called sociopsychological space-time. It is a combination of these patterns which we want to consider. A criterion for their recognition is order, structure, and form, and that is realized through the similarities and differences apparent in those patterns, for "any physical relationships between nature at different instants, and all that is left to connect nature at one instant with nature at another instant is the identity of material and the comparisons of the similarities and differences made by observant minds."[49]

Now there are two ways to analyze those patterns—*a priori* and logical or *a posteriori* and incuitive. Before going further we should clarify the role of these two (logic and intuition) in perceiving these patterns of order and form. "Logic, which alone can give certainty, is the instrument of demonstration; intuition is the instrument of invention."[50] The very definition of the two systems splits our definition of order and form. We should attempt to see whether we view order and form as *a priori* or, if they are to be experienced as viewed by Tolstoy.

Experience. . .has played only a single role, it has served as occasion. But this role was none the less very important; and I have thought it necessary to give it prominence. This role would have been useless if there existed an *a priori* form imposing itself upon our sensitivity, and which was space of three dimensions.[51]

To be sure, all components of environment (space, time, matter, and energy) have two characteristics depending on whether we look at them logically or intuitively. There is psychological as well as objective or physical space, time, matter, and energy. While the first is thought to be more qualitatively oriented, the second is viewed as quantitatively oriented. There is always the problem of transferring from one to the other. To clarify this issue we shall elaborate on each of the components separately.

A. PSYCHOLOGICAL SPACE

We do not know whether it is the duration of time which makes space meaningful to us or whether it is distance or space which gives the sensation of time. All we know is that they both exist, and without doubt they are either interrelated or one, "for the space revealed to us by our senses is absolutely different from the space of geometry. Is geometry derived from experience? Careful discussion will give the answer — no!"[52]

A major problem in dealing with psychological space is that it cannot be accurately measured and tends to involve a distinction between activities of the arts and sciences in dealing with environment. "Experience brings us into contact only with representative space, which is a physical continuum, never with geometric space, which is a mathematical continuum."[53] The characteristics of psychological space are as follows:

(a) It is formed in the mind as images or perceptions; it does not have anything to do with *a priori* mathematical space within the domain of pure science. One of the characteristics of psychological space is its involvement with visual comprehension. However, experience shows us that "there is no pure visual space."[54]

(b) Its "pieces" might overlap. "An increase of three inches in the spacing between two chairs. . .It means more than that. To the occupants of both chairs, actually there is a total increase of six inches from two viewpoints."[55]

(c) Its units are not equal. Experience shows that when one is hurriedly walking to arrive at a destination, the road seems to become longer.

B. PSYCHOLOGICAL TIME

Psychological time is fully comprehended through perception, not *a priori* knowledge. This is because its behavior and dimensions are, as Langer and Poincaré point out, beyond two-dimensional route-passage and length-measurement. "That is why subjective time seems to have density and volume as well as length, and force as well as rate of passage. The one-dimensional time of Newtonian physics, and its derivative, the time-dimension in modern physical theory, are abstractions from our experience of time."[56] Langer terms entities which are just for perception "vertical entities." "It is not unreal; where it confronts you, you really perceive it, you don't dream or imagine that you do."[57]

"So far as we do not go outside the domain of consciousness the notion of time is relatively clear. . .but we know perfectly well what we mean when we say that, of two conscious phenomena which we remember, one was anterior to the other."[58]

There are three characteristics which distinguish psychological time units from pure time units:

(a) They are formed in the mind and become meaningful through experience.

(b) Their duration can overlap. "When we say that two conscious facts are simultaneous, we mean that they profoundly interpenetrate, so that analysis cannot separate them without mutilating them."[59] "On the score, psychological time should be discontinuous."[60]

(c) Their units are not equal. *"We have not a direct intuition of the equality of two intervals of time."*[61]

C. PHYSICAL SPACE–TIME

It is said that the world surrounding us consists of matter, energy, space, and time. Space and time are the containers and we are actually dealing with matter and energy. The world is made manifest to us through orders and/or forms. This form is made of matter by energy in space and time. The continuity and eternity of space and time does not enable us to see at what point these orders and forms commence and how and when they terminate. Thus there is no absolute space (in the Euclidean sense) or time; nor are there absolute orders and forms. "Henceforth space by itself, and time by itself, are doomed to fade away into mere shadows, and only a kind of union of the two will perserve an independent reality."[62] A form or order appears to us as such, not because of what it is intrinsically, but because of its similarity to or dissimilarity from another form. As Moretti says "each form is not perceived by us in itself, but only by that assemblage of signs, of differences, which distinguish it from forms neighboring in space or memory."[63] There are two ways to search for an understanding of these forms, through the concept of atomism—through which we study the forms themselves—and through structuralism—through which we analyze the "differences" or interrelations of elements rather than the elements themselves. It is the second one that we emphasize here. "The association and interrelations of events are what matter most to us. We know that there are no isolated or spontaneous happenings, and we look always for the connections between them."[64]

Now the first question is where to look for these forms and differences and on what scale and level of hierarchical structure of the universe. This is a question with no single answer. We must investigate all the possibilities. As Novikoff says, "Knowledge of the laws of the lower level is necessary for a full understanding of the higher level; yet the unique properties of phenomena at a higher level cannot be predicted *a priori* from the laws of the lower level."[65] In classical physics, an atom was conceived of as being a unit which determines the lower level of the scale of the universe. The other end of the scale was conceived of in terms of three-dimensional Euclidean space. The intermediate scales, as well as the whole, was conceived of as the sum of its units (atoms). This idea was rendered obsolete by the theories of relativity and quantum. Since the advent of these ideas, the scale of these elements, like the form of their containers, seems to be indiscrete and without beginning and terminal points. These laws do not seem to be indiscrete and without beginning and terminal points. These laws do not seem to provide a satisfactory answer. There are "integrative levels" at which the "whole is not the sum of its parts." By forms I mean not only that each elementary unit of matter is a "point-matter" and the energy needed for one elementary act is one "point-energy," but that the time and place in which acts of energy exist are "point-time" and "point-space." Now a form is the assemblage (the patterning interreaction) of these point-energies while they are following the constituent rules of the forms at different levels and on different scales.

The most elementary form starts with two points of matter, since form is thought of as the interaction between the two entities. According to Newtonian laws:[66]

When there are only two elementary points the formula representing the form will be:

$$F = \pm\, G\, \frac{m\, m^1}{d^2}$$

When there are more than two elementary points, F the force between two continuous bodies is obtained by the formula:

$$F = \frac{1}{2}\, G$$

$$\frac{P(r_1)\, P(r_2)\, d^3 r_1 d^3 r_2}{|\, r_1 - r_2\,|^2}$$

$$F = \frac{1}{2} G \sqrt{\frac{m_i \, m_j}{|r_i \, r_j|^2}}$$

Thus all we perceive is the aggregate of these positive (tensive) and negative (repellent) patterns of energy. The answer to the Newtonian principle is given by Waddington:

The forces which hold the elementary parts in a certain orderly relation to each other are not derived from the affinities of just a few kinds of units but arise from the interaction of very numerous active entities.[67]

So the forms cannot be derived from the atomic module. Rather, they are actively and dynamically shaped at various "integrative levels."

Classification of the elements in space. In further elaborating on the concepts of environment, the characteristics of three-dimensional space should first be defined. To do so Poincaré's analogy for defining a "physical continuum" and the notion of "cut" is pertinent.[68] The total form, as stated above, is a set consisting of an assemblage of point—energy patterns, broken up into subsets (elements).

On the one hand, because of the conscious and semiconscious behavior of the mind and the problem of overlapping involved in units of psychological space-time, and on the other hand, because physical three-dimensional space is more concrete than psychological space, the integration of the two (physical and psychological) and the transformation from one to the other will be considered. We define psychological space-time on the basis of physical space-time. One arbitrary set is assigned to each unit of physical space-time to get a set representing psychological space-time.

D. POSITIVE AND NEGATIVE ENERGIES

We pointed out earlier how psychological space-time function and relate to the arts. Here these entities take tensive form (balance, rhythm) and are related to the pulse of our very lives. "A work of art is a composition of tensions and resolutions, balance and unbalance, rhythm and coherence, a precarious yet continuous unity. Life is a natural process of such tensions, balances, rhythms; it is these that we feel, in quietness or emotion, as the pulse of our own living."[69] Gropius also seems to agree with Langer and with the notion of positive and negative energies: "*Art must satisfy this perpetual urge to swing from contrast to contrast; the spark, generated by tensions of opposites, creates the peculiar vitality of a work of art.*"[70]

Taking into consideration the earlier definition of psychological space and time, we can argue that the pattern of our stimuli could not be a mathematical continuum in response to such patterns as space and time. Rather, like their counterparts, psychological space and time, they possess the three characteristics outlined above. Thus they are dense in some parts and spacious in others. This characteristic creates a potential energy between two states (density and spaciousness) with the inherent possibility of alternation between both states.

So far we have been talking about mental stimuli patterns with negative and positive signs. We can now reverse the situation (assigning the energies of mental stimuli patterns to those of space-time patterns which originally generated these mental stimuli patterns) and say that space-time patterns have positive and negative energies capable of being grasped by the mind. It should be made clear that neither positive nor negative energies are an ideal, but rather it is the composition and interrelation of these energies which is capable of creating an ideal pattern. "Architectural composition primarily calls for a happy combining of similarities and differences. The former furnishes ease of apprehension. . . .The latter creates change and interest. . . ."[71]

E. QUALITATIVE AND QUANTITATIVE ENERGIES

In defining psychological space and time we said that they are qualitative and not quantitative. Could the energies created by mental stimuli patterns, having originated in qualitative patterns, be quantitative? No, they are *qualitative*. For practical purposes we can convert those qualitative values into quantitative ones. This could be accomplished through the employment of sets of indices to the values which would then be tested against sociopsychological theories. However it would just be for the sake of deriving arbitrary answers. Poincaré in this regard has said that, "We therefore choose these rules, not because they are true, but because they are the most convenient. . . ."[72] Thus we can set up a standard for changing qualitative energies into quantitative ones or vice versa.

A tensive point would be one which creates a pulling effect toward us or another point in space. A repellent point would be one which creates a pushing effect toward us or another point in space. The same would be true of time.

Notes to Chapter Four

1. C. Shannon and W. Weaver, *The Mathematical Theory of Communication*, p. 100.
2. *Ibid.*
3. *Ibid.*
4. C. Cherry, *On Human Communications. A Review, A Survey, and a Criticism*, 2nd ed. M.I.T. Press, Cambridge, Mass. & London, 1957 & 1966, p. 170. Hereafter cited as *On Human Communications.*
5. C. Shannon and W. Weaver, *The Mathematical Theory of Communication*, p. 100.
6. S. Stevens, quoted by C. Cherry, *On Human Communication*, p. 170.
7. C. Shannon and W. Weaver, *The Mathematical Theory of Communication*, p. 102.
8. Myron Tribus, "Thirty Years of Information Theory," p. 3.
9. A. Newell and H. Simon, *Human Problem Solving*, p. 3.
10. *Ibid.*, p. 9.
11. *Ibid.*, pp. 20–21.
12. C. Jencks, *Modern Movements in Architecture*, pp. 167-183.
13. Christian Norberg-Schulz, *Intentions in Architecture*, M.I.T. Press, Cambridge, Mass., 1965, p. 31.
14. *Ibid.*, p. 78.
15. *Ibid.* p. 31.
16. Clark Hull, quoted by K. Lewin in *Field Theory*, p. 44, from E.R. Hilgard and D.G. Marquis, *Conditioning and Learning.*
17. R.P. Kilpatrick, *Explorations in Transactional Psychology*, quoted by E. Hall in *The Hidden Dimension*, p. 39.
18. K. Lewin, *Field Theory*, pp. 46-48.
19. *Ibid.*, p. 45.
20. Andres Paul Ushenko, *The Field Theory of Meaning*, Univ. of Michigan Press, Ann Arbor, 1958, p. vii.
21. *Ibid.*, p. 86.
22. *Ibid.*
23. *Ibid.*, p. 87.
24. *Ibid.*, p. 88.
25. *Ibid.* p. 98.
26. *Ibid.*, p. 90.
27. *Ibid.*, p. 95.
28. Franklin Fearing, "Toward a Psychological Theory of Human Communication," in *Foundations of Communication Theory* by K. Sereno & C. Mortensen.

29. A. Maslow, quoted by F. Fearing in *Foundations of Communication Theory*, p. 42.
30. F. Fearing, "Toward a Psychological Theory of Human Communication," p. 47.
31. Stephen Pepper, Introduction, *Dynamics of Art* by D'Arcy W. Thompson Indiana Univ. Press, Bloomington 1953.
32. *Ibid.*
33. *Ibid.*
34. K. Lewin, *Field Theory*, p. 34.
35. *Ibid.*, p. 35.
36. *Ibid.*, p. 32.
37. *Ibid.*
38. *Ibid.*, p. 45.
39. A. Whitehead, *Concept of Nature*, p. 27.
40. *Ibid.*
41. *Ibid.*, p. 31.
42. *Ibid.*, p. 43.
43. *Ibid.*, p. 32.
44. *Ibid.*, p. 44.
45. William Ralph Inge, "Platonism and Human Immortality," quoted by A. Whitehead, *Concept of Nature*, p. 48.
46. A. Whitehead, *Interpretation of Science*, Bobbs-Merrill Co., Indianapolis & New York, 1961, p. 59.
47. *Ibid.*, p. 63.
48. Teilhard de Chardin, *The Phenomenon of Man*, Harper & Row, New York, 1959, p. 12.
49. A. Whitehead, *Interpretation of Science*, p. 57.
50. Henry Poincaré, *The Value of Science*, trans by G.H. Halsted Dover Publications, New York, 1958, p. 23.
51. *Ibid.*, p. 70.
52. H. Poincaré, *Science and Hypothesis*, Dover Publications, New York, 1958, p. xxv.
53. H. Poincaré, *The Value of Science*, p. 70.
54. *Ibid.*, p. 52.
55. A. Chang ih Tiao, *The Existence of Intangible Content in Architectonic Form Based Upon the Practicality of Laotzu's Philosophy*, Princeton University Press, Princeton, 1965, p. 30. Hereafter noted as *Intangible Content & Laotzu's Philosophy*.
56. Susanne K. Langer, *Problems of Art*, Charles Scribner's Sons, New York, 1957 p. 38.
57. *Ibid.*, p. 5
58. H. Poincaré, *The Value of Science*, p. 26.
59. *Ibid.*
60. *Ibid*
61. *Ibid.*, p. 27.
62. Hermann Minkowski, quoted by Sigfried Giedion, *Space, Time and Architecture. The Growth of a New Tradition*, 5th ed., Harvard Univ. Press, Cambridge. Mass. 1967, p. 14. Hereafter cited as *Space, Time and Architecture*.
63. Luigi Moretti, "Form as Structure," in *Arena: Architectural Association Journal*, June 1967, pp. 22-24.
64. S. Giedion, *Space, Time and Architecture*, pp. 21-22.
65. Alex B. Novikoff, "The Concept of Integrative Levels and Biology," in *Structure in Art and Science*, ed. by G. Kepes George Braziller, New York, 1965, pp. 209-215.

66. R. Kronig in *Textbook of Physics,* Pergamon Press, 1959, p. 93.
67. C. Waddington, "The Character of Biological Form," in *Aspects of Form, a Symposium on Form in Nature and Art,* ed. L. Whyte, Indiana Univ. Press, Bloomington, 1951, p. 45.
68. H. Poincaré, *The Value of Science,* p. 55.
69. S. Langer, *Problems of Art,* p. 8.
70. Walter Gropius, *Scope of Total Architecture,* Collier Books, New York, 1943, p. 40.
71. Chang ih Tiao, *Intangible Content in Architectonic Form Based on Laotzu's Philosophy,* p. 41.
72. H. Poincaré, *The Value of Science,* p. 36.

5. Environmental Communication

5.0 Introduction–Abstract

In this chapter notions of Field theory and Information theory as well as the concepts of Communication theory are brought together into the framework developed in the first two chapters in order to define an *environmental communication system*. Within such a communication system, the originator of the messages is either man or the environment.

A designer, as communicator, uses "architectural language" as his medium to communicate to others—architects, builders, and users. His symbols are formulated in both personal and universal form and order. But the designer's message is not always interpreted as he intends. It is argued here that part of this miscalculation is due to differences in personal symbol systems, rather than through consistent use of universal objective communication systems.

Messages, on the one hand, are considered to have three general bases, *environmental* (physical, natural), *behavioral* (socio-cultural, psychological), and finally, *symbolic* (associative meanings relative to environmental and behavioral messages). Environmental messages, are seen in three groups: as a set of *a priori* geometrical elements, as a set of meanings, and as a set of messages. *A priori* and objective information corresponds to physical properties; meanings, on the other hand, carry along with them individual, as well as sociocultural values. The *environmental communication field* is then defined as consisting of complex fields of interaction between man and man, and man and the environment, using tangible and intangible environmental, behavioral, and symbolic cues. The *visual field,* as one example of such fields, is discussed as being composed of tensive and repulsive forces crating a dynamic field of interaction.

5.1 Components of Environmental Communication

Following are environmental communication components:

A. ORIGINATOR OF MESSAGES

The originator(s) producing the messages (sign-symbols) can be divided into two basic categories:

– man as originator of messages
– environment as originator of messages

In the first instance—man as originator of messages—human behavioral producers of messages or the "communicator," is a source (or sources) who produces signs and symbols with specific intent. He cognitively produces these event-patterns responding to an assumed set of receivers in the mind.

Thus man as originator of messages structures this field of interactions based on his own conditions (history, heredity, and environment) and his conception of receivers (interpreters) and conditions (needs and demands) and expresses himself through behavioral cues via environmental communication.

In the second case—*environmental as originator of messages*—similarities and differences observed in patterns of environmental entities also provide man with another set of messages, messages ranging from (1) symbolic values and meanings given to specific material configurations; (2) substantive elements such as properties of matter (color, light, material); and (3) structure of matter; i.e., the order and form by which its parts are joined together. There are two types of patterns, pure *a priori* and symbolic ones carrying some kind of meaning.

The difference between these two types of messages is that whereas the former is produced without intent, the latter is produced with intent. In the first case, an engine or a pot conveys messages; they say what they are, what they do, etc. In the second case, a mosque dome, the shape of a church, etc. not only say how they function, but also carry additional meanings beyond their physical properties.

In the case of either engine, pot, mosque, or church, a specific set of entities is put together in a specific way to perform a certain function. Thus the very form of each provides the interpreter with messages. This will be further discussed in detail.

B. RECEIVER OF MESSAGES

Each individual is considered a receiver or "interpreter" who perceives and is able to read into a specific set of signs and symbols produced by various originators, based on his needs, expectations, and demands.

C. MESSAGES

Messages are the content of communication which is conveyed from originator to receiver as stimulus in the form of similarities and differences, or signs and symbols. Signs and symbols can be "objects" (things), events (acitivities), concepts, properties of matter (structural) in a medium, statues, and personality of a person, etc.

D. MEDIA–ENVIRONMENTAL FIELD COMMUNICATION

Environmental field communication consists of the integration of all of the above components. Environmental communication occurs in environmental fields of sociocultural, psychological, and physical interaction among the three above mentioned types of forces.

The total environmental system should be examined when all its components reinforce each other in a comprehensive communication system. That is, any section of a building which modifies another, while itself a consequence of sociocultural properties, at the same time responds to natural determinism.

Comparing formal architecture with folk, indigenous, or vernacular architecture in the context of environmental communication of Information theory, we find that indigenous architecture provides us with much richer architectural qualities and experience than monumental, formal, geometrical architecture. The reason is that if contrast or existence of alternatives is the root of any information being conveyed, it would seem that probabilistic uncertainties inherent in irregular shapes and undulating networks of indigenous architecture are able to convey more meaningful alternatives, thus environments. In other words, the unexpected experiences received by spectators from an indigenous, irrational order leaves much more to expectation and curiosity than rational, preconceived patterns which are very much evident in formal architecture. According to Colin Cherry, "Signals have an information content by virtue of their potential for making selections. Signals operate upon the alternatives forming the recipient's doubt. They give power to discriminate amongst or select from these alternatives."[1]

Order and form is the overall framework tying together the totality of environmental elements (objects, events) and provides them with intelligibility, coherence, function, etc.

One discipline probably capable of dealing with tangible and intangible objective and subjective quantitative variables, as well as qualities, is the field of communication. On this ground, information and communication will provide architects and planners with a new perspective on the basis of which the totality of the objective-subjective environment can be seen within one single system.

Environmental communication field is considered to consist of tangible and intangible properties, of form and function.

Intangible parts or functions are presented to us in various event patterns of activity, performed in the space crated by cavities and voids within solids and objects.

The qualitative aspects of environment connected with human values transcend the physical boundaries of the objective world. Symbolism in the environmental sense can be considered the unwritten clues in a manuscript which ties the words together into a language. It is the way words are used or, in communication terminology, the ways objects and events are perceived by different cultures and societies. Symbolic information is the additional meaning added to an object or event relative to the way that *a priori* object or event is being used in a given culture or society.

5.2. Content–Messages of Environmental Communication

The historical approach to the aesthetics of form is, for the most part, based on *a priori* values and also symbolism, the study of prevailing ideas of form. In contrast, the new approaches (Information and Communication theory–message system) are a search for systematic studies of the materiality, as well as spirituality of aesthetic form. Here nothing is taken for granted. Attributes of form, order, and organization of the environment are in question, in addition to man's attitude toward the environment.

Thus the result is that we have to develop ways of understanding and defining the basic (universal) primary elements and then establishing rules and theories to enable us to compose these hierarchical elements into a meaningful whole. Let us look at these elements in the following order:

A. as a set of *a priori* geometrical elements
B. as a set of meanings
C. as a set of messages

Although necessary, this classification is rough and should certainly not be considered precise.

A. A SET OF A PRIORI GEOMETRICAL ELEMENTS

These types of elements of the environment, or in communication terms these sources of information or communication alphabets, i.e., "objects and events," convey universal messages. The messages are in an *a priori* form, the way an objective scientist sees the world, not as we see them in our daily experience. It is assumed here that information is intrinsic within the objective world (both objects and events), inherent in its very substantive nature and the structure of its components–which convey themselves directly regardless of context, creator, or receivers.

In an *a priori* sense there is no criterion for meaning. There is no beginning and no end of elements in universal space, thus no meaning for psychological or personal or sociocultural space. The criteria for measuring *a priori* spaces are defined within Euclidean geometry.

A posteriori space or conceptual space is defined by various physical or sociopsychological boundaries; boundaries which might vary from individual to individual or culture to culture.

Structural and construction engineers, as well as mechanical engineers, only deal with the objective parameters of spaces, pure matters of energy, and air circulation.

A posteriori or conceptual space is a product of the mind; although its existence is based on some physical configuration of physical realities, it goes beyond that, extending its boundaries to other disciplines, such as the social and natural sciences. Physical and conceptual space are two sides of the same coin. Their structural organization has to coincide.

These elements are either in the form of event patterns or object systems.

a. *Event Patterns.* The basic characteristic of these patterns is the isolated typology of event units and their linkage system. Owing to the fluidity of character of this type of phenomenon, and also man's incapability to perceive these patterns as well as tangible objects, the study of this aspect of the environment could be quite a task. This is probably the reason why this aspect of architecture, which primarily deals with the dynamic part of human life, has been very much neglected in the past. The architect of the past has only delineated static objects. Based on architectural field and communication, new systems of conceptualization, presentation, and representation must be developed to enable architect planners to deal with this vital part of environmental experience.

To deal with such phenomena, new horizons must be defined in planning and architecture which, inevitably, cannot be described by existing tools and technicians; i.e., plans, elevations, and plysical models. Rather it can only be defined by dynamic means which could describe the activities: "change," "movement," "process of formation and transformation," and finally, the "flow of life." In this respect, we should share experiences and develop our own theories in collaboration with sociologists, economists, anthropologists, psychologists, and political scientists who have been trying to deal with this aspect of human life. An example of such tools and techniques are those developed in the areas of musical composition, dance, and play notation systems. That is to day, the architect-planner must not be indifferent to the flow of life-events-patterns for which he is making a container. Rather the environment in which such a drama of life patterns is to take place, as well as the act itself, must be shaped as a consequence of the interaction and interplay of the two.

b. *The Object System.* There are two basic elements to be studied here: entities and linkages, or, in other words, the typology of different component objects and the structural properties which relate these components together.

A good example of such language is geometry, the *a priori* science of space. Geometry deals with form, shape, order, and the space typology of entities such as point, line, surface and volume, spatial characteristics of size, and spatial structure of the organization of the objective world. It should be noted that geometry in its *a priori* form falls into the domain of mathematics, but its application, as an *a posteriori* activity, is incorporated within the human value system and deals with "social objects" (symbol system) and is in the domain of architecture and planning; i.e., how to use pure, objective geometrical systems in shaping the human, objective-subjective environment.

With regard to the application of geometric properties to architecture, a considerable amount has been achieved in Euclidian geometry which deals with static three-dimensional space; e.g., proportions, rhythm, symmetry, etc. Very much remains to be done in the area of description of the dynamics of space, employing the properties of typology, probability, and stochastics.

To Alberti, the most perfect form for a church or city is a circle and polygon. Moreover he suggests formal buildings for public functions. Such concepts imply that he classifies the function to which an *a priori* form can be assigned. He thinks that "geometrical perfection reflects the cosmic harmony which the church-building should represent."[2] Thus an *a priori* approach deals with form in a formal manner characterized by pure geometrical properties in contrast to the other two categories which deal with man's experience of the form. Above a certain state (which we were just discussing), the analysis of matter and events within the atom is outside of our sense perception. But before this state of analysis, there is a level at which we can feel the atoms "as a whole occupying average positions, physics and sensation run parallel."[3] Before considering this level, let us see what the definition of form would be on this level. According to S.P.F. Humphreys-Owen, "To interpret form we say that matter consists of atoms, or, more generally, of groups of atoms (molecules) which are mutually attracted by certain forces, but which are mutually repelled when they approach more closely than a certain spacing."[4]

Now let us consider points and matter from a more specific point of view—one which is closer to our sense perception. This does not involve knowledge gained from *a priori* sources or instruments. This point of view is that held by Poincaré. In regard to the question of what a point in space is, he says that what we think of as a point is no more than an illusion. "Everyone thinks he knows, but this is an illusion. What we see when we try to represent to ourselves a point in space is a black spot on white paper, a spot of chalk on a black board, always an object."[5] He answers the question of what point in space is as follows, "For each attitude of my body my finger determines a point, and it is that and that only which defines a point in space. To each attitude corresponds in this way a point."[6] So one can say that real objectivity does not actually exist, meaning that even the objects of empirical science "are things and phenomena given in perception, space-time structures whose properties are described in terms of perceptible qualities and relations. The motion of bodies, the behavior of organisms and the relations between societies are initially described by concepts abstracted from perception."[7]

B. A SET OF MEANINGS

In the previous section, we dealt with information sources (objects and events) in an objective way, disregarding any subjective views or value system attached to such information sources. However, entities whether objects or events carry along with them individual, as well as sociocultural, values and meanings which transform an *a priori* object or event into a symbol. This category of messages is based on a set of conventions or "symbols" by which the creator's and receiver's minds are preconditioned.

With regard to man and his symbolism, Ernst Cassirer has stated that man has a symbolic, as well as biological, nature. The concept of the symbolic future is related to the prophets and to the idea of prophecy. The prophets, as opposed to the soothsayers, did not simply foretell future events. The concept of prophecy contains the hope of promise. To frustrate a man's symbolic future is to deny him that promise. Cassirer notes, moreover, that in the living world below man, the distinction between the possible and the real does not exist. To deny one the promise of his future, is to frustrate the fundamental human attribute of the understanding and hope for the possible. It is also to deny in oneself the existence of the possible, as well as to violate the ethical and religious task of the symbolic future. In architecture, much of the controversy over symbolism has resulted from a confusion of three related but distinct phenomena—icon, metaphor, symbol.

An icon would be an architectural form which by resembling another object, associates itself with that other object's attributes. Examples would be Saarinen's airport terminal in the form of a bird and LeCorbusier's Unité d'Habitation in the form of an ocean liner sailing in a sea of green. A metaphor in architecture would consist of a particular spatial experience where the psychological effect would associate a certain emotional state with the function of a building. One could, for example, conceive of a design for an airport terminal, which rather than alluding to an object, would impart the experience of flight, speed, spaciousness, etc. to the user. A symbol would be an architectural form that is given a particular sociocultural meaning. Sometimes, for example, circles and squares are given religious significance related to God and the cosmos.

The icon and metaphor are poetic images—they are not turned inward upon themselves; they allow and encourage individual interpretation and development. The symbol, though, if it is a poetic image at all, is the least open to expansion of poetic value by the individual. Consequently, icons and metaphors can be and have been successfully developed in modern architecture.

One might question however the relevance of the symbol in today's circumstances. In the past, the use of the symbol was associated with a relatively coherent worldview. Moreover, if one could discern a cosmological outlook today, it would be characterized by a fluidity and relativity that might render meaningless the concept of symbolism in geometric forms. To redefine symbolism for contemporary architecture and proposed environmental communication, one must first investigate attitudes underlying the contemporary architectural approach, and then search for universal meanings used in Communication theory—not isolated preconceptions, but interrelated message systems.

Considering architecture and planning as communication systems, the way the above mentioned objects and events are manifested to us in any meaningful symbolic life form is based on certain sets of order—structure or relationships—communication languages. The combination properties and relationships of various communication languages provide different sources of information in various contexts, the sum of which is environmental communication or architecture or planning. Symbols are also either in the form of objects or events:

a. *Symbolic Objects*. Any object conceived of by various individuals, groups, and societies receives special individual or sociocultural values and then enters man's field of endeavors and interactions, thus becoming an environmental communication component. As mentioned earlier, the study of objects in their pure, objective form is the domain of the physical sciences and mathematics and geometry, yet the symbolic values they embody make them part of the applied sciences and aesthetic and qualitative architecture and planning.

b. *Symbolic Events*. Intermingled in any act is the individual, as well as sociocultural, values of its creator and its recepients. Such values constitute the base of any symbolism. Any human endeavor, such as talking, dancing, even walking, etc. extends beyond physical properties and encompasses a full range of individual and cultural gestures and intricacies.

In addition to meaning and symbolism involved in environmental communication, one could also point out the potentials in relationships of objects and objects, events and events, and finally, the order and organization of pattern symbols and such patterns, which have the capability of awakening the receiver rather than transmitting preconceived messages. Accordingly, whereas the task in the previous symbol type was to answer the query, "What is a church?" ("symbol-milieu"), now the question is, "What is a church like?" ("physical milieu"), Norberg-Schulz argues that "a building only reveals its full meaning when seen as a part of a symbol-milieu, where all objects carry values as participants in human action which are *never* indifferent."[8] I do not agree with his argument that all objects are never indifferent; they are not because we have not thought of them as if they were not. Rigidly accepting his viewpoint of predefined symbols would lead us to live in the past rather than in the future or, in other words, to disregard the concepts of change. As Whitehead says, "The art of progress is to preserve order and change, and change amid order."[9] In speaking of a synagogue, Kahn said, "A symbol. . . .is not what you invent, but what it becomes. I cannot build symbolically. But I hope the new synagogue does become symbolic."[10] This statement is a good answer to the assertion that "It is the symbolic content which gives the concrete things their social meaning."[11] So there is always the question of what a church wants to be rather than what it is. Our goal in this theory is not to see what kind of a symbol a church is, but rather what made that form become a symbol or be used as a symbol: "they designate general human conditions, they may open our eyes to characteristic qualities inherent in the work of architecture, and thus give the architectural experience a point of departure."[12]

C. A SET OF MESSAGES (MESSAGE SYSTEM)

It should not be assumed that such messages are only physical. They have a variety of form and character. From an anthropological point of view, Edward Hall has called them "primary message systems." They are as follows: (1) Interaction, (2) Association, (3) Subsistence, (4) Bisexuality, (5) Territoriality, (6) Temporality, (7) Learning, (8) Play, (9) Defense, and (10) Exploitation (use of material).[13] Here we try to reach for an understanding of the principles involved in these types of form and order. It is fundamentally different from the historical approach explained above. This means that the emphasis should be placed on the objectivity and universality of architectural experience. That is to say, qualitative values of architecture can also be quantitatively measured, at least for the sake of simplifying their complexity and enabling them to be comprehended. Thus we have to understand art for art's sake. Both symbolically or purely mathematically, it is "isolationism," and we know that everything changes its values when it is put in new circumstances in the environment. "One of the most general heuristic procedures of aesthetics, based on the *materiality* of the work of art, consists in progressively *destroying* the work *by known,* perceptible qualities, and in following the variations in aesthetic sensation, value, and knowledge as a function of this destruction. This is a method of concomitant variations."[14] So "It is meaningless to talk about meaning as *a priori*, or to imagine that the work of art tells us something only by 'representing itself'."[15] Rather a work of art is perceived through the order of the manifestations of the disposition of its physical component systems. Our perception is conditioned by fundamental physical laws.

Thus our goal is to see how this disposition of the different elements (parts) of a system communicates different information, and thus different meanings. Our goal is not to determine what preconceived meaning is. As Norberg-Schulz has pointed out, Gestalt psychologists have noted that "shapes change according to the context in which they appear. Even without foreshortening, a square may look rectangular because of its environment."[16] This is a good answer to followers of the first and second categories. For example, Alberti, even though he thinks that "numerical and geometrical relationships may produce *architectural* order,"[17] believes that symbolically a circle is a perfect form for a church.

We said that to decrease the gap between the creator and the receiver, we should put the stress on objectivity and form and develop basic, universal elements in addition to analytical theories in order to compose the elements into an overall form. The degree of understanding of such forms depends on the complexity and simplicity of such rules and orders. "Greater or lesser knowledge of these rules determines, not only apprehension, but *comprehension* of the message, at least at the level considered."[18] Structurally, simplicity and complexity, or in other words the probability of redundancy of an element, are thus among the fundamental values of the theory. "In the perception of forms, originality opposes *intelligibility* because only *forms* are intelligible and they reduce unpredictability, hence originality."[19] "What is most intelligible is what has the most bonds (liaisons), and is thus what is most often encountered in the networks of thought."[20] In other words, intelligibility has a direct relation to banality: "the position of the mind between intelligibility and creativity is only a transposition of its position between banality and originality."[21] An exception to the above statement is those forms which are not original but permanent.

An architectural form is a set of meaningful parts, each consisting of a set of basic elements which are perceived as a set of points. The degree of similarities and differences apparent in a form measures the degree of similarities and differences apparent in a form measures the degree of complexity of that form. This theory can help us in ranking points on the basis of their similarities and differences.

Pythagoras found that musical harmony is based on numerical relations of the length of a sounding chord. This idea was later used by the Greeks in their architecture as "frozen music." Vitruvius, on the other hand, used numbers in a new language; numbers were not important, rather the ratios of numbers were thought of as the order of nature (as in the human figure). "Harmony presupposes the repetition of a *module,* in such a way that all the parts of a building are brought into simple numerical relations with each other. This idea is derived from the organization of the human body."[22]

Later during the Renaissance period, the ideas of Pythagoras and Vitruvius were further developed. Ideal forms for a temple, city, etc. were designed on the basis of numerical proportions. A circle appeared to be one of the ideas preferred by man and by nature. A perfect composition existed when "nothing could be taken away or added without destroying the harmony."[23] In summary, the "numerical composition of the Renaissance is based upon the theory of musical harmonies. . . ."[24]

During the Baroque period, all such ideas of numerical and geometrical components, such as *a priori* beauty, were overthrown by Hume, who claimed that "Beauty is no quality in things themselves: It exists merely in the mind which contemplates them; and each mind perceives a different beauty."[25] Such a point of view changed the whole spectrum of architectural values. One does not expect to see pure geometrical and numerical properties used as an *a priori* form in human experience. However we find that even LeCorbusier adheres to Vitruvius' concept of ideal proportions in the human figure. His ideal figure is as subjective as Vitruvius', although I agree with him that "the problem of form is of a geometrical nature and that the work of art is 'mathematical'."[26] Geometrical and mathematical in this sense of the word takes "material" and "spiritual" factors into consideration. Both " 'physical' and 'psychological' objects are logical constructions based upon phenomena which, as such, can neither be called physical nor psychological; they are only classified to allow for a convenient division of work within the sciences."[27]

LeCorbusier's point of choosing the actual size of man as a model for his buildings is valid as far as the physical laws of human activities are concerned, but it is not related to human experience. For such purposes, we have to work with the mind's activity patterns rather than the body. This is our task in today's and tomorrow's architecture. Considering form as sets or messages—due to the potential or matter in space and time—this theory works with (1) *matter* as its basic elements and (2) *fields* as the structuring relations of these elements.

5.3 Environmental Field Communication

Environmental fields can be divided into two groups: physical fields and nonphysical, sociocultural fields. Physical fields can be further divided into two groups: (a) a field between an individual and a physical set and that between two physical sets; this can be termed a "physical-field," and (b) a field between an individual at time t and a void (space)—his position at time $t + n$; this can be termed a "void-field." Due to the important role that vision plays in architecture, and because visual fields share characteristics of both physical and nonphysical fields, visual fields in addition to the above mentioned divisions will specifically be discussed.

A. NONPHYSICAL, SOCIOCULTURAL FIELDS

Every individual carries with him a range of fields from the "personal" to the "universal." The forces and characteristics of all are determined by one's history, heredity, and environment. W.H. Auden, has written the following in regard to one of these fields:

Some thirty inches form my nose
The frontier of my Person goes,
And all the untilled air between
Is private *Pagus* or demesne

Stranger, unless with bedroom eyes
I beckon you to fraternize,
Beware to rudely crossing it:
I have no gun, but I can spit.[28]

Lewin has developed some concepts of fields in the areas of sociology and psychology. Ushenko has developed concepts in the area of aesthetics and meaning, and Edward Hall's notion of the hidden dimension can also be related to the concepts of field. In order to demonstrate notions of conceptual fields in architecture Edward Hall's concept of "hidden dimensions" may be elaborated upon.

Due to the great dynamism and complexity of phenomenological fields (nonphysical), no single model or method is satisfactory. Whereas the components of physical fields can be studied by direct measurement, with conceptual fields this is not possible. Just as physical scientists work with what psychologists term "geographical environment," the latter group works with what they call a "behavioral environment." The first field deals with actuality; one can say that by the study of the geographical environment one is looking for the actuality of things—for example, how solid an object is, where it is located, what it is doing—and since such entities are measurable, the task is more easily completed than in the case of a search in behavioral environments where one deals with relatively immeasurable entities. In the second case, the search is not for how things are, but for how we *think* they are—how they respond to us and how we interact with them.

This is one problem which architects have always faced and have almost always overlooked (at least consciously). In dealing with the character of these two fields they have been overwhelmed by the physical dimensions versus the "hidden dimensions." Edward Hall is right when he says that "Architects traditionally are preoccupied with the visual patterns of structure—what one sees. They are almost totally unaware of the fact that people carry around with them internalizations of fixed-feature space learned early in life."[29] A good example of such an attitude can best be seen during the Renaissance. For example, Luca Pacioli says, "First we shall talk of the proportions of man. . .because from the human body derive all measures and their denominations and in it is to be found áll and every ratio and proportion by which God reveals the innermost secrets of nature."[30] Such notions of six-teenth century architecture are still around. What is missing in them is the concept of hidden dimension of man and nature, the dynamic dimension which does not appear on the surface—a consideration of the soul of man rather than the body of man. Of course, no one doubts the importance of physical proportions, but this is not enough.

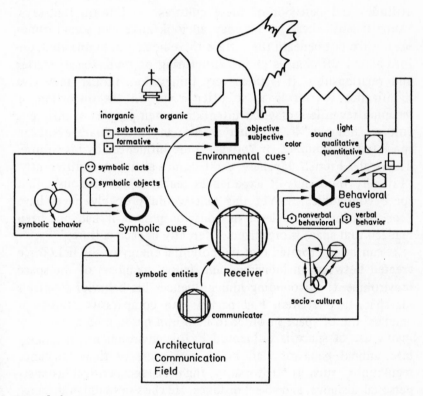

Figure 5–1

Architectural Communication Field Model

It is obvious that the case of a field between one man and another man (or men) is a general case of this kind of field. Edward Hall points out the existence of such fields carried by any living being besides his physical boundary. That is, "...another, non-physical boundary appears that exists outside the physical one. This new boundary is harder to delimit than the first but is just as real."[31] The study of such fields falls into the areas of cultural and sociological investigation. An architectural space enhancing these characteristics is not measurable solely as a physical one; rather, awareness of such space "goes far beyond cerebral activity. It engages the full range of senses and feelings, requiring involvement of the whole self to make a full response to it possible."[32]

An *a priori* analysis of man's sociocultural events-patterns would be superficial unless accompanied by a deep understanding of the attitudes and behavior of these cultures. As Edward Hall says, "Superficially, these groups may all look alike and sound somewhat alike but beneath the surface there lie manifold unstated, unformulated differences in the structuring of time, space, matter and relationships. It is these very things that, though they give significance to our lives, so often result in the distortion of meaning regardless of good intentions when peoples of different cultures interact."[33] In other words, any individual's events in space (either "public" or "private") are influenced by his culture. The Arabs, French, Japanese, and Eskimos all use space differently. "Literally thousands of experiences teach us unconsciously that space communicates. Yet this fact would probably never have been brought to the level of consciousness if it had not been realized that space is organized differently in each culture."[34]

It can be interpreted that the potential energy of the field force created between an individual and fellow members of the space (environment) surrounding him influences his behavior (controls his space-time events). Fall begins with comparative studies of animals' use of space in order to help him better understand how man's use of space is influenced by his environment. In looking into animal behavior Hall points out some of their "distance regulations" such as territoriality, flight distance, critical distance, personal distance, and social distance. He classifies human distance regulations into four types: intimate, personal, social, and public. Following Franz Boas, he develops the notion of "social and personal space and man's perception of it,"[35] and bases man's relationship pattern to the environment and to man on the communication pattern. "I hold that communication constitutes the case of culture and indeed of life itself."[36] Suppose, as Hall would say, communication constitutes life and culture constitutes communication. Then communication itself could probably be thought of as space-time events or processes of fields created between man and man and between man and nature. However, he states that space is the subject of any communication;

Spatial changes give a tone to a communication, accent it, and at times even override the spoken word. The flow and shift of distance between people as they interact with each other is part and parcel of the communication process. The normal conversational distance between strangers illustrates how important are the dynamics of space interaction. If a person gets too close, the reaction is instantaneous and automatic—the other person backs up. And if he gets too close again, back we go again.[37]

Hall goes further, saying that the substance of conversation could be subject to spatial relations between individuals of different cultures. "Not only is a vocal message qualified by handling of distance, but the substance of conversation can often demand special handling of space. There are certain things which are difficult to talk about unless one is within the proper conversational zone."[38] Later, we shall see to what extent these patterns are rooted in man's activity patterns in general (architecture).

Such communications are partly conscious and partly unconscious. "Communication occurs simultaneously on different levels of consciousness, ranging from full awareness to out-of-awareness."[39] Thus our environment consists of a set of complex patterns of field forces. Consciously or unconsciously we are being bombarded every moment with billions of bits of information. These patterns originate from many sources—generally those of a sociopsychological and physical nature. "Man's relationship to his environment is a function of his sensory apparatus plus how this apparatus is conditioned to respond. Today one's unconscious picture of one's self—the life one leads, the minute-to-minute process of existence—is constructed from the bits and pieces of sensory feedback in a largely manufactured environment."[40]

Another way of deriving concepts in field theory could be by using the notions developed by Fredrik Barth. One of the basic conceptual tools Barth utilized in his studies of cultures is that of "niche" as used in the biological sciences; i.e., the concept that the adaptation of an organism (or a group) to its total environment depends on the naural features of the particular habitat being exploited, as well as its relation to other groups in the habitat in terms of competition, cooperation, and symbiosis with each other."[41] Barth's concept of niche explains the mechanism operating which results in relationships which affect the disposition and structure of groups. One can also consider his concept as an example of the utilization of the notion of a conceptual field. That is, if different ethnic groups are utilizing the same ecological environment, the order of priority in the utilization of the niche or niches of that environment depends on the balance of power of the field created by each group involved based on the distribution and possession of political, economic, and social power. Thus in the case of inequality in the field of power of particular groups in a given niche, if the groups are to reside together the weaker is relegated to the marginal area, physically or economically (if it is able to utilize the marginal areas), or it is displaced altogether from the niche under consideration. Thus it is the field-power of each subsystem which determines the position of a subsystem within the total system.

One might also include Parsons' theory of action as another way of interpreting a conceptual field. In his theory of action (a theory of human social behavior), he bases the structure of interaction in a social system on a two-way process between man and objects: "an object may be significant in a given action process either because of its generalized properties independent of the specific relation to ego, the actor, or on the other hand, it may be significant precisely because of particular properties specifically deriving from its relation as an object to *him.*"[42] In comparison with our theory where man and his world are expressed by the structuring of matter-energy in the spatio-temporal world, he identifies two components, namely attitudes and objects. In his theory he tries to determine how the theory of symbolism can fit in with the theory of action. In so doing, he emphasized three points:

1. A distinction in kind cannot be made between cognitive and expressive symbols. Every symbol is characterized by both cognitive and expressive meanings.
2. All actions involve expressive symbols which presuppose the existence of conventionalized meanings attached to each expressive symbol.

3. the stabilization of the interaction process depends on the formation "of *complexes* of attitudes, symbolic acts, and objects with symbolic reference to each other. . . .It is the *patterning* of these symbolic references which constitutes the 'structure' of a system of action in the strictest sense."[43] Thus he states that the stability of the above organization depends on the "particular *relations* between the attitudinal and the situational components of a system of action. These types of relations, it appeared, could be formulated in terms of the combination of *one* pattern-variable component from the attitudinal side of the system with *one* corresponding component from the situational of *object-categorization* side."[44]

Thus Parsons seems to use Whitehead's theory of the abstraction of space, time, and material (touched upon earlier) as a basis for his theory of action. In this theory an object's basic cause of action (biophysical) is attitudes (cognitive, cathectic, and evaluative).

We said earlier that points (objects) communicate different meanings depending on their space-time structural location—the similarities and differences they possess with neighboring objects and elements contained in the memory storage. "A goal may be an existing object which could be attained (through perception or direct possession), or an imagined object which does not yet exist."[45] With such a definition of an object, value enters the object-system. Objects are perceived as wanted or not wanted. Hence they carry meanings depending on the different goals they are serving. Parsons and Shils have classified pure orientation to objects into three attitudes:[46]

1. The "cognitive attitude." This attitude classifies, analyzes, and describes objects.
2. The "cathectic attitude." This is the attitude which interacts with objects in regard to the "gratification" they give up.
3. The "evaluative attitude." This attitude creates norms for our interaction with objects. Whereas the cathectic attitude is subjective, this attitude is objective. It does not touch on personal values.

What Hall and Parsons are actually saying is that the space between a person and others, as well as the space between a person and his surrounding environment is not an empty space. Neither is it a solely geographical, massive space integral to events happening in it, but rather it is an active space carrying energies and information based on the properties of all the physical and nonphysical events-particles involved. This means that you do not stand in a similar situation with any person. You are independent of the form as well as properties of each participant, i.e., sex, cultural values, rank, appearance, etc. Rather the space in any situation takes on different dimensions carrying different dynamic states acting and reacting to find a state of equilibrium. When a young man is in a situation talking to a very attractive girl for the first time, depending on their appearances and the memory information of both, from the slightest interaction between the two, the space becomes bombarded with unique information-energy. Such information, depending on the knowledge, experience, sociopolitical, cultural situations of those involved in that space, information can be powerful. This also holds true between man and his environment (object-space). As Parson states in defining his theory of "action-space,"[47] objects take special form and characteristics by their users or by participating in sociocultural action spaces. This means that the coat you are wearing, the outfit and its color, shape, etc., would matter in activating the fields you create around yourself in relation to other people and the environments. The three characteristics of our natural, as well as man-made, environments-pure form, spiritual, and message system—would charge up their surrounding field spaces with relevant energy-information. This means that all the particles within a square space do not carry uniform energy, but every single point of space carries different types and qualities of load. The corners, as Louis Kahn says, have inherent in them, powerful attributes set to action due to their pure and symbolic form. They also convey messages to each individual regarding his stored information (sociocultural background). The center of a square, the center of each side, and even each single point along each side, and so on, carry different amounts and types of energy loads. The material, color and texture of each element of the space also adds new energies depending on the total characteristics of all the variables involved in the total system.

As stated earlier the messages meant to have been provided and received are often two different things, one in the mind of the creator (i.e., it is intentional) and another in that of the receiver. The two sets do not have to possess the same properties. And that is why the architect does not always correspond to the users' needs, perception, and criteria. To solve this problem two things can be done: educate architects to understand people, and educate people to grasp what the architect is attempting to do. Probably neither of the two would be successful because of the tremendous dynamism involved in the activities of each side. The only theoretical alternative left is what is actually stressed in this theory of architectural information field, i.e, work with the nature of *form* as the mediator between the two; that is, find the potentials hidden in form, the potentials which stimulate both the creator and the perceiver of the form. We should also try to define the building blocks of this form or information field.

Thus the result is that we have to develop ways of understanding and defining the basic (universal) primary elements and then establishing rules and theories to enable us to compose those hierarchical elements into a meaningful whole.

If that is the case, the author does not see any reason why, in addition to physical fields (developed by physicists) and socio-psychological fields (developed by psychologists), we cannot use the notion of Field theory in the study of mental stimuli responses to physical patterns in the environment, where the composition of these fields gives us architectural fields.

In phenomenological fields, as in field physics, it is expected that the parts, regardless of the subject matter, be integrated into a uniform whole by means of organized methods. An illustration given by Ushenko can clarify this point. Let us imagine a specific room furnished—in an organized method—so that one could hardly distinguish a chair from a table, table from television, etc. In such a situation the word "chair" or "table" would not be enough to locate an object. Instead, an object would be called a chair by virtue of its location, e.g., in this case, at the corner of the room. This illustrates that in such fields we do not recognize the components through their isolation, but through their structure and specific function and relation within the whole. In other words, it is with regard to such contextual fields that in disregard to the context of the room as a whole, we may identify the furniture, piece by piece, provided each piece is marked off from others by participation in some standard context.[48]

Furthermore, Field theory creates unity "(1) by a fusion of distinct field into one of a higher order of complexity, (2) by a reduction of particles to field, (3) by a reduction of matter to space, and (4) by a reduction of space to field."[49]

Norberg-Schulz states that "A *common order* is called *culture*. In order that culture may become common, it has to be taught and learned. It therefore depends upon common symbol-systems, or rather, it corresponds to these symbol-systems and their behavioral effects. Participation in a culture means that one knows how to use its common symbols. The culture integrates the single personality by giving him a feeling of security in an *ordered* world based upon meaningful interactions."[50]

B. PHYSICAL FIELDS

a. Tangible Fields

Although from the title of this section one might expect physical fields to be studies by physical scientists, this is not the case. Rather, this section deals with fields perceived by individuals and projected onto physical reality. "We can never be aware of the world as such, but only of. . .the impingement of physical forces on the sensory receptors."[51] Such forces are always present and affecting us. It is the consciousness and unconsciousness of our senses which brings them to the surface in the form of communication messages. "Each animal also inhabits a private subjective world that is not accessible to direct observation. This world is made up of information communicated to the creature from the outside in the form of messages picked up by its sense organs."[52]

A field between an individual and a tangible entity or set. In man's experience of the environment as sets of entities (objects, points) it can be said that the entity, depending on the order of the composition of its points (space, time, and matter), has a certain power (potential) to keep man in a certain relation to itself. His resistance against such a power creates discomfort which becomes resolved in a comfortable balance when the mover advances a certain distance from the entity.

A field between two tangible entities or sets. In a man's experience of two entities (objects, points) it can be said that each of the two, depending on the order of the composition of its points, has a certain power (potential) in relation to others. (This means that each point has a power on all its surrounding points.) The result of those two powers (forces) is a balance of the potentials of the participant's expectations. The best example of this type of field is a gravitational field. A good visual example is Michelangelo's rendition of the hands of Adam and God on the ceiling of the Sistine Chapel.

b. Intangible Fields

In an observer's experiences of space defined by the composition of tangible entities, it can be said that a void, depending on the order of the composition of its points, also has the power to locate the participant in a certain position. There is one difference between space-field force and mass-field force: we are within the space and outside the objects. Although space is made up of mass and conditioned by the mass enclosing it, it has something beyond that which can be defined by its enclosing masses.

C. VISUAL FIELDS

Two kinds of visual fields can be defined, the tangible and the intangible.

a. Tangible Fields (Mass-Visual Fields)

Any visual point of matter in space-time is thought to have certain potentials depending on its location in space-time or its relation to other visual entities. The greater its differences from its neighboring points or the greater the probability of its originality (H), the greater its potential (energy-density). The greater its similarity to neighboring points or the lower the probability of its originality, the lower its potential.

The reason why a visual, interacting process is called a field is clear. The change of potential $\frac{dx}{dt}$ at the time t depends on the situation at t and not on any other past or future situation. A visual field is obtained through the interaction of visual entities on

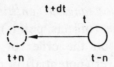

Figure 5–2
Visual Fields

the one hand and the observer and visual entities on the other. Michelangelo's painting of Adam and God is a good example of the first type of field (a), whereas the observer's interaction with an object is characteristic of the second type(b).

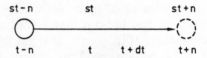

Figure 5–3
Visual Fields

b. Intangible Fields (Special Fields)

Any event is thought to have the following characteristics: In accordance with the principles of quantum theory and Hiesenberg's uncertainty principle, our attempt to see an isolated state representing an event is probably not possible. However we can think that an event starts (more or less) with a certain potential with a state $S + - n$ and ends (more or less) with another state $S + + n$ during which its potential (charge) changes its value (magnitude) depending on its relation to $S + - n$ and $S + + n$. In other words, its charge changes depending on its degree of proximity to or remoteness from its goal $(S + + n)$. The starting point

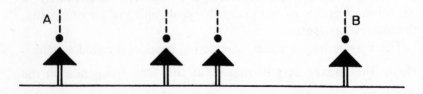

Figure 5–4
Spacial Field

(decision-point), climax, and discharge can be thought of as the highlights of such a process, each being at an extreme in the use of energy. The climax is followed by emptiness and discharge. Here also the change of potential $\frac{dx}{dt}$ at the time t depends on the situation at t and not on any other situation in the past or future. An example might be helpful. Suppose Mr. X wants to go from A (where he is now at $t - n$) to B (his seat at school where he is going to be at $t + n$). After the decision is made for such an event to take place, a pair of potentials is set up between P_A and P_B where the acting potential is $P(P_A - P_B = P)$. P is a funtion of P_A, P_B and the nature of the path available between $_A$ and $_B$. P_B can be thought of as a set (S) of probabilities of $_B$'s availability, acceptability of receiving the charge.

S is partly known to Mr. X as (S_1) and partly unknown as (S_2) where he does not have a knowledge of it. Path AB can also be thought of as a similar set (S) of probabilities $(S_1$ known and S_2 unknown to X) P_A, Mr. X's willingness to go ahead and take the risk between known and unknown determinants. Mr. X's getting to B is conditioned by many sets of variables generalized in history, heredity, and environment. In this study we are not going to deal with all of them. What we are concerned with here is learning something about the effect of the form of the environment as a physical determinant on man. One can easily argue that it is not fair to separate the physical from the nonphysical or provide any other break in the whole (human experience). However, there is no other alternative; we have to break the whole down into more simplified areas in order to be able to deal with it. Experimenting with the above theory certainly involves some limitations and assumptions. In making such assumptions on the part of Mr. X's behavior, we can follow the assumptions made by Zeigarnik in a series of experiments in the area of human will power. These assumptions are certainly helpful as determining factors for P_A. The experiments concerning association and " 'the measurement of will power'. . .suggested the theory that the effect of an intention was equivalent to the creation of an inner personal tension."[53] The theory makes the following assumptions:

Assumption A1–"The intention to reach a certain goal G . . . corresponds to a tension (t) in a certain system (S^G) within the person so that $t(S^G) > o$."[54]

Assumption A2–"The tension. . . $t(S^G) = o$ if $P \subset G$."[55]

Assumption A3–"To a need for G corresponds a force p, G acting upon the person and causing a tendency of locomotion toward G. If $t(S^G) > o \int P, G > o$."

Assumption A3a–"A need leads not only to a tendency of actual locomotion towards the goal region but also to thinking about this type of activity; in other words the force $\int P, G$ exists not only on the level of doing (reality) but also on the level of thinking (irreality); if $t(S^G) > o \int P, R > o$."[56] (R = recall)

Furthermore, if we represent a completed task by C and an unfinished task by U and their systems as S^c and S^u, "The tendency to recall interrupted activities should be greater than the tendency to recall finished ones."[57] On this basis $t(S^u) > o$, $t(S^c) = o$ and hence $P, U > \int P, C$.

Now that assumptions have been made concerning the nature of P_A, we should say a word about P_B and the path AB in the relationship $P_A - P_B = P$. First of all, P_B should be smaller than P_A, or in other words, the goal should be attainable. Secondly, suppose there are n states (Ei) between A and B $(A, E_1, E_2, E_3, . . E_i. . . , . . E_n, B)$. Earlier we talked about the quantum theory and Heisenberg's uncertainty principle in defining the boundaries of an event. The same uncertainty also exists for any state E_1 of the process from A to B depending on the flexibility of both the path AB(media) and Mr. X's activity pattern. The more rigid the activity patterns of the two, the easier it is to predict and vice versa. Thus the probability of predicting a state E_i of the path is a function of its time, T_i, as well as the fluidity of both the path and X. To deal with the high uncertainty involved in the full dynamic character of the field, assumptions must be made. Thus it should be assumed that some hierarchy of fluidity and rigidity can be established. As in the very beginning of geometry, one discriminates between the notion of solid and space. Such discrimination helps one perceive the nature, background (space), and foreground of objects located in space. "In order to be able to locate objects in space, we must *know* these objects, that is to say they must, roughly at least, preserve their identity."[58]

This assumption reduces the dynamism of objects which "were to appear to us changeable as the clouds, whose shape is constantly being changed by the effects of wind and sun."[59] Thinking of such dynamism gives us a space quite different from one bounded with assumptions. Either end of the scale seems useless—to think as a "bird that is moving in the midst of clouds. . . unable to perceive a fixed point on earth or in the sky. . . ."[60] or as a partridge who buries his head in the snow not to see outside, ignoring outside dynamism. It is a question of our experience and conception of space, and thus it depends on the mind conditioned by heredity, history, and environment.

Gestalt theory can be very helpful in understanding visual fields and the measurement of the potentiality of visual entities. "Gestalt theory deals with form only as the manifestation of forces, which are the true object of its interest. Physical and psychical forces can be studied only by their perceivable effects. Thus the overall direction of energy in a given system may appear as a visible axis in the observed pattern."[61] Although Gestalt psychologists stress the concept of form and its determination by "forces inherent in the object itself,"[62] they realize that "It is hardly true at all for the work of art. In the visual arts, except for the effect of such inherent qualities of the medium as the weight of stone, the grain of wood, or the viscosity of oil paint, form is imposed on matter by external force."[63] These forces are further described: "The psychological forces that determine artistic form operate essentially in the perceptual process of vision and in the area of motivation and 'personality'."[64]

Arnheim asks, If visual forces are not coming from physical objects, where *are* they coming from? He notes that "Gestalt psychologists refuse to describe them as an effect of empathy, that is, as a mere projection of previously acquired knowledge upon the percept. They assume that the sensations of push and pull are the conscious counterpart of the physiological processes which organise the percept in the neutral field of the optical sector, that is, the cerebral cortex, the optic nerve, and possibly the retina of the eyes."[65] Otherwise, those forces are not due only to subjective association, but also to geometric characteristics such as shape, size, line, and location. In other words, a visual artistic pattern is capable of forcing the observer to follow its necessitated articulation, even if his subjective "visual history" does not also follow. For example, let us consider the rules of visual grouping; i.e., the notions of similarities and differences among visual objects which Max Wertheimer has formulated. He suggests that "The relative degree of similarity in a given perceptual pattern makes for a corresponding degree of connection or fusion. Units which resemble each other in shape, size, direction, color, brightness or location will be seen together."[66]

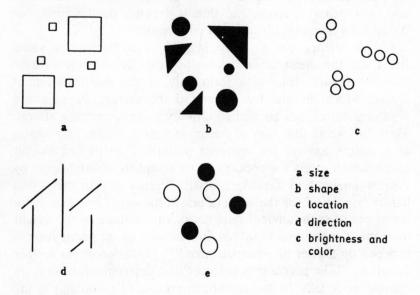

a

b

c

d

e

a size
b shape
c location
d direction
e brightness and
color

Figure 5–5
Visual Grouping

W. Köhler points out the relation between the notion of similarity and the theory of entropy saying that the principle of similarity is a special case of the general case in which the physiological and psychological forces are moving toward simplicity. In other words, in looking at a set of visual patterns, the observer tends to search for the simplest organization and order (this will be discussed later).

At this point I would like to mention some of A. Chang ih Tiao's notions of architecture which are based on Laotzu's philosophy. Such concepts can be seen as intimately related to Field theory concepts in architecture and especially to visual field in architecture.

Architectural composition primarily calls for a happy combining of similarity and difference. The former furnishes ease of apprehension and, because of uniformity of construction elements, is what an architect can easily have. The latter creates change and interest but, because of functional and material limitations, is what an architect ordinarily lacks.[64]

Because of such lack architects usually disregard man's experience as a full integration of all the senses. "Man's experience in space includes smell, hearing, touch and the interrelated sense of temperature and humidity. All these will contribute to man's sensation of distance between his position and the sources of sensation. None of these sensations, however, is as important as that of vision."[68]

D. VISUAL FORCES.

We usually think we see our world through our visual perception of masses, though in reality it is only light moving through voids which makes masses visible. The sensation of masses would probably not exist if it were not for voids. So the essence of vision can be found in the interrelation and interaction of masses and voids. In the past we have been more consciously occupied with masses and have been "space blind." However Bacon says the awareness of space "engages the full range of senses and feelings, requiring involvement of the whole self to make a full response to it possible." For this reason, "a conscious expression of space is essential to the highest expression of architecture."[69] Moreover Zevi says that the void in architecture is likely to be overlooked. Yet it is the most useful since it can always be filled by solid. The visual elements in one's surroundings include everything which transmits those surroundings down to a point in the participant's eyes.

a. Architectural "cuts" and visual forces.

We defined cut as the boundaries of an element of form These cuts play an important role in architectural forms, because physical form in architecture makes itself manifest only through the forces created at the points of contact between the forces of mass and the forces of space (void). Chang ih Tiao calls this interaction an organic experience. "The relation between man's experience and light in nature is an organic change between the tangible and the intangible. . . ."[70] So in actuality it is the architect's task to get to know the form of these cuts more than anything else. Here is where the drama of architectural sophistication appears. Cuts are the mirror of life and death in architecture. They reflect both the forces created by forms, mass, and space. These cuts are the musical instrument of the architect who is creating architecture, its notes being the set of its points and its sound being derived from the touch of each point of this set by man's sensations and carried along by light and vision.

b. Architectural cut and time.

"It is the natural picture frame, the emptiness surrounding an unfinished manifestation of physical reality, which makes a momentary being integrated and induces man's fluid continuity of clear vision in time. It is so because human mentality, as a part of unfinished nature, is provided for the experience of unfinished existence."[71] We just talked about cuts as the primary elements forming architecture. What would the role of time be in such a formation? How do we perceive a flashing speak of water or the dynamic growths of a tree or a flame of fire in the air? These dynamic cuts seem to be even more important than static ones, because our whole purpose in choosing a force as a basic unit for architecture is to enable us to talk about life rather than death, to analyze the dynamism of architecture rather than a static building, to picture the flow of life's events instead of a static existence. Life is a continuous flow of events. We are living within these events. "Nature is eternal because it does not manifest itself."[72] So to feel the movement of events passing by is the very meaning of life. How could we have architecture without life, i.e., without time? That is why I have over and over repeated that form is not the elements themselves but the interaction between these elements. So in architecture, as in music, it is not the sound of one note alone or the sum of the notes which creates music, but the experience of their interrelation; i.e., the perception of subsequent events while still being aware of those immediately preceding.

Psychologically we live in time and space, and time and space derive meaning from everchanging events. So time "although intangible, is more intimate to man because it is more sensible within the human organism itself and primarily makes up the continuity of life."[73] So consciously or unconsciously, as explained previously, architecture is based on time and can be defined as a "spatial expression of human life and experience in time."[74] These experiences consist of many conscious and unconscious memories and dynamic images already shaped in the mind, the domain of which is always beyond reach. This is because of our inability to grasp the unconscious and psychological domain, e.g. psychological time. Thus architecture as an exact applied science is meaningless. Objectivity could be valid to some extent by establishing some generalities rather than definite rules. The definite rules can exist in their fullest meaning only in the minds of individuals who apply the objective generalities involved for their own purposes.

"Visual objects are not as static as we might carelessly think they are. Actually they have life. They have life because their existences are complementarily interrelated to and influenced by each other; because they are subject to transformation due to the transfusion between brightness and darkness, and because they are experienced by life."[75] The above statement also reinforces the importance of not looking at objects in isolation for their own sake. The cuts must be seen as the most active parts of the environment which reveal those tensive and compulsive energies.

c. Color and its visual forces.

Color, light, and texture have visual forces. "Light, natural or manufactured, floods to every corner of an architectonic form. Darkness, which is preserved, is what makes depth be seen. If light be called the life-blood of an architectonic form, darkness could rightly be called its soul."[76]

There is a gradation between darkness and light; and any mass point has a quality depending on its darkness and light. Each has its own general characteristics:
1. Darkness creates a depth and so pulls the observer in.
2. Light, on the other hand, comes closer to the observer and hence its forces push him away.

The shadow of a white concrete entablature on a texture of dark brick moves the wall farther in and produces an inviting effect. The following are major factors which must be considered in reference to light:

1. The direction of light.
2. The scale and intensity of light.

The perception of the visual form of an object or a surface is influenced by the above two qualities.

d. Movement.

Man's perception and vision in motion concerns space and time. Things in movement do not appear to us as they are in reality or as they are when they are constant. An object moving away from us has the tensive power of pulling us with itself and vice versa. "Our motion in space and past experience helps us to understand that an object of normal size actually is bigger than what appears in our immediate perception from a certain viewpoint."[77]

Objects which vanish in space also seem to be moving away from us because they take us away with them. They help increase the distance, because the forces created in us in following them extend beyond the point at which they terminate. Thus when the object has come to rest we are still following it. The reverse is also true. Objects which are increasing in size seem to become greater than they are and come closer to us than they actually are. This is true because of the factors involved which are opposite to those mentioned above.

"Any existence occupies time, but no existence persists in time. When the speed of motion is high, the mind will be occupied by preceding objects and not capable of accepting a new independent image."[78] At the same time it cannot be said that since it is not accepting new images this means it is not aware of being influenced by them. This kind of unconscious experience is what makes existence complex and rich. Probably the richness is due to continuity and the overlap of elements; we comprehend something while something else is in our surroundings ready to get our attention.

e. Texture.

Texture also gives quality to surfaces. In texture we can fully see the value of points in architecture. The lightness, roughness, and darkness of points on a surface makes the energy within that surface "come out" and be visible. On a homogeneous, smooth surface without any texture the forces are always running on the surface out toward the edges. The reason is that one does not see anything on the surface to catch his attention. Consequently, he moves his eyes to the boundaries where he sees the energies going in and out. On a textures wall (e.g. one of the old brick walls) one sees patterns (of darkness and light, roughness, and smoothness), "attracting" him, They work as an abstract painting in which one seeks meaningful patterns. So texture breaks down the scale of large surfaces and creates closer contact, eliminating the distance between the receiver and the surface. Any surface and texture itself does not have definite value unless it is seen together with another texture, since in both conception and perception, one cannot conceive of white without conceiving of the existence of black. All is relative; white is white next to grey, whereas a grey can appear to be white next to black.

Texture also creates a certain depth and pulls one in as darkness does (the absence of darkness produces the opposite effect). The reason for this is that, first of all, texture creates dark spots, and secondly, it creates an abstract pattern which puts the conscious mind to work.

Notes to Chapter Five

1. Colin Cherry, quoted by Charles Jencks, in *Modern Movements in Architecture*, (Anchor Books, Garden City, New York), p. 172.
2. C. Norberg-Schulz, *Intentions in Architecture*, p. 89.
3. S. Humphreys—Owen, "Physical Principles Underlying Inorganic Form," in *Aspects of Form*, p. 9.
4. *Ibid.*, p. 10.
5. H. Poincaré, *Science and Hypothesis*, p. 85.
6. *Ibid.*, p. 86.
7. Victor F. Lenzen, *Procedures of Empirical Science*, University of Chicago Press, Chicago, 1938, pp. 55-56.

178   *Environmental Communication*

8. C. Norberg-Schulz, *Intentions in Architecture*, p. 88.
9. A. Whitehead, *Process and Reality*, Humanities Press, New York, 1966, p. 515.
10. L. Kahn, quoted in "The Philadelphia Architect," *Philadelphia Sunday Bulletin*, August 25, 1968, p. 30.
11. Gregor Paulsson and N. Paulsson, quoted by C. Norbert-Schulz, *Intentions in Architecture*, p. 88.
12. C. Norberg-Schulz, *Intentions in Architecture*, p. 90.
13. E. Hall, *The Silent Language*, Fawcett, Grennwich, Conn., 1959, p. 45.
14. Abraham Moles, *Information Theory and Esthetic Perception*, Univ. of Illinois Press, Urbana, Ill., p. 201.
15. C. Norberg-Schulz, *Intentions in Architecture*, p. 67.
16. *Ibid.*, p. 93.
17. *Ibid.*, p. 93.
18. A. Moles, *Information Theory and Esthetic Perception*, p. 161.
19. *Ibid.*, p. 197.
20. *Ibid.*, p. 197.
21. *Ibid.*, p. 197.
22. C. Norberg-Schulz, *Intentions in Architecture*, p. 91.
23. Rudolf Wittkower, *Architectural Principles in the Age of Humanism*, quoted by C. Norberg-Schulz, *Intentions in Architecture*, p. 91.
24. C. Norberg-Schulz, *Intentions in Architecture*, p. 91.
25. Laugier, *Observations sur l'architecture*, quoted by C. Norberg-Schulz, *Intentions in Architecture*, p. 92.
26. C. Norberg-Schulz, *Intentions in Architecture*, p. 92.
27. *Ibid.*, p. 82.
28. W.H. Auden, "Prologue: The Birth of Architecture," quoted by E. Hall, *The Hidden Dimension*, p. 107.
29. E. Hall, *The Hidden Dimension*, p. 100.
30. Luca Pacioli, *Divina Proportions*, quoted by R. Wittkower, *Architectural Principles in the Age of Humanism*, Random House, New York, 1962, p. 15. Hereafter cited as *Architectural Principles*.
31. E. Hall, *The Silent Language*, p. 146.
32. Edmund H. Bacon, *Design of Cities*, The Viking Press, New York, 1967, p. 15.
33. E. Hall, *The Hidden Dimension*, p. x.
34. E. Hall, *The Silent Language*, pp. 148-149.
35. E. Hall, *The Hidden Dimension*, p. 1.
36. *Ibid.*
37. E. Hall, *The Silent Language*, p. 160.
38. *Ibid.*, p. 162.
39. E. Hall, *The Hidden Dimension*, p. 4.
40. *Ibid.*, p. 59.
41. Fredrik Barth, "Competition and symbiosis in North East Baluchistan," *Folk*, 6:1 (1964), p. 15.
42. T. Parsons and R. Bales, "The Dimensions of Action-Space," *Working Papers in the Theory of Action*, Free Press, Glencoe, Ill., 1953, p. 70.
43. *Ibid.*
44. *Ibid.*
45. C. Norberg-Schulz, *Intentions in Architecture*, p. 64.
46. T. Parsons and E. Shils, *Toward a General Theory of Action*, Harvard University Press, Cambridge, Mass., 1951, p. 5.

47. T. Parsons and R. Bales, "The Dimensions of Action-Space," p. 70.
48. A. Ushenko, *The Field Theory of Meaning,* p. vii.
49. *Ibid.,* p. 88.
50. C. Norberg-Schulz, *Intentions in Architecture,* pp. 79-80.
51. E. Hall, *The Hidden Dimension,* p. 40.
52. *Ibid.*
53. K. Lewin, *Field Theory,* p. 9.
54. *Ibid.*
55. *Ibid.*
56. *Ibid.,* p. 10.
57. *Ibid.*
58. Emile Borel, *Space and Time,* Dover Publications, New York, 1960, p. 38.
59. *Ibid.*
60. *Ibid.,* pp. 38-39.
61. R. Arnheim, "Gestalt Psychology and Artistic Form," in *Aspects of Form,* p. 196.
62. *Ibid.,* p. 197.
63. *Ibid.*
64. Ibid., p. 198.
65. *Ibid.,* p. 199.
66. *Ibid.,* p. 201.
67. A. Chang ih Tiao, *Intangible Content and Laoizu's Philosophy,* p. 41.
68. *Ibid.,* p. 12.
69. E. Bacon, *Design of Cities,* p. 15.
70. A. Chang ih Tiao, *Intangible Content and Laoizu's Philosophy,* p. 12.
71. *Ibid.,* p. 17.
72. Lautzu, *Tao-te-ching,* Chapter 7, quoted by I. Chang ih Tiao, p. 17.
73. A. Chang ih Tiao, *Intangible Content and Laoizu's Philosophy,* p. 7.
74. *Ibid.*
75. *Ibid.,* p. 17.
76. *Ibid.,* p. 16.
77. *Ibid.,* p. 18.
78. *Ibid.,* p. 20.

6. Architecture as Communication Field

6.0 Introduction-Abstract

In this chapter architecture is defined as communication. In developing this viewpoint three sets of theories are put together: *System's theory, Field theory,* and *Information theory.* Here the objective is to look at the total environment as fields of "action" space having resulted from an interrelation and interaction among all sociophysical energy patterns. It is argued that architectural space is not to be thought of as the geographical boundaries of a sum total of its particles, but rather as the materialization of total environmental and human activity patterns.

Environmental communication is viewed as a system in which space-time events or the process of their formation in communication fields created between man and man and his environment and their characteristics give meaning to communication systems. An object or event may be significant in an environmental communication system either because of its properties independent of man or relative to particular properties derived from him. In other words, the space between a person and the environment is not empty space; it is active space carrying energy and information based on the properties of the physical and nonphysical, quantitative and qualitative disposition of energy patterns.

Similarities and differences perceived in the patterning of matter in communication field is considered to provide man with meanings, and therefore messages. Information is received where there is doubt; doubt is accompanied by the existence of an alternative choice. Organized and random choices, whether consciously or subconsciously originated, make the environmental message system. To measure the probabilistic occurrence of such message patterns, the principle of Information theory is used. Entropy is considered the key concept in measuring the information capacity of a set of patterns based on the degree of its randomness or order. Originality and variety are the criteria of information measurement. Higher originality and variety of the parts creates contrast and vitality resulting in rich information. Similarities and uniformity creates monotony and lack of information.

6.1 Communication Field—A Proposed Definition of Architecture

There are two basic concepts of architecture—the material and the nonmaterial or sociopsychological. These two have other subdivisions. Material aspects can be divided into mass and void—tangible and intangible.

The tangible and the sociopsychological aspect can be divided into an increasing number of subdivisions such as sociology, psychology, economics, etc. History shows that in the development of architecture, architectural concepts in the past were more shelter-oriented. Architecture was conceived of as providing man with protection against the inclemency of climate. The idea of space has always existed, though with different perception. Man's discrimination between masses and voids in architecture has its beginning in the first developments of architecture, where man used masses to provide protection against the weather and severe climate.

If we go back to the beginning of the twentieth century and look for the origin of modern architecture, we shall see how the whole history of architectural concepts could have been altered by a change in man's perception of nature owing to the advancement of science. Up to that time the conception of masses and voids as separate entities was not only typical of architects, but also of man's understanding of the universe in general. According to the classical atomistic view, matter and energy were two separate phenomena following certain deterministic laws of nature. The concept of relativity, quantum theory, and other related concepts changed this picture. Structuralism took the place of atomism and space-time became the new coordinate within which matter was conceived of as a new form of energy or as a new form of space. It is not the inherent quality of the units of an entity which make it manifest to us, but the structure of its organization. The scientist is also "concerned with groups of 'events,' rather than with 'things' that have changing tution of space-time for space and time."[1] By that time architects should have been aware of the fact that they could change the character and form of buildings from mass to void and from void to mass by means of a restructuring of the order and organization of its material; i.e., by having dynamism and fluidity, a building changes from one form to another. However great steps have been taken in this direction in the formation of the modern architectural movement; i.e., cubism, futurism, constractivism and its influence on this direction. These concepts not only proved to architects that mass and void are interchangeable and constitute one entity with different structures, but that matter is also represented as another form of energy. This notion is explained by the theory of relativity as follows; "energy can be converted into mass. . .all elemental particles are made of the same stuff—namely, energy."[2] What would this mean to architecture? It would mean not only that masses and voids are of the same matter, but that they both are a flow of energy. How can we interpret the results of this change in emphasis? Its development will probably someday prove that social and material phenomena are one and the same. Hence the whole dualism between the materialistic and social approaches in architecture would become one, and architecture would appear as energy patterns.

The intent of this book is to search for a new architecture based on the twentieth century concepts of the physical sciences. To achieve this we should go back and examine the line of development of science up to the transition from concepts of atomism to those of structuralism and quantum theory, and field physics. Thus we can look for the potential of matter and energy due to its order and structure, rather than seek the subjective preassigned values attached to different entities in isolation. Here we can find architecture as space-time events. Then we can hope to bridge the gap between the materialistic and social elements of architecture in a search toward common ground for both phenomena.

This is an interesting proposition, especially in light of the fact that creative and material processes traditionally have been consciously separated from each other. Thus Whyte[3] suggests that creative matter could be termed "formative structure." If this is the case, creativity would be seen, not as some mysterious, innate gift, but a product of the physical activity of the brain. Professor Perry also seems to think along the same lines as Whyte. He searches for an understanding of human values within a biological framework. Köhler discusses Professor Perry's theory of animal behavior as follows:

Animals . . . perform adaptive acts "in the *expectation* of . . . consequences." "Owing to the capacity of memory, life is circumspect and *prophetic*." The animal "acts not because of what is or has been, merely, but because of what he *anticipates*." His attitude is one of fear or hope "of something; which something is not upon the plane of past or present physical existence as ordinarily conceived.[4]

More acceptable at this time is Professor John Wild's point of view, expressed in discussing Merleau-Ponty's work:

Social scientists will be interested in his selection of behavior (*comportment*) as a central category, because of its neutrality with respect to the traditional distinction between mind and body. Human behavior is neither a series of blind reactions to external "stimuli" nor the projection of acts, which are motivated by the pure ideas of a disembodied, wordless mind. It is neither exclusively subjective nor exclusively objective, but a dialectical interchange between man and the world, which cannot be adequately expressed in traditional causal terms. It is a circular dialectic in which the independent beings of the life-field, already selected by the structure of the human body, exert a further selective operation on this body's acts. It is out of this dialectical interchange that human beings emerge.[5]

As stated earlier, some look down on any materialistic search into phenomenological fields such as architecture, asserting that there is nothing materialistic about such processes as creativity and aesthetics. It is worthwhile to elaborate on man's physical and mental activities—on creativity and its materialistic characteristics. Merleau-Ponty rejects the idea that the mind and body are two distinct entities. "He emphatically denies that what was called the soul is a separate, vital force exerting a peculiar, non-physical power of its own."[6]

Whyte has explained this creative process in further emphasizing the mind's physical aspects. Following a detailed discussion of man's plastic brain and its functions, Whyte notes the possibility that "the coming decades may see the creative powers of the human mind traced to the structural properties of the material fabric of the brain. This would imply that 'creativity' has been identified in matter'!"[7]

Thus far little attempt has been made to discover the mechanisms involved in the creative process. One reason could be the idea that the quantitative method with its precision could not be fruitfully applied to creative activity. "A metaphysical revolution is necessary to extend the traditional foundations of science, analysis, precision, and constancy, to include ideas which can do justice to combination, simplification, and a process leading toward novelty."[8] Of course this development has already begun in recent times. Whyte holds that the aesthetic creative process is a simplifying one in which material is not only selected and rearranged, but simplified as well. In so doing, the human brain distorts the material received as it does in other mental activities. This is true in all great art. Thus the artistic output is directly based on the plastic mechanisms of the brain, and more specifically, the cortex. To say that man does not add anything to what he receives seems illogical. As John Wild says, man has both "perceptiveness" and "originality." "This body, as I live it from the inside, is quite different from the objective body which is observed, though each perspective is legitimate and the two overlap at certain vital points, which introduces an essential ambiguity into the whole situation of man."[9]

Considering the mind's activity pattern as an extension of nature—material patterns—then architecture can be defined as *a dynamic process of structuring matter-energy in the spatio-temporal world.* The following is a statement of what architecture could be.

6.2 Architecture as Communication Field

The advancement of man's knowledge and understanding of inherent potentials of nature and technology during the eighteenth and nineteenth centuries has made tremendous changes in man's view of life and his concept of the universe, but considerably less change has resulted from environmental philosophy. Architecture is not and cannot be treated as the making of artifacts made by one individual. Today architecture is the product of numerous diversified disciplines and professions each of which thinks of architecture differently, looking at it from a specific angle. The bewildering variety of subdivisions in the study of man and his environment is due to two kinds of problems: (1) different interpretations of man and his relation to society, and (2) different interpretations of man and his society and their relation to nature. Today the advancement of science and technology has made us aware of, and has enabled us to use, the endless potentials of matter, and the decomposition of each particle's properties and potentials or its dispositional property and technology, in shaping our life and environment. Communication and Information theories have provided advances to the physical sciences, which enable us to transfer information regarding any event from any corner of the world to another. The unique characteristics of structural interrelationships of matter-energy in the spatio-temporal world have demonstrated that there is neither room for isolation of any constituent element, nor isolation of any change of state at any level; rather each part of the system is viewed as an integral part of the total system.

This is to say that our environment is built of a very complex communication system which, in contrast to the classical view of Newtonian physics, emphasizes structure rather than particles or events themselves. On the other hand, Newtonian physics and Euclidian geometry, similar to our present views of architecture which still follow them, emphasize the world as a mathematical sum of its particles. (In classical physics atoms are considered the final elements. Hence an atom is conceived as being a unit which determines the nature of things, and each event is conditioned by its origin in a deterministic way.)

However the world known to us today is a complex dynamic field of interactions, in which the whole is greater than and different from the sum of its parts. Each particle, element, is so totally integrated to the whole, that any change in its state of being is conditioned by the state of all the other parts of the system. Thus it can be said that each particle carries as much information as the whole. Each particle geographically takes a space and the sum of all particles makes up the total space. However, its dispositional potential (energy-information, due to transformation or dispositional properties) is not equal to its geographical size. Rather, its dynamic qualitative boundaries extend beyond the geographical quantitative boundaries of the entire system.

Taking this view of space, architectural space is likewise not to be thought of as geographical boundaries of a total sum of its particles, but rather the materialization of total human activity patterns, including the physical, metaphysical, natural, and socio-cultural flow of energy-events. Obviously the still used traditional definition of architecture as conceived by the Greeks and Romans, particularly the discrimination between mass and void and the awareness of static physical form and the apparent formation of masses, is no longer as useful.

To the Romans, architectural masses were the form and space was a finite representation of isolated parts. After the Greeks and Romans, the Renaissance approach to the aesthetics of form and architecture was, for the most part, based on *a priori* values and also the study of prevailing ideas and form. With the turn of the century advancements in the physical sciences brought up new horizons in man's view of nature, both in the sciences and the arts. Architectural concepts although affected by the new philosophies, have not been very much altered by this change in man's perception of nature due to the advancement of the sciences. Up to that time, the conception of masses and voids as separate entities was not only typical of architects but also of man's understanding of the universe in general.

After the 18th century, different branches of scientific awareness grew into disciplined areas. As a result, such disciplines as planning and design suffered for the universality of their outlooks, and for the combination of subjective and objective viewpoints. Historically the designer had a general notion about what was relevant to his work and thus took a holistic approach to problems based on intuition. In contrast, the emergence of specialized disciplines resulted in different scientific approaches, developing from the same specific issues.

In contrast to the traditional views of architecture, new approaches based on information pattern and message systems have been developed. These new looks in architecture are a search for systematic studies of the materiality of space and form. These new methods substitute quantities for qualities; quantities gained through probabilistic measurements of entropy and Information theory.

In the author's opinion, *architecture is not solids and voids, it is not building construction, it is not visual boundaries and empty space, but rather it is a dynamic continuous flow of all material and nonmaterial matter-energy events.* Architecture is an "action space"[10] in which each point-particle (energy-matter) has its unique properties conditioned by the structuring properties of all the points of the total field. The "action space" created is activated by "hidden dimensions"[11] resulting from cultural attributes as well as from socioeconomic values carried by different people and objects.

So the study, teaching, and finally, practice of architecture should be founded on an understanding of universal laws common to different disciplines related to environmental planning and design and a synthesis of intellect with feeling, quality with quantity, material with the nonmaterial, and the conscious with the subconscious, based on the understanding that architecture is a harmonic symphony that can emerge from the rational and irrational blending of these elements into meaningful order.

Developmental trends of our physical environment clearly demonstrate that our cities, once rich in spatial organization responding to the totality of units inherent in the conscious and subconscious activities of man and spaces, are turning into ugly uniformities, dictated by similarity of standard units and mass-produced elements created by man's conscious act to counterbalance the growth of the natural world, on the one hand, and the high diversity resulting from the expansion of the material world and resulting technology, as well as the problems received through the greater diversity of individual values on the other.

So today there is a great need for new philosophical orientation to environmental planning and design to seek the common unity of all factors and various elements within an environmental field. We know that there exist many diverse views affecting our picture of the environment and yet they end in the same unity in which they begin.

Let us think of architecture as the physical manifestation of culture (in its broadest definition) and define culture as a communication system in space and time, the media of which is man's total universe and the messages of which are formulated through the interaction of the physical and metaphysical in the form of symbols and values, the values being the manifestation of social interactions either on a conscious or subconscious level and the symbols being the disposition of matter in space and time in physical or biological forms. Whereas values are of individual as well as social origin, symbols take on either tangible physical form, e.g., the environmental symbol system, or intangible form, e.g., language, sociocultural interactions, and so on.

Let us also for the present think of the world around us as energy flows, i.e., energy associative as matter, and energy disassociative as radiation; matter presenting the material world, and energy the nonmaterial (sociocultural). Using these definitions, architecture can be defined as: *a dynamic process of structuring matter-energy in the spatio-temporal world.* In so doing, the above definition of culture and architecture will be used as a starting point, whereupon, in an effort to compliment this broad definition, a *general framework of man's relation to his universe* will be defined to further describe the above conceptual outline. Having defined the structure of universe and culture, communication systems are proposed as a reflection of the structure of the universe, and thus *culture,* and Field theory is proposed as a possible model for such communication systems and thus *architecture.*

Outlining this general framework, let us follow-up with Fuller's definition (mentioned in the first chapter) of *physical* and *metaphysical*: the universe consists of both the physical and metaphysical.[12] Every phenomenon which science can weigh, measure, and identify as energy, is a part of *physical reality.* Any and all of our thoughts are unweighable. They and their comprehensive family of concepts and generalized principles and our awareness of the interrelationship of experience and our progressively developed understanding of the interrelationship are altogether weightless and constitute what we speak of as the metaphysical part of reality. Starting with Fuller's definition of the universe we have further subdivided the divisions—the physical and metaphysical—as follows: 1) physical: material and natural (physiobiological, and 2) metaphysical: conscious and subconscious.

The nature of these four components as discussed in previous chapters has been analyzed by various disciplines, which have all developed their own theories, searching for a better understanding and an ability to predict more accurately.

Here we shall not basically make any subdivision in the material world, i.e., consider physical and natural components together in one category, and emphasize the second category, namely the nonphysical world. That is because the nature of the material and natural elements of the universe have been the subject of a great number of investigations, measurements, and developments and advances of the physical sciences. Therefore it can be readily evaluated, filtered, and transfered. The development of the intellect and knowledge has also advanced due to the measurability of its properties against various philosophies and the accumulation of intellect and knowledge which is tied both to the material world and its principle laws of nature and to the immeasurable dimensions of the qualities of life, and therefore subconscious behavior. That part related to subconscious behavior has no yardstick or standard by which it can be measured. So this is the crucial part which cannot be analyzed by means of any logical process but rather through society as a whole. The only measurement for such an evaluation is the dynamic process involved in the entire cultural process, in which every individual consciously and subconsciously plays a vivid and active role. As a part of this last component, aesthetic values should definitely be mentioned as one of the most significant indicators of man's sense of creation and change. They embody all the cultural values expressed through the active participation of culture's creative participants. Within such activities, different virtues and qualities related to the ordered-disordered senses of the participant are represented in such material form as color, form, proportion, and finally, beauty.

The major problems in disciplines dealing with aesthetics, art, and the humanities arise from our lack of knowledge and understanding of these properties. To point out the main basic problematic area of architectural study and design within the history of human experience and knowledge is to point out what parts rationality and nonrationality play in the process of experiencing architectural forms, and where and how they meet in conceptualizing a form of art. The two opposing characteristics of art form which satisfy the two outstanding principle desires of man are rationality and "order" (rational order) versus nonrationality and "disorder" (nonrational order, random patterns). The first category is *a priori,* objective knowledge based on conscious thought processes such as those of the mathematical, physical, natural, and pure sciences. The second category being *a posteriori,* is subjective subconscious experiences based on intuition, perception, and immeasurable innate emotional desire dealt with in the sociopsychological sciences and the arts.

Though emotional drives—as well as other qualitative and subjective values, i.e., the pattern and structure of the mind—are not measurable, they may be indirectly observed. In social terms one might say the subconscious behavior of members of society is reflected in "social relations,"[13] while conscious behavior is reflected in "social structures." Whereas social relations reflect empirical reality, social structures are those models derived from this reality. In contrast to the other three categories, no common ground can be found among different disciplines in discussing subconscious behavior.

As Poincaré has stated, "logic and intuition have each their necessary role. Each is indispensible."[14]

Consider the previously stated definition of architecture, *a dynamic process of structuring matter-energy in the spatio-temporal world.*

In order to arrive at a unified system which could integrate the universe's constituent components discussed above, and from which this definition of architecture could be drawn, one might suggest a field of communication system within which each of the four constituent components could be conceived of as a subcommunication system, where formation and transformation of events are formed through a discharge of information. Whereas ordered-disordered patterns express timeless formations of information occurring irrespective of any preconceived subsequent states—which are therefore rich and unexpected in nature, ordered patterns are specific cases in the system where predicted changes are presented with zero information. *Within this approach then the entire universal system, as well as culture, exists.* And any art forms can be described as one complex communication system consisting of such constituent systems.

Within such a communication system, information is transmitted via *ordered-disordered pattern systems of messages*: ordered-disordered patterns are measured against the laws of *entropy* and *centropy,* and thus considered to be information or noise, to be meaningful or meaningless, and the messages are shaped through media as well as sociocultural (and individual) content symbols and value systems.

In searching for a method to deal with difficulties between material and nonmaterial issues, the concept of Field theory in environmental studies is introduced, by which one can hopefully escape the problems of the "bifuration" of nature into the physical and nonphysical, "reality" and "appearances," matter and substances. Based on the concepts of communication fields, architecture is defined as the disposition of matter in space and time, where the position of each point in relation to the rest, as well as its similarities and differences with surrounding points gives it a special potential-energy. Models as representations of reality (physical and nonphysical) conceptualize the physical and non-physical phenomena in an integrative way. Matter carries along with it specific potential energy because of our perception of it. The quantitative character of energy (in the physical sciences) is here transformed to sociopsychological energies due to their behavior. In other words, in architectural communication models, the physical models are dealt with, any point of which carries a potential energy due to the nonphysical *a priori* and *a posteriori* values which have been assigned to it. The notions of probability and their application in Information theory are used to measure the degree of similarities and differences in architectural physical patterns (communication field properties) or, in other words, to measure the originality of a point (or element) in a set of points (or elements), or the degree of order/disorder of the set. Laws of entropy based on the theory of probability are used, both in the physical and social sciences, and are employed here to measure the energies related to both groups.

The theory begins with a simultaneous consideration of the physical and social aspects of the environment. Matter is conceived of as representing the physical aspects of human life, and energy the social aspects. The analysis of the physical form of the environment is based on the concepts of fields, with primary emphasis on the structure and interrelations among entities. Nothing is considered in isolation since each entity is what it is because of its relation to other entities in terms of similarities and differences.

Thus our goal is to see how this disposition of the different elements (parts) of a system communicates different information, and thus different meanings. Our goal is not to determine what preconceived meanings are. It is believed that to decrease the gap between the creator and the receiver of artistic expression, we should put the stress on objectivity and form and develop basic universal principles in addition to theories, as well as basic primary forms, structural frameworks, elements, and ways of composing the elements into an overall form. The degree of understanding of such forms depends on the complexity and simplicity of such principles and rules and orders. Greater or lesser knowledge of these rules determines *comprehension* of the message and their building blocks. Structurally, simplicity and complexity, or in other words the probability of redundancy of an element, are thus among the fundamental values of the method. In the perception of forms, originality opposes *intelligibility* because when *forms* are to be understood, rationalized, and reasoned, they are intelligible and they reduce unpredictability, hence originality and richness. What is not intelligible is what has the most uniformity, and is thus what is most often encountered in the networks of thoughts, not feelings. In other words, intelligibility has a direct relation to banality; the position of the mind between intelligibility and creativity lies on the area between rationality and nonrationality and, therefore, between banality and uniformity and originality and complexity.

An architectural form is a set of meaningful parts, each consisting of a set of basic elements which are perceived as a set of points (energy patterns). The degree of similarities and differences apparent in a form measures the degree of complexity of that form. This method can help us in segregating and finally quantitatively measuring their values on the basis of their similarities and differences.

From childhood we have become acquainted with these objects and whenever we needed something our actions took the form of "signs" in order to attain it and discharge the potential of the force created by our expectation. This is why Parsons sees "symbol-systems" as systems of socialization. The ways through which such socialization is expressed are "imitation" and "identification."[15] Imitation means accepting cultural determinancy, whereas identification puts us in contact with inborn values related to sign-object systems. This process is not a static one; it is continuously changing and substituting old expectations with new ones. So social structure is ordered through common values and expressed through symbol-systems and appears in object form. For example, language is a symbol-system, consciously or unconsciously structured and based on cultural values expressed through symbols and manifested in object forms, through the principle of similarities and differences. These patterns reach our understanding when filtered through our mind in an ordered form.

Pythagoras found that musical harmony is based on numerical relations of the length of a sounding chord. This idea was later used by the Greeks in their architecture as "frozen music." Vitruvius, on the other hand, used numbers in a new language; numbers were not important, rather the ratios of numbers were thought of as the order of nature (as in the human figure). "Harmony presupposes the repetition of a model, in such a way that all the parts of building are brought into simple numerical relations with each other."[16] During the Baroque period, all such ideas of numerical and geometrical components, such as *a priori* beauty, were overthrown by Hume, who claimed that "Beauty is not quality in things themselves: it exists merely in the mind which contemplates them: and each mind preceives a different beauty."[17]

This is our task in today's and tomorrow's architecture. Considering form as sets of messages—due to the dispositional potential of matter in space and time—this theory works with (1) *matter* as its basic element, and (2) *fields* as the structuring relations or forms relating these elements together.

A. MATTER

In architecture the final step is the crystalization of form. We assume that our form is in essence *made matter*. In actuality we use that as a unifying element with which to work. The world is composed of matter and energy. Matter itself is made of energy (Einstein's $E = mc^2$), and so we have only energy with which to work. The world is nothing but a "field" of energy patterns. Such patterns are both unknown to us and seemingly without a unit. Energies sometimes manifest themselves to us in the form of matter. At least for the time being we do deal with matter as being the clue. It solves some problems (causality, duality between the two units of measurements, etc.) and creates new ones (no exact unit with which to work, no perceivable order, etc.)

In architecture as well, we could use energy as a unifying element. In this way, all the disciplines could work with one another (physical, social, or psychological sciences). The problem of qualitative and quantitative, subjective and objective could thus approach a solution. One could assign quantitative values to relatively qualitative ones, not as an absolute answer but of necessity and in an effort to solve today's problems.

It would be helpful to touch on some of the studies of the social sciences and psychology in regard to Field theory.

B. FIELDS

In the physical world, $\frac{dx}{dt}$ is a change at the points n in time dt. The principle of field theory is that $\frac{dx}{dt}$ at t depends only on the situation at t and not on the past. In other words, any change in any point in space-time is not due to properties of any isolated space-time properties based on the structure or interrelationships of the elements. In Clark Hall's words, "As I see it the moment one expresses in any very general manner the various potentialities of behavior as dependent upon the simultaneous status of one or more variable, he has the substance of what is currently called field theory."[18] Any event can be considered a state of change in a conceived field, or as Stephen Pepper says, "The problem of potentiality—or, as some call it, of 'dispositional properties'—is probably the central philosophical problem of this and the next few decades. It is instanced in logic, in the problem of the 'conditional contrary to fact'; in scientific method, in the operational theory of truth; in ethics, in the emphasis on attitudes; in the general theory of perception; and here in the theory of aesthetic perception."[19]

The question of aesthetics or any phenomenological theory is that which has been discussed here, and can be divided into two levels, one of abstraction (phenomena), and the other of concreteness (pragmatism).

Such categorization is clearly demonstrated in the behavioral sciences working with "Field Theory." Here man and his environment are taken as a field. In that field the sociopsychological aspects are left, as much as possible, for the social scientists to handle. In working with the physical, we are again faced with the problem of the dualism between matter and energy. We choose to work with matter because the final form is going to be crystalized in matter. However in working with matter, specific assigned energies will be substituted, and thus could be thought of as energy-patterns as well.

Architects, like scientists, should endeavor to transform phenomena into "concepts," in order to work with them. We shall not get anywhere by sitting down and saying that art cannot be measured because it involves qualitative values. Granted, art is subjective and qualitative, but we need (1) to work with both qualitative and quantitative theories in a single system, and, (2) to perceive the basic, inherent universal laws of the phenomena. An example of such "elements of construction" can be seen in points of movement, the basic producers of a line, surface, etc. These methods, "generic definition," have been recommended by Cassirer as a means of coordinating qualitative and quantitative approaches to phenomena. He asserts that this method "is able, at the same time to link and separate; it does not minimize qualitative variables."[20] In addition, theories are needed (3) to break phenomena down into smaller elements so that they can be dealt with and also be put back together again, and (4) to develop means of evaluating and measuring both qualitative and quantitative values.

In further elaborating on this theory we should first define the characteristics of three-dimensional space. To do so we may use

Poincaré's analogy for defining a "physical continuum" and the notion of "cut."[21] The total form, as stated above, is a set consisting of an assemblage of point-energy patterns, broken up into subsets (elements). The following analogy is true whether the points are forming the subsets or the subsets are forming the set. It might happen that: (1) one of these elements (or points) cannot be "discriminated" from another element (or points); (2) one of the elements (or points) can be discriminated from another element (or point; this element or point is sufficiently different from that one); (3) two elements are indistinguishable from a third one and are distinguishable from each other. Suppose A and Z are two distinguishable points of a subset K, and suppose there are n points (E_1, E_2, E_3, . . . E_n, etc.) between A and Z indistinguishable from one another and from A and Z. In this case we say K is "one piece." The total form is the assemblage of these "pieces" which are "divided" by a "cut or cuts." So the cut or cuts are also a set of parts forming the boundary of the subsets.

In the above subset K, if none of the parts (E) is distinguishable from any parts of the cut, we can say that one can go from one side to the other without cutting the "cut." If there are some points of the subset K which are distinguishable from the points of "cut or cuts" we say that one can't go from one side to another without cutting the "cut or cuts." Rather, one has to go out of "the pieces" and out its boundaries.

An individual and his environment form an interacting unit. This interaction is expressed in a set of messages composed of similarities and differences reached as combinations of various cuts characterizing the external world. Such messages are not simplified, isolated entities. As explained previously, they are superimposed and constitute integrated levels. Points, lines, and surfaces are the elements, and a message is grasped by an observer on the basis of that scale at which a set of points or elements are meaningful to him. Because of the superimposition, one element might simultaneously participate in the formation of different messages on different levels. The repertoires are known to the "perceptor" (R_1, R_2, ... R_n).

To each point in psychological space and time could be assigned specific qualitative energies, the quantitative values (density) of which could range from $-\infty$ to $+\infty$ depending on the similarities and differences between it and neighboring points and throughout the total pattern; the lower the absolute value of the density of a point, the greater its similarities to neighboring and other points. These energies would characterize the architectural qualities of any given point; in visual terms positive energies, possessing a pulling power, would first create a psychological tension. Then negative energies, possessing a pushing power, would create a psychological repellence. Architectural form would thus be a harmonious, pleasing combination of ordered patterns of tensive and repellent energies. The same principle holds true for other energy-information patterns, in any information field.[22]

We could employ any event or sets of units of energy-matter able to convey messages to us by segregation on the patterning of its units or their state of change. Such information systems could be considered a work of art. This would mean that the very nature of segregation in our minds would not be there unless a pattern of energy and information had been transferred to them by our minds. We can now reverse the situation (assigning the energies and information of mental stimuli patterns to those of space-time patterns which originally generated these mental stimuli patterns) and say that space-time patterns have positive-negative energies and a store of information capable of being grasped by the mind. Effected by such energies, a work of art is a combination of tensions, balance, rhythm, etc.

In order to use Field theory in environmental studies for both matter and mind, we can divide environmental activities into two parts—one physical and the other nonphysical (this pertains to mental activity and is phenomenological). The study of architecture as an aesthetic experience, as well as a sociopsychological interaction, would be the combination of both types of fields. In other words, the holistic characteristics of phenomenological fields are much more important than they are in physical fields. In phenomenological fields, as in field physics, it is expected that the parts, regardless of the subject matter, be integrated into a uniform whole by means of organized methods. Consequently, in keeping with the above discussion, we can compare the physical and nonphysical aspects of the environment in consideration of Locke's and Descartes' theories of material substances, Northrop's normative social theory, Parsons' theory of action, Lévi-Strauss' structuralism—formulations of the structure of mind in relation to the structure of culture—and Edward Hall's theory of man's pattern of behavior in relation to spatial factors as a manifestation of "communication fields."

6.3 Measurement of Field Properties

The similarities and differences perceived in the patterning of matter (energy) in the environment by man provide him with meanings, and therefore messages. The disposition of matter in space-time also creates changes which add new messages to the former ones. Any events (disposition of properties) in space-time creates messages, that is, "procedures," by which the mind is affected in communication.

Since our task here is not the study of man but the environment, man's behavior (as a sender of messages) is considered one aspect of the environment, and his behavior is conceived of materially by the receiver. In this theory everything is regarded as a change of states in matter.

Information is received where there is some doubt; doubt is accompanied by the existence of an alternative choice. We constantly make choices among alternatives, but they are not all conscious ones. A painter chooses colors and places them on a canvas consciously and subconsciously. Discrimination is the simplest and most basic operation performable.

A pointillist painting which consists of a set of n colors arranged in a specific way is an example of the above. Let us take a very simplified case in which the painter is only using pure unmixed colors, not letting them overlap so that the result is dots on the surface of the canvas. Let us say there are eight colors and in this very specific situation the painter has decided to paint (put the dots next to the other from left to right and from top to bottom). The process of his painting is as follows: There are eight sources (colors) in each act of choosing a color and putting a dot on the paper. The painter should choose one of the eight colors. The *a priori* probabilities of the choices are all equal, i.e., 1/8.

1st	2nd	3rd
1	1	1
1	1	0
1	0	1
1	0	0
0	1	1
0	1	0
0	0	1
0	0	0

Figure 6–1

In choosing a color in any act of placing dot on the canvas the painter should first answer three questions by either "yes" or "no." They are as follows: Is it among the first four colors: 1, 2, 3, 4? (Let us say the instructions say, Yes, in this example; see fig. 6–1). The second question is, Is it in the first two colors of the first four or in the first two colors of the second four? And finally he can divide the second group of double-choices to make a single choice. In the above alternative between two measures, a zero (*0*) signal is given for a nonchoice and one (*1*) is given for a choice. To be somewhat more specific, the amount of information is defined, in the simplest cases, to be measured by the logarithm of the number of available choices, it being convenient to use logarithms to the base 2, rather than common logarithm to the base 10.

A two-choice situation is characterized by a unit of information. This in the case of a unit is called a "bit" in a "binary digit" system, i.e., when the digits are only 0 and 1. If one has 8 alternative messages from which to choose, $8 = 2^3$ and $\text{Log}_2 8 = 3$ and the situation has 3 bits of information in the above examples; or, 3 bits of information are needed for the painter for the selection of each dot-color among 3 equal choices.

The notion of similarities and differences and one's conception of such patterns seems to be greatly based on the theories of probability. One's prediction of the location of specific matter or the occurrence of an event depends on the chaotic or orderly nature of the pattern. The higher the order of such patterns the higher the probability of prediction or understanding of the behavior of the matter. Thus not only is probability essential, but the concept of entropy is as well. The principles of entropy are principles at which most of the sciences have arrived, and even some artists. Arnheim has stated that "while Gestalt theorists recognize a tendency to 'good form' or 'well organized structure,' the physicists see a development from order to disorder."[23] According to the principles of entropy, when the situation is highly organized, in deterministic systems, it is not characterized by a large degree of randomness or of choice—that is to say, the information (or the entropy) is low.

A set of patterns in which the sequences occur according to specific probabilities, is termed a "stochastic process." The special case in a stochastic process in which each situation depends on the previous situations is called *Markoff's chain*. Markoff's process is a mathematical tool which predicts new patterns on the basis of their past behavior and in regard to their entropy. Thus entropy is the key concept for meeting the requirements for setting up information. It is based on the degree of order of pattern and the degree of their occurrence. The concept of entropy could be the most helpful theory for the measurement of information where the physical systems are always directed toward less organized systems.

To state the mathematical sequences of Information theory, I shall use Hancock's logical steps. The most simplified communication system is one which deals only with discrete symbols. All the symbols are of equal duration. For example, consider a source which is producing English letters at a uniform rate. The measurement of the information of such a discrete message system is usually as follows: to take the logarithm of the probability of occurrence of the message $x = - Log\ P$, where x is the measure of information, P is the probability of the occurrence of the message.[24] The base of the logarithm shows the units of information associated with the message.

The logarithm usually has the base 2, and x is carrying units of bits.

$$X = - Log_2\ P\ bits$$

When we have only one single occurrence with a probability of *P*, its information can be measured by the above formula. Suppose we have more than one source. It is often desirable to compute the average information per symbol in the case of a long sequence of symbols.

We can conclude that when we are dealing with one source with a *single* event which is producing a long sequence of symbols, there are two basic state-characteristics of the process which assist in attaining a higher degree of power (degree of attraction) and richness in a composition: (1) originality and (2) variety. Originality in the parts of a composition provide it with foreground and highlights. In the case of a lack of originality a composition is monotonous. A higher originality of parts helps establish contrast of sequences. However variety tends to create richness and greater dynamism. In any case, there is no way to give any value judgement concerning originality or contrast. It is the harmony of the whole which makes any composition good or bad.

A general formula of the above special case can be as follows: Suppose that there are *m* different points with the probability of choice of occurrence of each $P_1, P_2, \ldots P_m$.

$$H = -(P_1 \log P_1 + P_2 \log P_2 + \ldots P_m \log P_m)$$

$$H(x) = -\sum_{i=1}^{m} P_{(i)} \log P(i) \quad (1)$$

The addition of a constant *K* before the summation amounts to a choice of a unit of measurement where the source *x* is producing *m* independent symbols, and where the symbol *i* occurs with a probability of *P(i)*, and where *H* is called the *entropy* of the source.

So far we have been dealing with a discrete source with independent symbols with a one-event situation. Let us now consider the same situation but with two events. Let us say that we have an event *x* with *m* possibilities and an event *y* with *n* possibilities where *P(i, j)* is a joint probability of occurrence:

$$H(x,y) = -\sum_{i=1}^{m} \sum_{j=1}^{n} P(i, j) \log P(i, j) \quad (2)$$

$$H(n, y) \leqslant H(n) = H(y)$$

As said earlier the probabilities are equal, H is the maximum. If symbols are not independent:

$$H(y/x) = - \sum_{i=1}^{m} \sum_{j=1}^{n} P(i, j) \, Log \, P(j/i) \qquad (3)$$

$H(y/x)$ of y means the conditional entropy that is the entropy of y when x is given.

Let us now look at the previously mentioned case of a painting consisting of elements (points) from a different point of view, that is, as a continuous set of points. Any discrete set can be thought of as a simplified set of continuous sets, the elements of which are continuously variable and undefined. In other words, when the number of elements of a discrete set increases toward infinity, the discrete set becomes continuous. In contrast, when the size of each entity in a discrete set is broken down into a number of smaller and smaller entities the set changes its character from a discrete to a continuous set.

In the case of discrete sets we saw that

$$H = - \, Pi \, Log \, Pi$$

Now in the case of continuous sets, instead of using the probability of each entity, we use the density distribution function of each $P(x)$ and as Shannon suggests:

$$H = - \int_{-\infty}^{+\infty} P(x) \, log \, P(X) \, dx$$

Suppose that x has a distribution of $(1, 2 \ldots \ldots n)$, we have $P(n_1 \ldots \ldots n_n)$.

$$H = - \int \ldots \int P(x_1 \ldots \ldots x_n) \, log \, P(x_1 \ldots \ldots x_n) \, dx_1 \ldots \ldots dx_n$$

Accordingly the joint probabilities, conditional probabilities, could be calculated.

To define and produce architecture through architectural basic elements based on Field theory, we deal with probability and entropy as the measurement of qualitative properties of architectural fields. We use such methods as were first developed and used in physics mathematics. "To consider qualitatively different geometrical entities (such as circle, square, parabola) as the product of a certain combination of certain 'elements of construction' (such as points and movements) has. . . been the secret of this method."[25]

If qualitative entities are dealt with through *a priori* topological and vector concepts, it "(a) makes each situation open for quantitative treatment, (b) does not handle these qualitatively different situations as entirely separate entities, but conceives of them as a result of certain quantitative variations or of variations in the distribution of forces."

Notes to Chapter Six

1. Bertrand Russell, *The Analysis of Matter*, Dover Publications, New York, 1954, p. 286.
2. Werner Heisenberg, "Problems of Atomic Physics," in *Space, Time, and the New Mathematics*, ed. by Robert W. Marks, Bantam Books, New York, 1964, p. 124.
3. L. Whyte, chapter on "His Creative Activities," *Accent on Form. An Anticipation of the Science of Tomorrow*, Routledge and Kegan Paul, London, 1955, p. 17 ff. Hereafter cited as *Accent on Form*.
4. Wolfgang Kohler, *The Place of Value in a World of Facts*, The New Amerikan Library, New York, 1966, p. 59.
5. John Wild, Foreword to *The Structure of Behavior*, by Maurice Merleau-Ponty (Bonson: Beacon Press, 1963), pp. xiv-xv.
6. *Ibid.*, p. xv.
7. L. Whyte, chapter on "Creative Activities," *Accent on Form*, p. 155.
8. *Ibid.*, p. 158.
9. J. Wild, Foreword to *The Structure of Behavior*, by M. Merleau-Ponty, p. xv.
10. T. Parsons and R. Bales, "The Dimensions of Action-Space," in *Working Papers in the Theory of Action*, p. 70.
11. E. Hall, *The Hidden Dimension*.
12. R. Fuller, "Architecture as Sub-Ultra-Invisible Reality," unpublished paper, p. 2.
13. C. Lévi-Strauss, *Structural Anthropology*, Doubleday & Co., Garden City, New Work, 1963.
14. H. Poincaré, Science and Hypothesis.
15. T. Parsons, *The Social System*, Free Press, Glencoe, Ill., 1951, p. 211.
16. C. Norberg-Schulz, *Intentions in Architecture*, p. 91.
17. Luca Pacioli, *Divina Proportione*, quoted by R. Wittkower in *Architectural Principles in the Age of Humanism*, p. 15.
18. C. Hall, quoted by K. Lewin in *Field Theory*, p. 44, taken from E.R. Hilgard and D.G. Marquis, *Conditioning and Learning*.
19. Stephen Pepper, Introduction, *Dynamics of Art*.
20. K. Lewin, *Field Theory*, pp. 32-35.
21. H. Poincaré, *Value of Science*, p. 55.
22. A.T. Minai, *Art, Science, and Architecture*.

23. R. Arnheim, "Gestalt Psychology and Artistic Form," in *Aspect of Form*, p. 202.
24. John C. Hancock, *An Introduction to the Principles of Communication Theory* (New York: McGraw-Hill, 1961).
25. K. Lewin, *Field Theory*, pp. 30-33.

7. Architectural Communication Field's Building Blocks

7.0 Introduction—Abstract

In this chapter environmental communication field components are discussed. In the context of Systems theory, environmental communication field consists of a set of parts; each part or element is a finite ordered set of points perceived by individuals in different sets of structures. We define "point" thinking as the smallest element. Before there are any dimensions in the mathematical sense, we can assume that there is a definable place represented by a point, although such a point which can be grasped by the mind does not exist in reality. The idea here is to specify the importance of the classification of such a range of complexity in magnitudes and characters into certain typologies. System's theory and concepts of modulization provide a basis for such classification; i.e., where and how to cut the systems into subsystems.

In defining such typologies, not only are the objective views of the physical sciences used as criteria, the subjective views geared to the qualitative aspects of hidden dimensions of environmental communication which have resulted from a psychological and sociocultural symbol system are also used. In this regard, then, modulization in art and science is discussed separately. For example, with the exception of those called "objective artists," modulization does not mean anything in the plastic arts. Thus the views of artists such as Cézanne, Kandinsky, Mondrian, etc. which represent the first viewpoint are broadly discussed. Nevertheless, also mentioned are the opposite view points of aesthetics, e.g., Hodgarth who rejects any congruity between mathematics and beauty, or Hume who views all probable reasoning as nothing more than a species of sensations.

And finally, in the last section of this chapter, there is discussion of the building blocks of architectural field, including points, line, surface, and volume.

7.1 Modulization

In the search for understanding nature through art and science, one area of common ground is found: form and its related principles—structure, order, organization, and subdivision (modulization). Such form does not change its character for scientists or artists, for the intuitive approach or the logical approach, or for qualitative or quantitative measurements. It is we, looking at it through different eyes, who change our perception of it. "We do not say: there is a form where angles seem to total 180°, it has three sides, etc., therefore this form must be a triangle. On the contrary, we say intuitively, with hesitating, even with reflection, this is a triangle. Form therefore appears to constitute a bridge between art and science."[1]

Now let us look at the concepts of modulization from both points of view—art and science.

A Modulization in science
B Modulization in art

A *Modulization and measurement in science.* Scientists have always dealt with the notion of modules and measurement, yet they have shifted their interest from one area to another. At one time an understanding of the units was considered the final goal in comprehending the law of nature. Now the form and interrelation of parts are the area of investigation.

That was a hundred years ago; science then was the manipulation of exact measurements. Now, in the twentieth century, the stress has shifted. Measurement and precision are still necessary, of course, but we now recognize them to give only the raw material for science. The aim of science, we now see, is to find the relations which give order to this raw material, the shapes and structures into which the measurements fit. We are no longer preoccupied with the mere facts, but with the relations which the facts have with one another — with the whole which they form and fill, not with the parts. In place of the arithmetic of nature, we now look for her geometry: the architecture of nature.[2]

In discussing the nature of biological forms and their modulation, Waddington states that in the deepest sense, biological form "can never be modular in the sense in which an architectural or pictorial design may be."[3] Hence architectural form might be categorized as a specific case of biological forms. He further states that there are of course many other biological forms which are built up of units, where these units are much larger than cells and also composed of a large number of cells. The same thing is true in the modular units in a building which is constructed of numerous bricks. Kepes also elaborates on the modular principle of having two characteristics. The first characteristic is the use of some standard unit of length or volume as the basis for the whole. The second characteristic is the adoption throughout the whole of certain definite series of proportional relations. As stated previously, in an architectural spatial system composed of units, the smaller the number of its units, the larger the units and the easier it is to comprehend and manipulate. But this far from represents the flow of life, since the greater the number of units, the smaller the units and the more efficient their ability to respond to the dynamics of human psychological and biological needs.

Thus it is in parts, as well as in the whole, that we see nature. "The awareness of nature essentially requires both factors, namely, the sense of the whole and the discrimination of parts."[4] Now, the point is that when this number of units (in this theory, points) increases, some people may ask apprehensively whether it is meant that we have to consider every single point of a building. Actually, there is no cause for apprehension because we are not dealing with each point separately. Rather we are dealing with groups of points, point types characterized by the order and rhythm in organization and structure, found in nature as well as in man's activity pattern. Hence this rhythm and order (i.e., the standardization of physical and biological form) would cancel out a great number of these points. We can be thankful for the existence of structure, order, and rhythm. As Whitehead says, "The essence of rhythm is the fusion of sameness and novelty; so that the whole never losses the essential unity of the pattern, while the parts exhibit the contrast arising from the novelty of their detail. A mere recurrence kills rhythm as surely as does a mere confusion of differences."[5]

The next question concerning standardization is the nature of its units and elements. Are they equal in size, function, and character? The answer is no. This might have been the notion of classical physics, but,

to the modern scientist simple number and geometric shape as such are not the ultimate principle; they are only the formal manifestation of physical forces holding each other in balance. The atomic model is, of course, the prize discovery of the rationalist. If at the foundation of all matter there is no regular, simple, and symmetrical pattern as any order-loving mind could dream up, then it may seem sensible to expect that the shape of things around us is based on rationality.[6]

The scale of these units and the behavior of each level of organization is different and special for that specific scale. The notion of points in this theory is also based on rationality. There are in nature global patterns appearing and disappearing, shaping and reshaping, similar and dissimilar, large and small, constantly deceiving us with their similarities and differences. "The spherical surface of the raindrop and the spherical surface of the ocean (though both happen to be alike in mathematical form) are totally different phenomena, the one due to surface energy, and the other to that form of mass energy which we ascribe to gravity."[7] In the areas of organisms, "the forces which hold the elementary parts of a certain orderly relation to each other are not derived from the affinities of just a few kinds of units but arise from the interaction of very numerous active entities."[8] So there is no single unit and no single scale and level for these units of nature and the environment. Rather there is a set of different scales and levels of organization involved— "integrative levels."[9] Thus the order of integration and the nature of the units cannot follow the classical concepts of atomism (as purely additive). Rather the modern concept of integrative levels is involved.

In an effort to establish building blocks or basic elements for the physical environment, we see that both the scientists and the artist have developed theories. "Standardization aims at facilitating the functional relations between things. Since most manufactured objects are 'either containers of man or extensions of man' . . . ."[10]

Suppose we agree that there could be a set of units or basic elements forming the physical form of the environment. Then the questions would be: (1) what is the tool by means of which we detect these patterns, and (2) how are they patterned? If in answer to the first question I assert with Plato and Pythagoras that "everything is arranged according to numbers."[11] I have gone too far. There is a difference between saying that everything is arranged according to numbers (like they did in classical mechanics as if they understood nature as well as its laws) and saying that the number is our only tool for tracing patterns (however inadequate to represent phenomena). The second question is how these units and elements are organized and ordered in the totality of the whole. We see that this should be answered in a form which is not number but its greatest complex form—a numbered number.

B *Modulization and objectivity in the arts.* In contrast to scientists, some artists think that art cannot be explained or analyzed. So Francois Molnar says, "The work of art, on the other hand, cannot be explained. Its beauty may or may not reveal itself, but it does not explain itself. It is possible to help someone become permeable to this beauty, but we certainly cannot explain it to him, for there is nothing to explain."[12] I think Francois Molnar would agree with me that by his last few words he means that we cannot (consciously) find anything to explain, rather than that there is nothing to explain because we do not know whether there is or there is not anything in reality. All we do know is that we do not see anything. Yet if we believe there is nothing there we had better forget the whole thing. However, this is not the case because our very life has made us search rather than close ourselves off.

We see, therefore, that if we do not want to shut ourselves up within a blind mysticism, subject ourselves to a dangerous illusion, we cannot *a priori* accept any mathematical modular that excludes man. Such a rejection of the priority of mathematical formulas over aesthetics by no means signifies an *a posteriori* renunciation of mathematical formulation. If the foundation is man, and his sensitivity alone, it is easy to slip into a subjective idealism. To be sure, art is the only terrain where one can eventually accept a subjective realism. But—to paraphrase C. Cherry, 'Speaking language, and speaking about language'—to look at painting is one thing, and talk about painting another. When we confront a work of art in order to analyze it, we must have a scientific attitude; we have to distrust idealism.[13]

As was explained earlier, artists have sometimes been interested in an *a priori* understanding of the objective and "universal principle" governing the concept of aesthetic phenomena.

In the 17th and 18th centuries a great deal of emphasis was placed on the mathematization of the universe in terms of harmonic ratios. Examples are Kepler, Galileo, and Shaftesbury. They followed Plato and saw order and harmony in music, as well as in man's nature. "Virtue has the same fix'd Standard. The same *Numbers, Harmony*, and *Proportion will have place in Morals; and are discoverable in the Characters* and *Affections* of Mankind."[14]

Philibert de l'Orme, a follower of Vitruvius, writes, "in truth, a sound piece of good Art, where the *Materials* being but ordinary Stone, without any garnishment of Sculpture, do yet ravish the beholder. . . by a secret *Harmony* in the *Proportions*." He further examines the intentions of Vitruvius, saying that there is "no superficial, and floating *Artificer*; but a *Diver* into *Causes*, and into the *Mysteries* of *Proportion*." Moreover he explains how to change "*Symmetry* to *Symphony*, and the *Harmony* of *Sound*, to a kind of *Harmony* in *Sight*."[15]

The same concepts can be found in Reynolds' work. "To pass over the effect produced by that general symmetry and proportion by which the eye is delighted, as the ear is with music, architecture certainly possesses many principles in common with poetry and painting."[16]

Later a new notion was introduced which was primarily a British movement whose followers completely rejected the notion of *a priori* mathematical order in the human experience of art and architecture. For example, Claude Perrault broke away from the concept that certain ratios possessed *a priori* beauty and declared that proportions which follow "the rules of architecture"[17] are agreeable for no other reason than that we are used to them. Consequently he advocated the relativity of our aesthetic judgement. However it does not seem logical when he maintains that musical consonances "cannot" be translated into visual proportions. The reason for this is that when one talks about experience, any *a priori* reasoning cannot be valid.

Hogarth rejected "any congruity between mathematics and beauty."[18] Hume noted that "all probable reasoning is nothing but a species of sensation." So he turned objective aesthetics into subjective sensibility. He rejected the classical theories of art and held that "beauty is inherent in the object provided the latter is in tune with universal harmony." He said that "beauty and deformity, more than sweet and bitter, are not qualities in objects, but belong entirely to the sentiment. . . ."[19]

Burke also rejects the notion that beauty has "anything to do with calculation and geometry."[20] He defines proportion as a quantitative entity which does not have anything to do with the mind.

Notions of objectivity have continued since the beginning of the twentieth century. The notion began with Cézanne. He "wished to exclude this shimmering and ambiguous surface of things and penetrate to the reality that did not change, that was present beneath the bright but deceptive picture presented by the kaleidoscope of the senses."[21] Thus he was in favor of *"structure* at any cost, that is to say, for a style rooted in the nature of things and not in the individual's subjective sensations, which are always 'confused.' "[22] He thought that an artist by doing research and analysis could bring order to this confusion. Moreover he felt that "art was essentially the achievement of such a structural order within the field of our visual sensation."[23] He opened a new vista toward objectivity in art, i.e., toward an understanding of nature, not through an individual's mind order (which varies from person to person) but through the order and structure in nature which is constant. He was trying to create an order in art following the order of nature. Of course, such an order in art has a life and logic of its own.

Cézanne's notion of objectivity was experimented with by others. For example, Seurat became increasingly interested in scientific research on the above order and structure and searched for a "scientific basis of aesthetic harmony." He developed a method of painting which Paul Valéry calls pointillism—"a unified system of human sensibility and activity."[24] Seurat himself states that "If with the experience of art, I have been able to find scientifically the law of pictorial colour, can I not discover an equally logical, scientific, and pictorial system to compose harmoniously the lines of a picture just as I can compose its colors?"[25] The above notions of modern painting thus began with Cézanne and later were further developed into new phases.

Around 1914 the ideas of Cubism and Futurism appeared on the scene. In Cubism the generalization and standardization of pattern took geometrical form. "Those conceptions of the spatial experience and of the plastic volume which are committed to expression can be detected in the smallest units of the geometrical image. . . ."[26] The ideas of Cubism later developed into structuralism or constructionism where the basic notion is still objectivity in art and the intention is to reach beyond the individual's interpretation of relationships, colors, and forms. Finally a school was founded on these concepts; namely, the de Stijl school, whose followers are "in search of the absolute: universal harmony."[27] One of the followers of this movement, Malevitch, found that "additive elements" provided a base for "the origin of an artistic structure" where "the artist is intent on bringing the additive element into a harmonic norm, into conformity. . . ."[28] The same notion is expressed by Kandinsky: "the work of art is a construction of concrete elements of form and colour which become expressive in the process of synthesis or arrangement: the form of the work of art is in itself the content, and whatever expressiveness there is in the work of art originates with the form."[29] Moreover in his book *On The Spiritual in Art*, one finds that

The leading idea of this book. . . is that a harmony of colours and forms 'can only be based on a purposive contact with the human soul' and that 'composition is a combination of colored and graphic form which exist independently, which are summoned up by an inner necessity and, thus living together, come to form a whole that we call a picture' but this does not preclude the possibility that the inner vibration may be provoked by a represented object. . . .[30]

Thus he is saying that he is not going to "render the visible, but make visible" through the "principle of internal necessity."[31]

Kandinsky and Malevitch have called these elements primary signs or "non-situational," "non-environmental" signs: "non-objective art was a matter of making explicit those 'feeling states' which are separable from a particular situation because they are found in all situations."[32] Thus this group is more interested in the analytical conscious act of painting than in its subconscious aspects. "The contents. . . are indeed what the spectator *lives* or *feels* while under the effect of the *form and color combinations* of the picture. ... This entire description is chiefly an analysis of the picture which I have painted rather subconsciously in a state of strong inner tension."[33]

Picasso however does not agree that the purpose of art is only to analyze. The realization of form is his aim. He defined Cubism as "an art dealing primarily with forms, and when a form is realized, it is there to live its own life."[34] He further states that "we have introduced into painting objects and forms that were formally ignored," but "mathematics, trigonometry, chemistry, psychoanalysis, music and what not, have been related to Cubism to give it an easier interpretation. All this has been pure literature, not to say nonsense, which brought bad results, blinding people with theories."[35]

We can thus conclude from our discussion of modulization— either in art or in science—that it seems essential to understand and work with nature's order and structure. It is all the same and a part of a greater totality, no matter whether the order and structure are seen by artists or by scientists; they all originate in man and nature. As Philip Morrison states,

just as all our prose might indeed appear from his mindless but modular frame, so our pictures, fabrics, devices, formulae—all knowledge—share the modular nature. The whole even of our world—radiant energy and protean matter, crystals and cells, stars and atoms—all is built of modules, whose identity and simplicity belie the unmatched diversity of the works of man and nature. The world is atomic, which is to say modular; our knowledge is modular as well. All can be counted and listed; our very analysis implies atoms of knowing, as the material itself is atomic. The prodigality of the world is only a prodigality of combination, a richness beyond human grasp contained in the interacting multiplicity of a few modules, but modules which nature has made in very hosts.[36]

He further indicates that "the world is modular, yet it never repeats, nor does it supply meaning randomly. The possibility of the typewriting apes and the script of *Hamlet* is no more than an arithmetical joke, a game with logic."[37]

Architects have also been searching for *a priori* theories in architecture. The scientific approach in architecture put forth by Alberti and Leonardo in the 15th century was the first firm step toward the mathematization of nature and architecture based on spatial units.

Architecture was regarded by them as a mathematical science which worked with spatial units: parts of that universal space for the scientific interpretation of which they had discovered the key in the laws of perspective.
Thus they were made to believe that they could re-create the universally
valid ratios and expose them pure and absolute, as close to abstract geometry as possible. And they were convinced that universal harmony could
not reveal itself entirely unless it were realized in space through architecture
conceived in the service of religion.[38]

Such attitudes were too idealistic; absolute and divine beauties
were sought after rather than the reality of real beauty in man's
experience with its change and dynamism.

In the concept of modulization as seen by LeCorbusier, "man
and the world he builds are an indivisible unity. Just as man
is an outgrowth of nature, so the building, the furniture, the
machine, the painting or statue, are outgrowths of man. The
builder and his work are interdependent like the snail and its
shell."[39]

The notions of modulization in art and science were discussed in order to understand something about the order and structure
of the relationship between the parts and the whole in different
systems. The result shows that there is no one unit in either
biological, physical, or natural forms. As Waddington has suggested, there are integrative levels. In the first part of this book,
it was also stated that there is no one level or scale of ideological
theories which can integrate man's behavior within a single scale
or law. So the form of our environment should also follow the
rest with a set of scales and integrative levels. Now let us delve
into this problem of the organization of the parts and the whole.

Ackoff has suggested two types of adaptation: Darwinian
and Singerian. In Darwinian adaptation, biological forms are,
by definition, those which change to be more efficient in a changing environment. (In the organization of the environment, we
deal with people and include the use of machines as extensions
of man's body.) In Singerian adaptation, higher organisms are
more intelligent and posses the ability to change the environment to suit their needs. It does not seem quite right that any
organism follows either Darwinian or Singerian definitions alone.
Both are followed.

The author suggests that a higher organism in not one which is more sensitive, but rather one which *can be* more sensitive. This sensitivity means the degree to which an organism can respond to its environment. In the organization of the form of the environment, a system with more flexibility will be less sensitive to error in prediction because the consequence of decisions are not entirely foreseeable. The question is how to subdivide a system and its activity vertically (through time) and horizontally (within space) into subsystems and processes to get an optimum or higher organism. Higher organisms can be defined as those which are more aware and capable of responding to changes (to be changed or to change) now and in the future, partially or totally. Subdividing and studying parts would help us better understand the system. However the whole is not merely the sum of its parts. Thus neither composing and studying the whole nor decomposing it and studying the parts would suffice. A two-way, dynamic feed-back process between the parts and the totality should be explored for the sake of the present and the future.

As Harris has said, engineers, planners, operations researchers, and some scientists have a psychological dislike for open systems. They do not like loose ends. Mathematics however now deals (in axiometric systems) with open systems—consider Godel's theorem for example. Modern physics, like mathematics, is using a semiaxiomative method, in contrast to the humanities where there is not a trend toward *closed* systems. In a search for environmental form, we should attempt to develop more open systems because in working with closed systems, "if one does not understand how the large scale system works, redesigning a part of it can be dangerous or even disastrous."[40]

In terms of time-range form-making and scale of organization of the form of the environment, makers of form cannot be too concerned with precision because the flow of time and range of scale, as well as the diversity of systems involved, do not allow them to define boundaries accurately. Even if they were able to do so, the next instant would bring new changes and their endeavors would be wasted.

Since we cannot develop total system models at once, and since the most important job of the designers is the problem of aggregation, the best we can do is assemble part models. This job of assembling will not be successful unless we not only place our emphasis on the study of the part (for its own sake), but also on the organization, interrelation, and structure between parts. To do this we should provide open-ended systems which are flexible and adaptable.

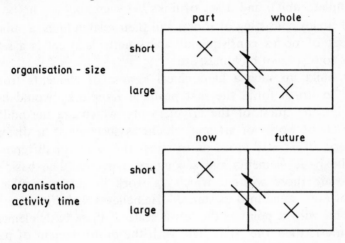

Figure 7–1

Relationship of Sizes and Times Ranges in Organization

7.2 Architectural Field's Building Blocks

A. POINTS

Points are visible to us when they are lines; lines are visible when they are the boundaries of surfaces; and surfaces are visible when they are the boundaries of objects of pieces of space which form a "continuum" (a set or sets of points), each separated from its surroundings by a "cut or cuts"[41] (dividing a set or sets). An example would be the set of points of line AB, the two end points of which (A and B) are distinguishable from each other and from the rest of the points of the line, although there exist n points (E_1, E_2, ... E_n) between these end points which are indistinguishable from one another and from A and B. Architectural or urban form is made up of many pieces of either mass or space. However this form could be thought of as sets of nodes (architectural elements equaling pieces of mass or space), with the related connecting sets of links in "integrative levels" forming an overall pattern of the environment. A room is a set of nodes consisting of objects, space (entities which constitute a complete unit), and a set of links between nodes; a house is a set of nodes consisting of rooms and their related links; a building is a set of nodes consisting of apartments; a street is a set of nodes consisting of buildings, etc.

To build up such a hierarchical system of elements from a point to urban form, the first problem Kandinsky would begin with is "the quest of the art elements, which are the building materials of works of art and which, as such, must be different in every art."[42] He proceeds to stress the need for differentiating the basic elements and secondary elements. The basic elements are those without which "a work in any particular art cannot even come into existence." He believes that it is important to begin with a point as the lower scale of these basic elements: "We must, therefore, start here with the proto-element of painting—the paint."[43]

The definition of a point is different if it is conceived of in *a priori* terms or as seen by the eye. Russell analyzes Whitehead's concept of "points" as,

systems of finitely-extended events. In advocating this method, it is not necessary to maintain that mathematical points are *impossible* as simple entities (or 'particulars'). . . . What we know about points is that they are useful technically—so useful that we must seek an interpretation of the propositions in which, symbolically, they occur. But there is no ground for denying structure to a point. . . .[44]

There are various ways of arriving at points. One way is Whitehead's method, "in which we consider 'enclosure series.' Speaking roughly, we may say that this method defines a point as all the volumes which contain the point."[45] That is to say, he assumes that "every event encloses and is enclosed by other events. There is, therefore, for him, no lower limit or minimum, and no upper limit or maximum, to the size of events."[46] Another way of arriving at points is Russell's method, whereby the flow of events is not as smooth as in the above case (Whitehead's method) Russell defines "instants" and uses another method; namely, "partial overlapping." In this theory he differentiates between a psychological time-order which is one-dimensional and free from the change of relativity, and a physical "point-instant" which, for its location, requires a "completely definite position in space-time."[47] Hence he assumes that two events may overlap in space-time. He terms these relations "compresence." For example, when music is played, if one note

is heard beginning before the other has ceased to be heard, the auditory percepts of the hearer have 'compresence.' If a group of events in one biography are all compresent with each other, there will be some place in space-time which is occupied by all of them. This place will be a 'point' if there is no event outside the group which is compresent with all of them. We may therefore define a 'point-instant,' or simply a 'point,' in one biography, as a group of events having the following two properties: (1) any two members of the group are compresent; (2) no event outside the group is compresent with every member of the group.[48]

Whitehead has stated the most advanced and adequate logical statement which can be made about the nature of the universe and the flow of events and life. However his assertions have not yet been verified by experimentation and his theories belong more to the areas of logic than experimentation. The furthest that an experiment could go is dealing with the concept of quantum theory, where "events could not have less than a certain minimum spatio-temporal extent."[49] But this view is also now encountering doubt in favor of the theories of subquantum.

B. TWO POINTS

To have a form, at least two points of matter which could create one interaction are necessary. This interaction is not a "thing," constant, static, and unchangeable, but rather a "set" of "pure relations" among elementary differentiable and undifferentiable elements. Thus the very meaning of form embodies the concept of time. However it is not necessary to think of time as a fourth dimension in space. In other words, in each form there exists a past and future, and what we see is only the relation between its points at a given moment and its transformation from past to future. The more complicated the set of integrative levels of scales, distances, and times, the more complicated and vital the form becomes. Since we see the form as the set of inter-relations, the elements cannot be any more important than the dynamic flow of changing order between these elements. Moretti says,

it necessarily and clearly appears that every elementary assemblage of differences must be replaced by other assemblages, because if the first one remained static, beyond a certain level of memory its perceptions would weaken and the assemblage itself would subside into an undifferentiated and null element. Thus a continuous flux of assemblages is necessary for the knowledge of a complex form, whether due to the succession of the assemblages themselves, as in the cinema and in music, or to the eye's displacement, as in painting and architecture.[50]

The perception of each form is the result of and dependent on the energy-pattern of neighboring and successive past and future, not what is there but what is in the memory of the perceiver.

According to the earlier definition of architecture and of tension and repulsion, two points do not rest in a visual field or in other fields. Rather they are in a dynamic field of interaction. In the study of physical fields we said that the first step in a search for understanding charge (energy) and field distribution is a knowledge of how a force acts on a charge. Here we should know the force between two points in an infinite uniform medium architecturally.

The definition of an energy-point as energy-density (q_1 = charge in electric field) comes first. The energy density or *power* of a point can be thought of as the power of its attraction (either as tension or repulsion in the visual space) or the absolute value of its energy-density. Such power can also be thought of as a function of its "originality" (developed earlier) either in the medium or in our memory. In general, with regard to the role of originality in a system, we can say that the originality of a part of a system is the power of that part (needed the most) in the organization of the system.

To measure the *a priori* originality of a situation, the only procedure offered us by logic is to reckon its improbability. If a given message or event is certain, it teaches the receptor nothing and cannot modify his behavior. An unexpected event has to be defined as a zero probability; hence it substantially modifies the behavior of the receptor. This is the essential, well-established point of every study of behavior.[51]

Thus we can say that the power of a point, according to its originality, is a function of the improbability of its appearance either in the environment (medium) or receptor memory storage. Abraham Moles has considered this improbability as the "received physical excitation" and has connected information (originality = energy-density of a point in our study) H to improbability I by means of Fechner's relations, saying that "the sensation, here information or originality, is proportional to the logarithm of the excitation, here the improbability."[52] This improbability is analogous to Boltzmann's formula of *entropy* ". . . as the *proportion of disorder* of a phenomena (*sic*)."[53]

$$H = k \log I$$

The comparison of the above formula to Boltzmann's formula of entropy (5) in statistical thermodynamics is as follows:

$$H - K \log W \text{ or } S = K \log W$$

This is obtained by substituting the probability of occurrence (W) with improbability (I) in the above formula. W is the "probability of a given state" either as "matter" or a "message." According to Moles, the *a priori* probability of an answer to a question such as "did or did not Miss X wear a hat when you met her? "is one half. Of course, it must be considered that with a change in the system of logarithm, K changes as well as the unit of originality. So this unit can "correspond to the choice between two mutually exclusive choices which are *a priori* equiprobably for the receptor. . . ."[54] Thus, the probability of

$$W = \frac{number\ of\ favorable\ cases}{number\ of\ possible\ cases}$$

Therefore, $H = -K \log \frac{1}{2} = K \log 2$

It is important to notice that only when the probability of W is $\frac{1}{2}$, *i.e., when there is "an a priori equi-probable hypothesis" in receiving yes or no* in Miss X's case, can we write the above equations in the following forms:

$$H = - Log_2 W$$

Moles gives the following formula (given by Wiener and put into useful form by Shannon) more general form:

$$H = - Nt + \sum_{i=1}^{n} p_i \, log_2 \, P_i$$

We looked at this earlier in our study where pi's are the probabilities of occurrence of favorable events (points) along n possible events (points), assembled in a space-time dimensional sequence of NT (N representing space distribution and T, time distribution).

Let us go back to our discussion of two points and their interaction. In the case of two points set in an infinite uniform medium which are different from the points of the medium, each point would have its highest energy-density (originality), because there is no similarity at all between the two points and their surrounding points (medium).

C. A LINE

A line is next to point in the hierarchy of elements. It is a particular set of points sitting next to each other in some specific order; mathematically, it is the first element with dimension. The study of a line is accompanied by two distinct concepts.

a) Atomism—where a line is the sum of a set of points (A, E_1, E_2. ... E_n, B). The identify and constituent character of each point is the most important character of a line.

b) Structuralism—where a line is a set of interrelations between a set of points (A, E_1, E_2, ... E_n, B). The identify of structure and organization between the points is more important than the points themselves. David Bohm in defining structure states that,

structure is in essence a hierarchy of orders, on many levels. Consider, for example, a house. The basically similar elements are the bricks. But these *differ* in position and orientation. When these are *ordered* in a certain array of similar differences, they make a wall. But now, the wall is an element of a *higher order*. For the different walls, arranged with suitable similarities in place and orientation make the rooms. Likewise, the rooms are ordered to make the house, the house to make the street, the streets to make the city etc. etc.[55]

Although according to the physical and natural sciences (discussed earlier), the notions of structure and order in nature now have different meanings in the 20th century than in Palladio's time, Palladio's statement in regard to the form of a building is still valid. However parts and wholes should be defined. Palladio says "Beauty will result from the beautiful form and from the correspondence of the whole to the parts, of the parts amongst themselves, and of these again to the whole; so that the structures may appear an entire and complete body, wherein each member agrees with the other and all members are necessary for the accomplishment of the building."[56]

I think these two lines could be representative of the two concepts. In Fig. 7−2.a, one should know the characteristics of each point in isolation, the sum of which makes the line. So E_4 is what it is, not because of its location, but because of its own inherent nature, However, E_4 in Fig. 7−2.b has that character (potential) because it is located in that relation to the rest. Although the structural approach is much more emphasized today, both could be helpful in their proper place. Russell in this regard says "I shall give the name 'particulars' to the ultimate terms of the physical structure—ultimate, I mean, in relation to the whole of our present knowledge. A 'particular,' that is to say, will be something which is concerned in the physical world merely through its qualities or its relations to other things, never through its structure, if any."[57]

I think we are still following the Greek concepts of geometry without any consideration of the new conceptions of structure in danger. The following is an explanation of the Greek perceptions of the geometry of a line as pointed out by William M. Ivins.

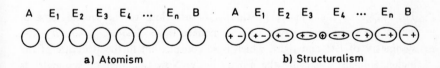

a) Atomism   b) Structuralism

Figure 7−2
Line: Atomism and Structuralism Notions

In their geometry the Greeks measured segments of lines, angles, areas, and volumes, and worked out many of the relationships between those measurements, but, just as in their art they never really studied spatial organization, character, or movement. In their geometry they paid no attention to the inherent structural qualities of lines and never discovered such notions as those of duality and geometrical continuity. I have not discovered that any Greek ever thought to wrestle with the problem presented by the order of the points on a line. Basically the Greeks thought about their geometry in terms of an unexpressed chalk line or yard stick which they held in their two hands.[58]

The reason for following the Greek concepts is probably due to the fact that man hesitates to question those things which are taken for granted. We should remember that Greek lines are different from those of modern times. Whereas theirs represented static, finite, and metric concepts, today we are talking about infinite, transformational, and relational concepts. As A.N. Whitehead says, "In those days, mathematics was the science of a static universe. Any transition was conceived as a transition of static forms. Today we conceive of forms of transition. The modern concept of an infinite series is the concept of a form of transition, namely, the character of the line is such a form."[59]

If one compares the characteristics of Greek mathematics, geometry and notions of line in the two above quotations with conceptions of modern architects, we realize that we have not advanced too far in our understanding of spatial properties since Greek times. What is needed is what Whitehead stated—an understanding of form as transition. We should also recognize the problem of Greek geometry, which has been pointed out by Ivins; namely, that the Greeks never bordered on thinking of a line as the order of its points.

A line, like any other geometrical element, has two sets of values attached to it: that of a purely geometrical nature, as well as that created in man's experience.

The image of the balance provides a natural link to the second sense in which the word symmetry is used in modern times: *bilateral symmetry*, the symmetry of left and right, which is so conspicuous in the structure of the higher animals, especially the human body. Now this bilateral symmetry is a strictly geometric and, in contrast to the vague notion of symmetry discussed before, an absolutely precise concept.[60]

Hermann Weyl deals with the question of whether artists have discovered the symmetry inherent in nature and have copied it, or whether symmetry has an aesthetic value of its own. He agrees with Plato that "the mathematical idea is the common origin of both."[61] The author is inclined to agree with Kant that we cannot have an idea about anything unless it goes through the filter of the mind and is colored by it. Hence in comparing the two notions with reality, one feels that there is a third dimension between the two. This third dimension should be called perception, whereas the other two could be called conception and custom. The following is Russell's point of view

It was only through Kant, the creator of modern Epistemology, that the geometrical problem received a modern form. He reduced the question to the following hypotheticals: If Geometry has apodeictic certainty, its matter, i.e., space must be *a priori*, and as such must be purely subjective; and conversely, if space is purely subjective, Geometry must have a apodeictic certainty.[62]

This may be viewed as the third dimension of symmetry. *A priori* and subjective concepts could be a greater help to such disciplines dealing with human experience. The reason is that the *a priori* deals with a kind of knowledge which, though "perhaps elicited by experience, is *logically* presupposed in experience. . . ."[63] And subjectivity deals with mental attitudes of an internal nature. We have to find room for Kantian discipline as a link between subjectivity and objectivity. This would not only limit the subjective activities but also free us from *a priori* preconceptions concerning nature. It would also help us see the attributes of nature and geometry and learn how physical phenomena behave.

Thus the search for attributes of form and geometry in this theory follows the path set by Helmholtz rather than Euclidean notions of space and geometry. The difference between the two has been illustrated by Hermann Weyl. In the Euclidean coordinate system, spatial forms are described by the set of its parts; e.g., ABC forms a straight line, $ABCD$ forms a plane, and AB is congruent to CD. Helmholtz, on the other hand, uses the idea of "congruence" of figures. "A mapping S of space associates with every point p a point $p^1 : p \rightarrow p^1$. A pair of mappings S, S^1 : $p \rightarrow p^1$, $p^1 \rightarrow P$, of which the one is the inverse of the other, so that if S carries P into P^l, then S^l carries p^l back into P and vice versa is spoken of as a pair of one-to-one mappings or transformation."[64] Thus in Helmholtz's approach, spatial form which "carries any two congruent figures into two congruent ones—is called an *automorphism*. . ." As Leibniz notes, "this is the idea underlying the geometric concept of similarity."[65] The reason why left and right "are of the same essence is the fact that reflection in a plane is an automorphism."[66]

Although Helmholtz's notion of congruence has just been explained, it would probably be helpful to explain further the notion of isomorphism, since the concepts of similarities and differences are central to this theory and an understanding of form. Ralph Crouch defines isomorphism in the following terms: "Let (G, O) and $(H, +)$ be groups. Let f be a one-to-one function from G onto H. Then f is an *isomorphism* of (G, O) onto $(H, +)$ if, and only if, $(aOb)f = (a) f + (b) f$ for all $a, b \in G$. The groups (G, O) and $(H, +)$ are *isomorphic* if there exists an isomorphism form (G, O) onto $(H, +)$."[67] In more simplified terms, if we have set G with operation O and set H with operation $+$ and f is the function by which one can go from set G to set H, then f is an isomorphism of (G, O) onto $(H, +)$. Automorphism, on the other hand, is the function by which one goes from set G back to itself. In other words, automorphism is an isomorphism from a set to itself. By this then one can define the correspondence between the differences in two sets or forms.

Such an attitude toward form is geometrical. In areas of human experience we have stated that subjective attitudes are necessary. Another approach involves taking into consideration matter and its qualities which are fundamental in the structure of spacetime. Without this is the perception of space is impossible, as perceived in human experience, which dictates the following study of a line as well as the other architectural elements in this theory. These three attitudes are creating a new geometry.

A line perceived as a straight line is not straight in reality. *A priori* geometrical properties only belong to pure science and not architectural experience. A truly st aight line does not appear straight in one's perception as it d es in *a priori* geometry or mathematics. Let us restate the above statement. The points of a set making a straight line $(A, E_1, E_2, \ldots E_n, B)$ are not all the same as in mathematics and geometry. Rather each point, depending on its relation to the rest, has a special value (potential) of its own. (A point in a line of n points could have $n!$ value, depending on its location in relation to the rest. Of course, it is $n!$ when we do not consider the symmetry of a line but $n!$ because $\frac{n}{2}!$ *considering symmetry.*)

How are these values determined? The following three analyses elaborate on the above hypothesis:
1) *a priori* geometry and mathematics
2) physics and physical analysis
3) perception
1) Using *a priori* geometry (graphical analysis), we can draw a line, *AB,* and say it consists of points $A, E,1, E_2, \ldots E_n, B$. (The distance between each two points is supposed to represent a point). Let us assign an artificial value to each point, depending on its location on the line. Suppose we think that the two end points, because of the highest differences from the rest, have the highest value and let this be 9 units. The value of the other points can be determined through the following diagram.

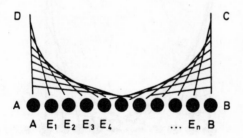

Figure 7–3a
Line and Its Potential

The resulting curve represents the character of the line *AB* due to the assigned values of *A* and *B*. The assigned values of *A* and *B* depend on the length of *AB* (and the distance of the observer from the line in visual experience). Now let us analyze the visual experience of the line. If the line is so large that the observer cannot relate *A* to *B* or *B* to *A* at one glance, it is clear that its characters are not going to be as in Fig. 7–3 (a). The opposite is true when the line is very short. The following graph also points out the same times. There are three cases, $BC = \frac{AB}{2}$, $BC > \frac{AB}{2}$ and $BC \leq \frac{AB}{2}$. Fig. 7–3 (b) shows when $BC = \frac{AB}{2}$, Fig. 7–3 (b) shows when $BC > \frac{AB}{2}$, Fig. 7–3 (b) shows when $BC < \frac{AB}{2}$.

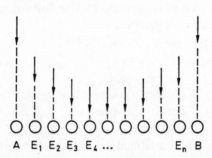

Figure 7–3b
Line and its Potential

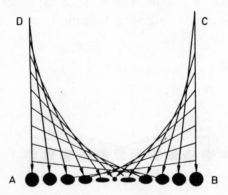

Figure 7–3c
Line and Its Potential

The notion of the mathematical analysis of nature and its elements is not new. When discussing modulization and objectivity in art earlier in this part, we outlined some of the highlights of the development of these notions. Now the views of Pythagoras and Plato will be considered. Pythagoras' concept of "all is number" was emphasized by Plato, both of whom were "convinced of the mathematical and harmonic structure of the universe and creation. If the laws of harmonic numbers pervade everything from the celestial spheres to the most humble life on earth, then our very souls must conform to this harmony."[68] Although Alberti followed geometrical and mathematical rules toward an ideal form, he was still concerned with the sensation of perception. According to him it is an inborn sense, due to the mechanization of our brain, that makes us aware of any harmony. He maintains in other words that,

the perception of harmony through the senses is possible by virtue of the affinity of our souls. This implies that if a church has been built in accordance with essential mathematical harmonies, we react instinctively; an inner sense tells us, even without rational analysis, when the building we are in partakes of the vital force which lies behind all matter and binds the universe together.[69]

Alberti's statement also shows how conception and perception, although different, emanate from the same sources. Whereas Alberti once just explained the importance of the senses, now he stresses pure forms. In explaining the ideal form of a church (during the Renaissance), he emphasized that "Nature herself. . . enjoys the round form above all others as is proved by her own creations such as the globe, the stars, the trees, animals, and their nests, and many other things."[70] He indicates that "we must therefore conclude that the harmonic perfection of the geometrical scheme represents an absolute value, independent of our subjective and transitory perception."[71] It was the artists, lead by Alberti and Leonardo, who were responsible for the development of a mathematical approach to nature. Searching for the answers in a scientific approach, they "found and elaborated correlations between the visible and intelligible world which were as foreign to the mystic theology as to the Aristotelian scholasticism of the Middle Ages. Architecture was regarded by them as mathematical science which worked with spatial units."[72]

Through the eyes of Einstein we see the field of gravity acting on all bodies "independently of their nature, and only according to their position in space and time."[73] As a result, "gravitation. . . becomes one of the geometrical properties of the

universe, a geometrical property which in four-dimensional geometry is nothing but the generalization of what we term curvature
in ordinary geometry."[74]

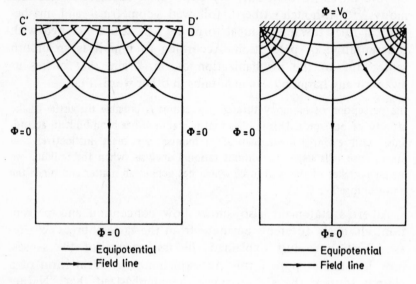

Figure 7–4

Line and Its Potential

Desiring to locate an entity or a point in space and time, we
can say "it is located at a certain point of the universe, and the
manner in which it behaves depends solely upon the curvature
(or rather curvatures) of the universe at this point."[75] With
this viewpoint of space—time relations as a field, our straight
line within such a field is also conditioned by that field. Riemann's geometry, in contrast to Euclidean geometry, gives particular evidence in this case. According to Riemann's geometry,
in the concept of the curvature of space, the curvature can be
classified into positive, zero, and negative curvatures. In a space
of positive curvature, a line cannot be drawn parallel to a straight
line. In a space of zero curvature (Euclidean) only one line can
be drawn parallel to the straight line, and in a space with negative
curvature "more than one" line can be drawn parallel to the
straight line. "Riemann developed further a discovery by Gauss
according to which the shape of a curved surface can be character-

ized by the geometry within the surface."[76] Since the curvature of space varies from one point to another due to the change of

variation in the curvature, $\frac{dx}{dt}$ is not a function of past and future, but of dt.

2) *Physics and physical analysis.* Let us now consider Fig. 7—4. We see that although potential distribution is sustained through a straight line, *CD*, the equipotential lines appear not as parallel lines with *CD* but as curves, as in the following figure. The line *AB* in this diagram could represent our own line *AB* discussed above.

An angle's experience perception is not an angle. Following the same graphical method as we did for the straight line, we get Fig. 7—5.

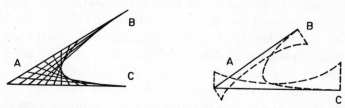

Figure 7—5
Corners (Angles) and Field Near Them

It can also be proved mathematically as in the case of a straight line. To see how an angle acts on equipotential lines in an electric magnetic field, we can look at Fig. 7—6.

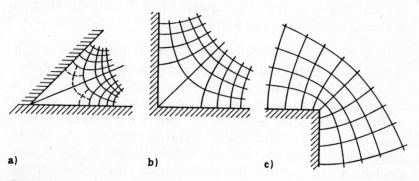

a)   b)   c)

Figure 7—6
Corner (Angles) and Field Near Them

The mass and void of a line should be mentioned here. The qualities of the mass and void of a line do not change its general character. The potential of each point (either physical or spatial) on a
line is a function of its position on the line rather than the nature
of its matter. (Of course, we are only comparing two homogeneous physical and spatial lines.) A comparison of three lines
AB, DC and *D'C'* in fig. 7–4 provides good proof for the above
statement. Whereas *DC* is a spatial line, *AB* and *D'C'* in the same
figure are physical lines. The curves of the equipotential lines
as well as field lines are there in either case, whether we consider
them as part of and originated by *DC* (nonphysical line) or *D'C'*
(physical line). Of course, in the case where we compare *AB* and
D'C' (two physical lines), the direction of curve changes depending on the direction of the field.

3) *Perception.* Before we begin dealing with the perceptual analysis of a line, we should define what perception is. A comparison
of the two definitions given by Russell and Bohm would be
helpful. According to Russell, "perception is the process of
acquiring knowledge of dated events at times closely contiguous
to them. . . . We wake up and find it is daylight. . . ."[77] Event
and knowledge occur simultaneously. Bohm believes that perception is the recognition of order through the principle of similar
differences. It is the awareness of similarities and differences
between "what actually happens and what is inferred from previous knowledge." Sensitivity to the differences between the two
leads to a new perception which explains the differences. Thus
"one first becomes aware. . . of a new set of relevant differences,
and one begins to feel out. . . a new set of similarities, which do
not come *merely* from past knowledge. . . ."[78]

It is not that they believe in different things, they simply
emphasize different parts of the same process. Whereas Russell
talks about percepts in the memory, Bohm talks about perception
as recognition of order—or *"similar differences* and *different
similarities."* In other words, while Russell discusses the process
of acquiring knowledge, Bohm seems to stress events, the recognition of which is called perception. It appears that Russell
emphasizes the part of the process under man's control, and
Bohm stresses the part of the patterning of events perceived by

man. If the problem of forming the environment is left to two groups—architects and sociopsychologists—in choosing one of the two above points of view (Russell's or Bohm's), I would say that the sociopsychologists would probably take Russell's perspective and work with man's understanding of the pattern, while the architect should take Bohm's point of view and search more into patterns and their similarities and differences, rather than into man, the perceiver of these patterns. Of course the architect would use the results of the sociopsychologists. That is to say, he should look for what a phenomenon wants to be rather than what we want it to be.

To define a line let us look at Kandinsky's definition of a geometric line. His definition can be applied to the concept of field because he does not speak of a stretch of line, but rather a dynamic line as "becoming" and "changing" rather than being static. "The geometric line is an invisible thing. It is the track made by the moving point; that is, its product. It is created by movement—specifically through the destruction of the intense self-contained repose of the point. Here the leap out of the static into the dynamic occurs."[79]

The measurement of the Parthenon is a good example of Doric architecture, revealing that the edge of the steps and the lines of the entablature are not straight as it was thought before the measurement. Rather they are convex curves, parallel to each other. This probably shows that the Greeks were aware of differences between perception of a line and its conception.

Penrose has quoted Vitruvius' statement,

The stylobate ought not to be constructed upon the horizontal level, but should rise gradually from the ends toward the center, so as to have there a small addition. The inconvenience which might arise from a stylobate thus constructed may be obviated by means of unequal scamilli. If the line of the stylobate were perfectly horizontal, it would appear like the bed of a channel.[80]

He goes further and says that,

In placing the capitals upon the shafts of the columns, they are not to be arranged so that the abaci may be in the same horizontal level, but must follow the direction of the upper members of the Epistylium, which will deviate from the straight line drawn from the extreme points, in proportion to the addition given in the centre of the stylobate.[81]

Another example of such a use of curvature is in the architecture of the Theseum, where vertical and especially horizontal curvature has been used. As Penrose notes,

The inclined lines of the Pediment of this temple are found to have a delicate vertical curvature, to which we may assign an increment of about .025 in 25 feet, which is nearly the same ratio to the length of the arc as in the other instances of curvature in this temple. This curvature seems to be a refinement peculiar to the Theseum.[82]

He further states that "we see that the pavement of the Theseum, like that of the Parthenon, is convex, and that the horizontal lines of the entablatures are nearly parallel to those of the stylobate."[83]

4. *Surface.* We are not defining architectural physical form in the traditional sense of mass, volume, "empty space," and the representation of surfaces. Rather we define it as the disposition of matter in space-time or space-time events. With this definition in mind, it is not only surfaces (as in traditional architectural form) which make the whole of architecture, but rather that which is going on (the events) within the space. Surface can be defined as a set (S_2) of mass-points (cuts obtained by contingent sets of points: space S_1 and mass S_3). The potentials of these configurations (as a consequence of their space-time location) present architectural physical form. Such sets of points also follow the boundary of space. Although the architect's goal is the formation of S_1 and S_2, since S_2 is obtained as a consequence of S_1 and S_3 (S_2 is the union of S_1 and S_3) and since S_3 is more tangible to work without the formation of S_3 the form of S_2 is unfeasible and turns out to be the architectural end. But it should not be forgotten that the full organization of S_2 and S_3 is sufficient but not necessary, but it is S_1 (space as a field) which is necessary and sufficient.

Thus surface—the transitional part—is a more critical part of architecture where the events have more specific characteristics. For example, it is the origin of visual forces where the rays of light bounce off; it is the natural characteristics of matter change, etc. Finally, it is where the presentational conceptualization of architecture takes form. Mass and space would be meaningless without the existence of a surface where the two are contingent.

Furthermore, from childhood our sensory experience has taught us to discriminate masses and voids. Thus this sensory experience further reinforces that discrimination—between mass and void—obtained due to the physical change at the surface area.

Although vision is fundamental in architecture (it of course does not constitute all of architecture), architecture is not what we see but what we experience. It is the purpose of this book to shift the emphasis from visual architecture (surface architecture) to field architecture or all-senses architecture. All-senses architecture should step beyond the actual dimensions to the hidden dimensions and take into consideration man's subconscious behavior (social, cultural, psychological), as well as his conscious behavior. We not only see the spaces and masses, but we also sense them by smell, temperature, sound, etc. Not only vision but also other senses are influenced by the effect of a surface due to the very nature of a surface. For example, auditory signals reflected from a surface change their audibility according to their distance from that surface. This is also true of the effect of the reflection of heat waves from surfaces.

Notes to Chapter Seven

1. C. Shannon and W. Weaver, *The Mathematical Theory of Communication*, p. 9.
2. Jacob Bronowski, "The Discovery of Form," in *Structure in Art and in Science*, p. 56.
3. C. Waddington, "The Modular Principle and Biological Form," in *Module, Proportion, Symmetry, Rhythm*, ed. by G. Kepes, George Braziller, New York, 1966, p. 20. Hereafter cited as *Module*.
4. A. Whitehead, *Interpretation of Science*, Bobbs-Merrill Co., Indianapolis & New York, 1961, p. 59.
5. A. Whitehead, *Principles of Natural Knowledge*, quoted by C. Waddington, in "The Modular Principle and Biological Form," in *Module*, ed. by G. Kepes, p. 23.
6. R. Arnheim, "A review of Proportion," in *Module*, pp. 225-226.
7. D'Arcy Thompson, *On Growth and Form*, Cambridge University Press, Cambridge, 1966, p. 57.
8. C. Waddington, "The Character of Biological Form," in *Aspects of Form*, p. 45.
9. A. Novikoff, quoted by R. Arnheim in "A Review of Proportion," in *Module*, p. 226.
10. R. Arnheim, "A Review of Proportion," in *Module*, p. 222.
11. Francois Molnar, "The Unit and the Whole: Fundamental Problem of the Plastic Arts," in *Module*, p. 204.

12. *Ibid.*, p. 207.
13. *Ibid.*
14. Shaftesbury, quoted by R. Wittkower, *Architectural Principles in the Age of Humanism*, p. 142.
15. Philibert d l'Orme, quoted by R. Wittkower, *Architectural Principles*, pp. 143-144.
16. Sir Joshua Reynolds, quoted by R. Wittkower, *Architectural Principles*, p. 144.
17. Claude Perrault, quoted by R. Wittkower, *Architectural Principles*, p. 144.
18. Hogarth, quoted by R. Wittkower, *Architectural Principles*, p. 150.
19. D. Hume, quoted by Wittkower, *Architectural Principles*, p. 151.
20. E. Burke, quoted by Wittkower, *Architectural Principles*, p. 151.
21. Herbert Read, *A Concise History of Modern Painting*, Frederick A. Praeger, New York, 1959, p. 13.
22. *Ibid.*, p. 16.
23. *Ibid.*, p. 17.
24. Paul Valéry, quoted by H. Read, *A Concise History of Modern Painting*, p. 28.
25. Georges Pierre Seurat, quoted by H. Read, *A Concise History of Modern Painting*, p. 28.
26. Richard P. Lohse, "Standard, Series, Module: New Problems and Tasks of Painting," in *Module*, p. 146.
27. H.L.C. Jaffé, "Syntactic Structure in the Visual Arts," in *Structure in Art and in Science*, p. 146.
28. Kasimir Malevitch, quoted by Margit Staber, "Concrete Painting as Structural Painting," in *Structure in Art and in Science*, p. 166.
29. H. Read, *A Concise History of Modern Painting*, pp. 194-195.
30. Vasily Kandinsky, quoted by Morse Peckham, *Man's Rage for Chaos: Biology, Behavior, and the Arts.* Schocken Books, New York, 1967, p. 156. Hereafter cited as *Man's Rage for Chaos.*
31. H. Read, *A Concise History of Modern Painting*, p. 195.
32. M. Peckham, *Man's Rage for Chaos*, p. 154.
33. V. Kandinsky quoted by M. Peckham, *Man's Rage for Chaos*, p. 154.
34. Pablo Picasso, quoted by H. Read, *A Concise History of Modern Painting*, p. 78.
35. *Ibid.*
36. Philip Morrison, "The Modularity of Knowing," in *Module*, ed. by Kepes, p. 1.
37. *Ibid.*, p. 3.
38. R. Wittkower, *Architectural Principles in the Age of Humanism*, p. 29.
39. R. Arnheim, "A Review of Proportion," in *Module*, ed. by E. Kepes, p. 222.
40. Notes from City Planning 841, a course given by R. Ackoff and B. Harris at the University of Pennsylvania. 1966-67.
41. H. Poincaré, *The Value of Science*, p. 55.
42. V. Kandinsky, *Point and Line to Plane*, Solomon R. Guggenheim Foundation, New York, 1947, p. 20.
43. *Ibid.*, p. 21.
44. B. Russell, *The Analysis of Matter*, p. 290.
45. *Ibid.*, pp. 291-292.
46. *Ibid.*, p. 292.
47. *Ibid.*, p. 294.
48. *Ibid.*, pp. 294-295.
49. *Ibid.*, p. 292.
50. Moretti, "Form as Structure," in *Arena* in *Architectural Association Journal*, June 1967, p. 22.

51. A. Moles, *Information Theory and Esthetic Perception*, p. 22.
52. *Ibid.*
53. *Ibid.*, p. 23.
54. *Ibid.*
55. David Bohm, "On Creativity," in *Arena* (*Architectural Association Journal*), May 1967, p. 293.
56. Orazio Palladio, quoted by Wittkower, *Architectural Principles*, p. 21.
57. B. Russell, *Analysis of Matter*, p. 277.
58. William M. Ivins, Jr., *Art and Geometry, A study in Space Intuitions*, Dover Publications, New York, 1946, pp. 39-40. Hereafter cited as *Art and Geometry*.
59. A. Whitehead, quoted by W. Ivins, *Art and Geometry*, p. 101.
60. Hermann Weyl, *Symmetry*, Princeton Univ. Press, Princeton, 1952, p. 18.
61. *Ibid.*
62. B. Russell, *Foundations of Geometry*, Dover Publications, New York, 1954, p. 1.
63. *Ibid.*, p. 2.
64. H. Weyl, *Symmetry*, p. 18.
65. *Ibid.*
66. *Ibid.*
67. Ralph Crouch and Elbert Walker, *Introduction to Modern Algebra and Analysis*, Holt, Rinehart and Winston, New York, 1962, p. 14.
68. R. Wittkower, *Architectural Principles*, p. 27.
69. *Ibid.*
70. *Ibid.*, p. 3.
71. *Ibid.*, p. 8.
72. *Ibid.*, p. 29.
73. E. Borel, *Space and Time*, p. 35.
74. *Ibid.*, p. 36.
75. *Ibid.*
76. H. Reichenbach, *The Philosophy of Space and Time*, p. 7.
77. B. Russell, *Analysis of Matter*, p. 173.
78. D. Bohm, "On Creativity," in *Arena* (*Architectural Association Journal*), May 1967, p. 291.
79. V. Kandinsky, *Point and Line to Plane*, p. 57.
80. Francis C. Penrose, *Investigation of the Principles of Athenian Architecture* (London: MacMillan, 1888), p. 23.
81. *Ibid.*
82. *Ibid.*, p. 73.
83. *Ibid.*

8. Planning As Communication System

8.0 Introduction—Abstract

In this chapter, following the general orientation of the book, total planning process is viewed as a complex mega-system, a system where all environmental physical and nonphysical determinant factors are fused together into a gigantic system of systems. Each system represented in a matrix form consists of vertical and horizontal forces. The vertical forces represent a multiplicity of views in a variety of disciplines, interest groups, and assorted sociopolitical interpretations, all relating to interaction and intervention in the environment. However, the horizontal forces represent a multiplicity of overlapping and interwoven hierarchies of scales ranging from molecules to universal dimensions, i.e., territorial, national, regional, urban, rural, and even architectural and subarchitectural.

Planning is viewed here as an optimization of the environmental communication system. Within this context environmental form and its form-making process is viewed as the structure of energy patterns (social, political, material, etc.) and its planning as the optimization of some combination of system's function; i.e., reduction of tension, maximization of entropy, etc. Likewise the planning process, in order to conform with this process, cannot be anything but *structured patterns of decision points over space and time.* The system's approach in environmental planning and design is then viewed as the means by which the multiplicity of horizontal and vertical forces involved can be brought together into one common system.

The Esfahan case study (presented in Appendix I) is an example of an adaptation of System's theory into regional planning. Two models are introduced: (1) originality, (2) probability. Planning the region is considered a structuring of its energy pattern through optimization of originality or probability or a combination of any such models. The rationale behind such a theory is that it is not the isolated value of any entity, whether social or physical, which contributes to the well-being of the total function of the region, rather it is its relative value measured against other elements throughout the total system. Based on these assumptions the two models are provided as examples of such an approach to planning regions.

8.1 Background

The process of environmental form-making is a dynamic one, involving the change in a set of instantaneous decision points over space and time. In other words, it is the pattern of decision points over space and time which illustrates this process. Teilhard de Chardin's point of view in this regard seems highly significant, for he suggests that "The different branches of science combine to demonstrate that the universe in its entirely must be regarded as one gigantic process, a process of becoming, of attaining new levels of existence and organisation, which can properly be called a genesis or an evolution."[1]

Planning and design of the environment does not necessarily need to follow the traditional approach related to the boundaries of architecture, decoration, and interior design. Rather it should be seen as the structure of energy patterns social, political, material, physical, etc.) toward a reduction of tension, maximization of entropy, maximization of originality, maximization of probability, and maximization of the efficiency of communication systems and their information. These are some of the planning approaches which are going to be undertaken as Esfahan regional planning is introduced as a case study at the end of this chapter. The author believes that the structure of these patterns can be identified with Parsons' and Bales' system of action-space where,

a system of action is involved in what may be called developmental phases. The system or any given unit of it is, from the perspective of what may happen or be about to happen, in a 'state of tension'. This means that if certain conditions of motivation are given and not changed the system may, in the relevant ways, undergo a process of change which is directionally defined, that is, other things being equal, it can change *only* in the direction of 're-duction of tension'. Secondly, there is the phase of actual process of change which, according to the point of view, is formulated as affectivity or as performance. Finally, there is the state of completion of the change which, form the point of view of what has happened in the system, of the new state, is a set of qualities of the objects which compose it; from the point of view of what *may* happen in the next phase of process, on the other hand, it is a neutrality aspect of the motivation system, it is a tension not yet released into action.[2]

8.2 Urban-Environmental Form

In addition to its soul or content, the environment or a city as a compact activity system also has a body. This body is structured in space. In the city a tremendous variety of activities take place in a highly dense area. Planners, in an effort to maintain this concentration of peoples and services, have made various proposals. Common to many is the conception of the urban community as an independent "spatial unit" set apart from the surrounding land. Planners aim to confine the urban area and set boundaries, thus reinforcing the distinction between urban and rural areas. In the words of Wingo, it is important to understand "space as a resource to meet future requirements for the growth and development of American cities, about how social and economic activities get efficiently structured in urban space. Both the *resource* and the *structural* dimensions of urban space are tied up in the bundle of issues we refer to as the urban problem. Cities exist in space; their activities occupy space; space contains the interaction among their activities."[3]

Planning and design are disciplines which need a rational method to explain the nature of urban form and, subsequently, its form making process. A form is usually a physical or nonphysical object or event. It can only be an extension of the human mind and feeling. At the same time, a physical form usually has a more or less common ground of definition in the eyes of the general public. Traditionally, the city has been defined in predominantly physical rather than sociocultural terms. However, with the passage of time new forces have been exerting a profound influence to bring about an unconscious alteration in the meaning of a city form and the forces operating within it; i.e., the dynamics of economics, sociology, politics, and the natural sciences. Today's environmental planners are absorbed in the task of devising a city form. As has already been mentioned, the idea of this book is to see just what the environmental form is and how it can be devised. Jesse Reichek has explained what this form is: "Form in architecture is a statement of an understanding of the content of life. Life is not an art; it is the content of art. A city is not art; it is life. Its form is a multidimensional tracing of the content of the life of individuals of the society."[4]

In dealing with environmental form and the proponents of the various determinants of its form, we see that each group advocates a different cause, depending on its particular viewpoint, knowledge, and background. To an economist, the city is a complex of input and output factors economically based on supply and demand, exchange, equal sharing, etc. Through the eyes of the sociologist the city represents a form which provides wide opportunity in terms of social interaction between individuals and society. To a politician the city is an organized group of people engaged in a contractual agreement with one or another political groups of force. Of paramount interest to a natural scientist are the physiological, biological, and natural forces operating as primary determinants of the content of city life. Finally, a physical designer conceives of the city primarily in terms of a physical form which is the result of planning, design, and foresight.

In today's city design, the total system of forces involved is neither one nor the sum of all the forces proposed as major causes of the form taken by a city. It is an even more complex entity (*Gestalt,* configuration) which takes on new proportions which are much greater than merely the additive value of all the forces. What we see in operation is an interacting system of systems within which it is impossible to determine where one starts and the other ends. This interaction is precisely to determine where one starts and the other ends. This interaction is based on a wide range of links from the smallest elements involving only a narrow segment of the environment to those elements encompassing the totality. We can understand this as a feedback system operating among the diverse elements and scales, the total outcome being dependent on the total system in space and time.

In the past, environmental or city form-making was not conceived of as a dynamic process. The form was a result of the static concepts of individual designers. If a designer commenced a design which was later left unfinished, the design would remain forever incomplete; no program remained to carry on the work. Such a technique is impractical because form-making is a process with an immediate concern for *time and change*. This diversity of interaction has been expressed very well by Webber:

> Among the various subpublics within a given urban population, there is a wide diversity of interests, life styles, and values. The preferences of any one group may be in direct conflict with those of other groups; indeed, the diverse values held by any given group may also be internally incompatible. Hence, government progress that might satisfy one group within the community might harm another; or if they satisfy some wants of a given group, they may simultaneously deprive the same group or others of its values.
>
> This value-pluralism makes the planning of governmental services an extremely complex undertaking, since democratic governments are obligated to foster the welfare of all members of the community. The task is all the more difficult in that it becomes necessary explicitly to identify the value sets of the various subpublics. As every psychiatrist knows, no individual, much less group, is consciously aware of all his (or its) wants. He therefore cannot rank his preferences for various goods and services; and we would certainly be hard pressed to say what combination of goods and services we would prefer at some date in the distant future, especially since his preferences are likely to change over time. And yet, long-term public commitments must be made for educational, medical, housing, transportation, and other services that will intimately affect future levels of social welfare. We therefore cannot avoid an attempt, consciously and explicitly, to identify social goals, if the actions we take have reasonable probabilities of inducing the consequences that are desired.[5]

Dealing with this great diversity of interest groups has become quite important in our century. It would take volumes even to begin to say what each group (social, economic, psychological, political, etc.) is after. All we know is that, in different ways, all are after one thing, "human desire and need." Webber sees the situation as "order in diversity." Although he is more socially oriented, one can still understand the interests of other groups through his work. In emphasizing social values, he stresses man's institutions. He goes even further than just criticizing physical designers for stressing "space as a basis for urban form" and considers the issue "no place" rather than space. He says that regardless of what planners may do to prevent it, the urban complex is gradually expanding and diversifying. Technical advances now allow easy access between centers and related peoples, and as a result the city and country are becoming one. He asserts that we have mistakenly confused "urban chaos" with what in reality is a new way of life. Instead of considering today's changes opposed to our ideal goals we should work within a framework "in which space is distinguished from place, in which human interaction rather than land is seen as the fruitful focus of attention, and in which plans limited to the physical form of the urban settlement are no longer put forth as synoptic statements of our goals."[6] Instead of projecting past plans into the future there should be a fluid process flowing between spatial and social changes in our environment. *Planning would thus become a continuing process instead of a fixed, static goal.*

I think it is the job of the planner to stimulate the interrelation of the individual to society and his environment and vice versa. This is not an easy task. Dyckman notes that, "The rationality of social choice and group decision has been even more difficult to demonstrate than that of individuals. The stumbling block has been the determination of the appropriate value scale. In any representative political system we try to construct the social-value scale from the values of individuals, and this poses some difficult aggregation problems."[7] The interconnection between the individual, his society, and his environment is possible only through a series of laws and values, formulated in standard values which are based on a series of decisions made on different levels of the societal hierarchy. Such planning should disregard traditional planning characteristics which have tended to narrow it, and should emphasize those values which stress connecting relationships between interdisciplinary values.

8.3 Spatial Planning–Environmental Physical Planning

In analyzing the reality of the urban physical form as a dynamic phenomenon, we obviously reach a point where we need a comprehensive design language based on a systems approach regarding the hierarchical order of the environment in which the elements are skillfully composed into a whole, and which would correspond to human relations and activities. Our task here is to create a form which introduces a system for the values of life in place and time, for the body of social life. The question is whether the planner or designer should deal with space as a confined area and set man in the middle or whether he should take man and his behavior and define them by establishing a physical setting around them. In other words, Is our end the space and physical forms or the events occuring within that physical space or form? Is the physical form of a static space our end, or the dynamism of space which involves our sensitive interaction within that static form? Our goal is definitely the events and life within that framework. Our aspiration is toward understanding the soul of space rather than the space itself. This involves man's institutions and interactions with his total environment. The environmental designer is the one through whom society translates, however imperfectly, social needs into physical form.

The reason that we have not been able to conceive of the flow of life (individuals or society) as it is in reality and have conceived of it as a collection or composition of defined, separate, self-centered events is that we have not had the means to create the physical form in which the flow of events or life proceeds as in one's mind.

In reviewing urban life we find that such continuity of flow of life's unity and structural qualities were more apparent in a medieval rather than 20th century urban environment. The medieval city consisted of fewer elements, objects, and activities. It was more unified and structured. The unity of urban form and life resulted from an underlying sociocultural structure. Messages were more meaningful, not because of the nature of isolated forms, but due rather to the creators and users of the messages—cultural values shared by both the creators and users of the messages. In today's cities we have a greater diversity of forms and types, without however a common structure which provides a unifying framework.

Today most planners talk about growth, change, adaptability and flexibility because they are aware that when the above mentioned nonphysical forms or events change, the physical forms should likewise change. *Unfortunately, most of the emphasis is on the physical form rather than on the meaning behind the form.* Before a physical form exists, the idea and function of that form exists. The designer's job is not to base his designs on the concepts of traditional definitions, but on his interpretation of the dynamism and change of life. As time changes, technology and knowledge improve. We should not use today's technology to solve the problems of yesterday, but rather to check the ideals and goals of today in advance to see if the goals formulated yesterday are still valid. We should think in terms of achieving today's goals and their definitions instead of simply reevaluating the physical forms. The important consideration is *not the adaptability and flexibility of physical forms, but instead the adaptability of the definitions of functions and events.* It is the social, cultural, and psychological characteristics of human beings which interact and result in definite functions. The definite physical form serves or follows that function. Our task is not to make a neutral form capable of adaptation, but a flowing, positive conception. I think that designing neutral forms is worse than designing ones which are not capable of adaptation. With the possibilities inherent in today's technology, we should break down some of the definitions of the past and rebuild new ones which come closer to reality. In so doing, we should avoid superficial adaptations. We should not even separate such things as shopping, the street, the home, public spaces, life, and nature from each other.

With respect to growth and change, the designers' difficulty is that they have not been able to create a flowing form for the flow of life. This is because they give social events a more precise definition than is needed.

Some think of the form-making process as having distinct stages, one formally following the other, and as beginning with cultural values and policies and terminating in physical form. Having passed through the planning procedures, architects are called upon. Since the architect is the last step in the process of formulaging urban form it is he who transforms the nonphysical forms, which have already been defined by the planning process, into physical reality.

To express the inseparability between the physical form of the environment and its nonphysical-social (moral, social, cultural, etc.) form and to arrive at a new way of looking at the environment, I shall compare the traditional and modern city-making processes. Traditionally, to build a new city or building, for example a palace, the master architect was summoned by the king. Following the king's orders the architect would formulate the physical form according to his subjective concepts. The actual physical action of constructing the building would commence with the appearance of the physical body of the building. By the actual movement of laborers to the site of the new building the public would be made aware of the plan. With the physical setting in place of each stone community values were reinforced. However if the architect's concepts were not parallel with society's values, the placement of each stone disrupted the social values and created tension.

In contrast, in today's planning process there are numerous stages beginning with concepts and leading to actuality. I think that the moment in which the decision maker is making his decision, the bricks forming the new building are already abstractly in the air, moving back and forth to find their physical stability according to the nonphysical cultural values on which the decision is made. That is to say, the dynamism involved in the total environmental mega-communication system is so interwoven and interrelated it becomes impossible to find any root for a single isolated event. Although formal contractual processes are defining the boundaries of stages and subdivisions of the continuum of various daily activities, the underlying dynamic flow of "force processes" in political, social, cultural, or economical, etc. form are constantly at work.

Thus this planning process cannot be a sequentially defined, closed-ended subsystem. Rather it should be a flow of interrelations and interconnections between the subsystems and the overall system. (This is again the concept of Gestalt psychology.) If we care about the individual parts without understanding the whole, or vice versa, it will be disastrous. My response to the process goes even further, to the extent that I see each physical unit accompanied by energy (accumulated cultural values).

8.4 System's Approach in Planning and Design of Environment

The dictionary definition of a system is an "assemblage of parts forming a complex whole." Organism refers to an "individual animal or plant." We can extend this meaning to refer to the total environment. A composition is "combining parts to form a whole" or "the manner in which such parts are combined." The environment as a whole (not as a collection of cities or buildings or forces) is an organism, not a system, composition, or collection. By organism, I mean a coordinated totality. It is a fundamental unity in which the proper functioning of each element is dependent on the working of the whole. We have not been able to create an organism and having failed, designers have attempted to create systems or compositions (these two terms are almost the same in content). By system I mean the network of interrelations of a set of elements, each of which has definite boundaries and functions. This is in contrast to an organism where there is not such a distinction between elements, rather there is an overlapping process involved in the function of the elements. That is, there is a totality within which there is a flow of coordination of parts with no beginning or end for each element.

" 'Structure' should be understood to mean a network of relationships of elements or of elementary processes. Structures appear wherever elements combine into a meaningful whole whose arrangement follows definite laws. The wholeness in which we discover and examine structures, we call a 'system'. Thus there are inorganic, organic, sociological, and technical systems. . . ."[8] Moreover, we should certainly be fully aware as are Kant, a philosopher, and Wieser, a biologist, that "structure is not some rigid condition, but that it creates itself, that it develops out of different kinds and differently interpretable forces."[9] It is a fundamental unity in which the proper functioning of each element is dependent on the operations of the whole.

The reasoning has been that since it is impossible to create an organism with the parts in an undefined, flowing relationship to the whole, then it is better to be satisfied with a composition or system. Historical illustration would further amplify these two concepts in the case of, for example, hunting and sleeping. For sleeping, man devised a physical form as well as an oral definition; i.e., a physical room in which to sleep. The expression of other activities, e.g., hunting, remained in oral form. (They took place in "no-place" and at the same time someplace.) In actuality, both activities should be expressed as flows, each to a greater or lesser degree, rather than as static forms. However, since man was unable to devise a physical form defining the function and event of hunting, he abandoned the attempt and only made a shelter for sleeping.

The same applies in a more complex way today. It is our responsibility to give these events flowing, physical definition in terms of form. A composition is man's attempt to crate an organism. In order to accomplish this end, man first classified and defined the events. The smaller he is able to make the units of the whole in terms of size and function, the better an organism he will derive and the better he can define it. The larger he makes the elements, the easier it is to handle, while at the same time the further it is from his goal which is to make the needed organisms. After the designer has defined the elements of a composition (based on a composer's conception and traditional definitions of different functions) he can compose these elements in the best manner possible. The result will be close to the organism if he is able to compose these elements to follow life's pattern.

Because of the lack of overall organization, past cities did not achieve an organic unity. They were usually a repetition of some basic form with the individual entities connected to one another. The overall pattern was the sum of individual "cities," with each defined by its own boundaries based on physical, economical, political, and topographical considerations. The concept of the city as separate entities is no longer valid with today's complex life. The city of today should be an inseparable element of a hierarchical organism.

In the first two chapters we have seen what the individualistic attitude toward art in relation to the harmonization of different disciplines in planning and design is. In this regard science provides methods for measuring and compiling different values, i.e., the scientific approach which is based on establishing measurements and methods for evaluating goals and controls. For example, such a planning process could be the following which is explained by Davidoff and Reiner: "The choices which constitute the planning process are made at three levels:

1. the selection of ends and criteria;
2. the identification of a set of alternatives consistent with these general prescriptives, and the selection of a desired alternative; and,
3. guidance of action towards determined ends."[10]

Ackoff is an example of a planner who thinks in terms of a scientific approach. He realizes that determining the needs and desires off future generations is an almost impossible task when we consider our rapidly changing culture. The techniques employed should not be utilized to determine what a future generation will want, but to attempt to give them the capability to satisfy their own needs and desires, whatever they may turn out to be. As Ackoff says, "There is one desire common to all men, the desire to have the ability to satisfy their desires. The desire for the ability to attain objectives is universal. If this ideal were satisfied, all others would be. Men pursue objectives (ends or goals) by various means (courses of action) which incorporate a variety of conceptual and physical instruments. The capability for obtaining any objective presupposes the attainment of four ideals: the scientific ideal of perfect knowledge... the politico-economic ideal of plenty of abundance... the ethical-moral ideal of goodness... the aesthetic ideal of beauty."[11] To satisfy such requisites Ackoff seeks a new order by which he can deal with the complex of urban planning. His solution is system decision.

For simplicity Ackoff thinks that the system should be broken into subsystems. He believes that "Planning has three essential characteristics. First *planning involves a system of decisions*. That is, it involves a set of two or more decisions each of which is dependent on at least one other decision. Hence, "planning consists of a set of interdependent decisions."[12] Furthermore he says that "the set of decisions required in planning is so large and complex that it cannot be dealt with all at once. It must therefore be broken into subgroups of decisions which are small enough to handle, but these subgroups cannot be formed so as to be independent of each other. Hence, there is a need to review previous subsets of decisions in light of subsequent ones."[13] Though we agree that planning is a system of decisions, the scope of which is too large to be dealt with, we should not forget that the most important question is how to divide it into subsystems.

I think that an ideal subdivided system should evidence certain characteristics: (1) The more distinguished the subsystems are from each other, or in other words, the more black and white the differentiations we have between the subsystems, the further away from reality the totality of the system becomes. A flow of subsystems into each other would be ideal because of their strong interdependence. (2) The larger the subgroups (one system without subsystems) the easier it is to have a system-totality, but the harder it is to handle. (3) The smaller the subsystem (individualism) the closer it is to reality and the harder it is to arrive at a system-totality. However it is easier to handle for practical purposes (e.g., voting).

To create a better system the three above ideals should be satisfied. There should not be a sharp break between subsystems which would produce an interlocked set of subsystems. To me, the answer to the situation is to have a hierarchical range of scales in subsystems, with a span from an individual scale to one encompassing the totality of society and environment.

Following Waddington's view of a billiard ball, one could classify the nature of interaction among elements of an "open system" versus classical views and closed system. When one ball is shot, the behavior of any ball coming in contact with this ball is circumstantial and a function of the total movement system rather than an isolated, predictable, deterministic motion. "The world of billiard ball atomics exists at definite times in simple three-dimensional space dissolved into the esoteric notions of quantum mechanics and relativity."[13]

Thus far the available comprehensive theory which deals with this quality of open systems and environmental dynamics is "General System theory," and thus for the time being it could serve the role of providing the necessary framework. Following the principles of Systems theory, Field theory, cybernetics and Information and Communication theory, can be incorporated into a unified framework.

Many critics state that systems approach to issues related to human endeavors is problematic. One problem, they suggest, is that human beings are seen mechanically. The second problem is the concept of subdividing the totalistic and holistic character of life continuums into subcomponents. The third they claim to be oversimplification of mathematical representations of reality. But adherents to this approach have their own justifications. They say that science has to be simplified in order to ease the understanding of a multitude of variables. Their aim is not to reduce reality, but rather to dig into what is essential. Thompson, one of the adherents, is not confined within the narrow limits of current viewpoints. He analyzes biological forms and processes in light of their mathematical and physical characteristics. His approach can aid us in realizing that there is not such a vast difference between science and the humanities as we often imagine, especially in today's world of specialization. As he has put it, "Without something of the strength of physics philosophy would be weak; and without something of philosophy's wealth physical science would be poor."[14] Of course, science is undoubtedly much more current, whereas the human ties are historical as well as current. The merit of his work lies in his amazing correlation of biological forms and processes with mathematics. He defines simple organic forms in mathematical terms. For example, whereas a zoologist would ordinarily look upon a honeycomb as a product of animal instinct, Thompson regards it as the result of mathematical or physical forces or laws.

But of the construction and growth and working of the body, as of all else that is of the earth earthy, physical science is, in my humble opinion, our only teacher and guide. . . my sole purpose is to correlate with mathematical statement and physical law certain of the simpler outward phenomena of organic growth and structure or form, while all the while regarding the fabric of the organism, *ex hypothesi*, as a material and mechanical configuration.[15]

Thompson analyzes many organic forms and tries to determine how and to what extent living things can be explained by physical and mathematical consideration. For example, he finds that the shell of a snail or nautilus is quite similar to a sphere or spiral and can, within this context, be explained by mathematical laws.

Growth, he studies in relation to form. He speculates as to whether growth is a product of mere increase in size without marked change of form or whether it results in a gradual alteration of form and development of a complex structure to a greater or lesser degree. The resultant form he views in terms of forces acting on the organism which enable it to retain its configuration. "In an organism, great or small, it is not merely the nature of the *motions* of the living substance which we must interpret in terms of force (according to kinetics), but also the *conformation* of the organism itself, whose permanence or equilibrium is explained by the inter-action or balance of forces, as described in statics."[16] In light of such an approach he uses physical methods to examine the active movements of, for example, an amoeba, and then interprets its motions and the form or forms it displays in terms of a mathe-matical concept of force. These forces are products of various energies. The amoeba, he holds, is held together by the inter-molecular force of cohesion. In its own movements of itself and with those of other organisms it meets friction which it must oppose in order to continue its own movements. Moreover, the force of gravity presses down on the amoeba (admittedly due to its small size and the little difference between its density and the fluid in which it exists, this force is small) to keep it weighted down to the surface on which it is moving. The surrounding fluid and outside pressure, too, are exerting forces. Thus the amoeba reacts to all of the forces exerting pressure and, in response, changes its shape. Moreover, chemical and electrical forces on a molecular level are operating and producing an effect on the form taken by the organism. "Indeed we shall manifestly be inclined to use the term growth in two senses. . . on the one hand as a *process*, and on the other as a *force*."[17] Celldivision and attraction and repulsion of parts both involve the effects of forces which are closely related to physical phenomena.

Morphology does not deal solely with physical laws. "Mor-phology is not only a study of material things and of the forms of material things, but has its dynamical aspect under which we deal with the interpretation, in terms of force, of the operations of Energy."[18] If we look at the environment from a completely physical or biological point of view we shall reach a dead end because we cannot completely separate physical and nonphysical forces involved in organization and behavior. I agree with Thompson that since the nature of these forces is largely unknown and it is difficult to demonstrate their existence through observational experimentation, we can at least examine those parts to which the ordinary laws of physical forces apply.

Notes to Chapter Eight

1. Julian Huxley, Introduction to *The Phenomenon of Man*, by T. de Chardin, pp. 12-13.
2. T. Parsons, R. Bales and E. Shils, "The Dimensions of Action-Space," in *Working Papers in the Theory of Action*, p. 83.
3. Lowdon Wingo, Jr., "Urban Space in a Policy Perspective," in *Cities and Space: The Future Use of Urban land*, ed. by L. Wingo, Johns Hopkins Press, Baltimore, 1963, p. 7.
4. Jesse Reicheck, "On the Design of Cities," in "The Architect and the City," in *American Institute of Planners Journal (AIPJ)* (May 1961), p. 141-170.
5. Melvin Webber, "Order in Diversity: Community Without Propinquity," in *Cities and Space*, ed. by I. Wingo, p. 25.
6. *Ibid.*
7. John Dyckman, "The Changing Uses of the City," in *The Future Metropolis, Daedalus*, ed. by Lloyd Rodwin, G. Braziller, New York, 1961, pp. 144-170.
8. M. Staber, "Concrete Painting as Structural Painting," in *Structure in Art and in Science*, p. 181.
9. *Ibid.*, p. 183.
10. Paul Davidoff and Thomas A. Reiner, "A Choice Theory of Planning," in *A.I.P.J.*, Vol. 28 (May 1962), p. 103.
11. Russell Ackoff, *Scientific Method: Optimizing Applied Research Decisions*, John Wiley and Sons, Inc., New York & London, 1962, pp. 1-8.
12. R. Ackoff, "Toward Strategic Planning of Education," Unpublished paper, pp. 1-2.
13. *Ibid.*
14. D'Arcy Thompson, *On Growth and Form*, pp. 9-10.
15. *Ibid.*, pp. 8-9.
16. *Ibid.*, p. 11.
17. *Ibid.*, p. 13.
18. *Ibid.*, p. 14.

9. Design of Environmental Communication Systems

9.0 Introduction–Abstract

In this chapter it is argued that, contrary to traditional architectural design, the architecture of tomorrow will find its roots in a harmony between subjectivity and objectivity, consciousness and subconsciousness, rationality and nonrationality; i.e., in the human sciences and cybernetics, on the one hand, and the advancement of technology, on the other. Consequently this architecture will search for the structure of the random behavior of man's activity patterns and the technology which would enable man to give shape to such a dynamic complexity of structures, and thus the formulation of its relevant spatial organization and order.

The objective of environmental design is to create a harmonic order among a set of communication field cues: behavioral, environmental, and symbolic. Two factors must be analyzed: 1. harmonic order, which has to do with structural properties of the space-time relationship of objects-events patterns; and 2. the nature of cues, which are defined in physical and conceptual terms.

Then the harmonic order, as the law of opposites, is demonstrated by increased uniformity and regularity through reduction of entropy of certain functions (e.g., rhythm), and at the same time increase in randomness and diversity occurs through increase of entropy of opposite functions (e.g., climax), within the context of certain constraints. Finally, "originality" and "probability" techniques are introduced as tools for optimizing certain random functions such as design axioms (rhythm, climax, balance, proportion, harmony, and functional expression) to thus produce "harmonic order."

Contrary to the traditional architectural design process geared to subjectivity and value judgement, or dogmatic rationalism, the architecture of tomorrow will fine its roots in a harmony between subjectivity and objectivity, consciousness and sub-consciousness, rationality and nonrationality. It will draw upon the human sciences and cybernetics, on the one hand, and the advancement of technology, on the other. Consequently, this architecture will search for the structure of the random behavior of man's activity patterns and the technology which would enable him to give shape to such a dynamic complexity of structures, and thus the formulation of its relevant spatial organization and order. Our objective is to: 1. outline a new definition of architecture as environmental field communication, and 2. outline the relevant design process: a communication systems approach.

9.1 Environmental Design–Problem Identification

In looking at the present state of architecture and comparing it with the development of other disciplines, we can identify two types of inherent problems. The first type of problem relates to the way we conceptualize architectural ideas and concepts, how they are transformed, and finally, how they are turned into design, design process, and implementation. The second type of problem is involved with the identification of a definition of architecture and its subcomponents.

In the following pages, we shall address these two sets of problems in order to see the shortcomings in the present system and thus be able to formulate new theories.

A. PROBLEM OF CONCEPTUALIZATION, TRANSFORMATION AND DESIGN

Developments in the natural and behavioral sciences in the nine-teenth/twentieth centuries brought us to understand that there are two ways through which we see the environment: object- event phenomena revealed through purely *a priori* logical and scientifc investigation, and *a posteriori* detached and mundane, daily experimentations with the environment. Based on the above two methods, we find a dichotomy between the two observation processes and, thus, products; namely, the *tangible* or physical and the *intangible* or perceptual. The physical refers to how a structure, as far as we can humanly determine, actually *is* from microscipic atoms to the macrocosmic universe. The perceptual refers to the normal behavior patterns of our sensory receptors; i.e., our everyday touching of the world and the meaning we construct out of these encounters.

The dynamics of change and complexity of ever increasing diversities of life patterns has made it tremendously hard to come up with any formula capable of forseeing the transformation involved in such changes. Another obstacle is the lack of evidence in finding any permanent origin and destination, and nonchanging reference points or coordinate systems to which such life patterns could be related. Answers to these two major questions facing planning and design activity could be useful in formulating any forseeable solutions. This entails a coordinate system (origin and destination of life), the nature of the primary basic elements of life forms (from the Newtonian viewpoint), and its way of change from one combination and shape to another. Lastly, one must consider the direction and purpose of change. Theoretical conclusions provide the only way out; they simplify planning and design objectives and criteria into a much smaller number of relatively known facts and principles.

Man is thought to be rational and nonrational. Rational behavior on the part of man is exhibited when he can justify what he does and provide some logical reasoning for it. To be able to reason any behavior one must be able to repeat, and one must have a full conscious comprehension (cognition) of such repetive behavior. There are certain behaviors of man and his perception of environmental patterns which seem to be chaotic and unrelated as far as the consciousness is concerned. However the structure of this same behavior might be considered ordered in relation to the subconscious, as it is tied to the subconscious structure and nonrational behavior of the mind; thus it is ordered on a higher level of comprehension. Your behavior when you enter a classroom, trying to find a seat for example, or when you wander in an urban space in your free time, or your speech or gestures while talking or acting, are all subconsciously ordered.

Art works created by artists could be the result of rational and/or nonrational behavior. By the same token the object−event patterns perceived in the environment could be seen as rational or nonrational patterns, based on the perceiver's ability or inability to make a logical order out of them. Your pattern behavior while wandering around an urban space is conscious-subconscious. The decision process during such a period of time−elimination of one route versus another and so on−is not considered totally conscious or rational. The physical representation of such a pattern, whether the path of your footmarks or visual contacts with the environment, are also rational-nonrational. Random pattern could have some complex order beyond reasoning or even comprehension. Such random and probabilistic forms could only be seen by the subconscious behavior of the mind.

Let us look at an architectural piece−an object or picture. What you see in your mind's eye is an awareness which constitutes all the properties (let us say points) of that picture which could fit into a matrix of n times n points. It could be said that you would holistically see or have an awareness of all of those points, as well as the relationship of each point to the others−an immediate intuitive judgement or subtle discrimination of these properties and relationships. Now let us try to look at the same picture differently, that is, through the intellect and cognition and try to analyze, know, and reason properties of our mental picture, its parts and their relationships. It becomes obvious that not only is it impossible to know all the properties of an intuitive form, it is also impossible to see what you could see, simultaneously. In other words, only some properties of an intuitive picture can be seen in cognitive and, thus, analytic terms. That is to say, our logical mind cannot simultaneously see and thus analyze, compare, design, and act upon all the elements of a mental picture at once, rather it views them in some sort of linear fashion, in simple groupings and relationships and by drawing some logical relationship among some sequences of perception in order to make a comprehensive overall picture. So this is the problem of architecture and design: the linkage between the senses and the intellect and its functions are unknown. Consequently, unless such factors become known, our policy formulation regarding design process, design method, and their implementation might fail. In developing any theory of design, we deal with creativity and thus with emotions and feelings, as well as with the intellect, employing cognition and intuition at the same time. In this process we deal with two different characteristics of mental activity; i.e., the objective and subjective, rational and non-rational, thinking and feeling, and so on. The issue is the nature of the relationship of these distinct behaviors of man.

In this regard Karl Popper[1] draws a distinction between logic and empirical science, as well as a distinction between these and design. To mix design theory with logic and empirical science, is wrong. Logic has its base on abstract *a priori* pure forms; science searches for concrete real and existing forms, but design originates generic novel forms. Popper also rejects any solely subjective theory of probability in which our rational beliefs are not guided by an objective frequency statement. In design, the main form of reasoning is inductive or synthetic rather than analytic. A good design idea is chosen in the expectation that it could succeed on a trial-and-error process. Since design is thought to be unique, Probability theory, to be of any use, cannot be bound by the interpretation of probability in the long run.

Peirce, in order to distinguish the nature of inductive reasoning and its relationship to other modes of plausible reasoning, asserts that any human being with enough information and thought on any question will be able to arrive at a certain definite conclusion, which is the same that any other mind will make under sufficiently favorable circumstances.

Now, whereas the major goal of scientific endeavor is to establish general laws or theories, the prime objective of design is to realize a particular case or design. Both require deduction, the quintessential mode of mathematical reasoning for analytical purposes. Yet science must employ inductive reasoning in order to generalize, and design must use productive interference so as to particularize. In attempting to draw distinctions between induction and productive reasoning or, for that matter, science and design, nothing could be more confusing than the fact that the word hypothesis has become its own antonym. *In science, "hypothesis" is commonly used to mean a tentative general statement about a class of cases,* though it originally meant a particular case of a general proposition. This semantic ambiguity accounts for widespread confusion and misunderstanding. It has also led to the use of the term "induction" to cover a variety of Peirce's synthetic models.

To start with the very basics, let us begin with the conscious and subconscious activities of mind described in the first two chapters. These two activities, as earlier explained, are the bases of the above mentioned mental behavior. The rational thought process, as a conscious activity of the mind, functions in a linear, two-dimensional manner. Conscious and rational behavior is predictable; transferable, and restorable. However, the intuition and the subconscious comprehend the space-time event pattern in a holistic way and do not have the other mentioned characteristics.

To simplify these ideas, let us regard the picture or object just analyzed without any reasoning or even thought processes. Then the conscious rational perception enters; it resists the unknown, so one begins comparing the pattern with relevant comparative information in the scene, as well as in the memory storage, for logical, rational comparison. One tries to understand and reason it. Moreover when you perceive, your perception covers the total picture, whereas, as soon as you try to understand logically the relationships of the parts, you only see those relationships in a linear, simplified way.

Human physiology also functions in the same way as man's rational behavior. That is, one could not walk in all different directions at one time; one cannot even think of being in several places at a time. Due to this very reason, in architecture man has historically utilized three dimensional space, though not entirely, but rather in a combined two-two dimensional manner; that is to say, vertically and horizontally. Consequently we see our architectural forms as consisting of horizontal plus vertical dimensions, not a combination of the two. Elevations, plans and their parts, windows and their subdivisions, brickwork and its patterns are all additive components of horizontals and verticals.

On the basis of the above, we conclude: the two processes, namely, intuition and cognition, are basically different and *cannot* be matched. Any attempt to replace either one for the other or completely integrate the two has not yet been successful. A comprehensive approach, attempting to incorporate both processes is needed. Consequently, design activities, if they must be reasoned in a logical and analytical way, should be considered in sequence, step by step. This can be achieved through the conceptual analysis of simple relationships at one time, then by the synthesis of subrelationships into a total set.

The dilemma of design processes rests on these very issues:

1. The end product a designer creates is supposed to bridge the senses and the intellect and satisfy both the *intuitive* and *cognitive* minds and the conscious-subconscious experience of its creator and users; thus it is transformed, materialized, and expressed with the same form characteristics into a real and concrete shape.

2. During the course of the creative process, from the moment the creative piece is conceptualized and transformed into presentation material for builders or users, through to its implementation, there is failure to match precisely the conceptual pictures of the creators and users.

3. Intuition carries n degree of freedom; i.e., emotions and feelings simultaneously travel in n dimensional space-time, whereas intellect, and also the physical body, moves two-dimensionally. Rational thought processes cannot keep up with the complexities of dimensions and freedom of choice that intuition and human experience have and require.

Thus the dilemma is the inadequacy of environmental communication media or the materialization of environmental ideas and concepts in physical form. Any form of creation has to lose its complexities as well as freedom of choice, after it is originated, while in the process of transferring it to any other form which can be understood by others and/or materialized into concrete forms.

Finally, the materialization of environmental physical form is a cognitive act whereas the communication language of creators and users is a mixture of feelings and emotions, as well as the rational and logical. That is to say, a building is a concrete form, built in definite and finite parts and pieces and analyzed in the same way; but the same building is experienced holistically and not in parts.

To improve this communication process we begin with man as creator and user, whose characteristic behavior we do not want to change to fit the capabilities of the communication media, but rather to improve our media to fit him.

Hence, to overcome the above mentioned dilemma, we should try to look for means of bringing our intermediary processes closer to the two end-processes; i.e., the conception, intuition, and experience of the creators and users.

In the traditional form of architectural presentation and re-presentation, drawings and models are the only medium used. However, since they represent already-simplified complex, dynamic, and infinite properties of the designer's concepts into a fixed, finite dimension of space, they are not able to keep up with the complexities experienced on either end of the scale. Drawings and models are incapable of presenting activities or the flow of intangible infinite properties of human experience and communication. They are incapable of representing any state of change and growth. They are incapable of presenting the probabilistic or random qualities of active space,[2] and finally, they are neither capable of exploring all existing, alternative sets of possible compositions and orders, nor capable of easy correction and transfer to somewhere else unless physically carried.

In an attempt to solve some of these problems, the proposed environmental communication field theory is used to:

1. minimize the problem of bifurcation between physical and nonphysical environmental properties by using common primary units such as environmental, behavioral, and symbolic cues in order to avoid viewing architecture as mere masses or buildings;
2. conceptualize architecture as communication which results from the tangible and intangible properties of the environment;
3. deal with the unknown properties of environmental quality by incorporating the notion of random and probabilistic forms and patterns into architectural conception, presentation, and expression; and
4. expand the logical and analytical capabilities of mental activities through the use of computer-aided analytical methods and the environmental communication systems approach.

9.2 Environmental Communication and Components

A ENVIRONMENTAL COMMUNICATION

The world as known to us today, is a complex dynamic field of interactions in which the whole is greater than and different from the sum of its parts. Each particle, element, is so totally integrated into the whole that any change in its state of being is conditioned by the state of all the other parts of the system. Thus it can be said that each particle carries as much information as the whole; i.e., the dispositional potential (energy-information, due to transformation or dispositional properties) of each particle, though geographically assuming a space, the sum of which forms total space, is not equal to its geographical size. Rather its dynamic qualitative boundaries extend beyond the geographical quantitative boundaries of the entire system.

So the study, teaching, and practice of architecture should be based on an understanding of universal laws common to disciplines involved in environmental planning and design, the synthesis of intellect with feeling, quality with quantity, material with non-material, and conscious with subconscious, with an understanding that architecture is a harmonic symphony emerging from the rational and nonrational, having blended both into a meaningful order.

However, in communication terms, objects can be seen not by virtue of their associations within our conceptual framework as to what, for example, a tree is or what a table is, but rather by environmental field properties. This implies looking at the environment as if you could not distinguish one tree from another in a surrounding environment, table from chair, etc. Instead, a tree is identified by virtue of its structural properties in a spatio-temporal continuum; i.e., its structure of matrix, location, and order among complex sets of environmental, behavioral, and symbolic cues.[3] In such a case tress or tables are not isolated sets of matter. Their boundaries are affected and thus expanded to external space-time; i.e., they are part of a continuous continuum of space and time which is impossible to subdivide and segregate fully; they must be dealt with in relative and probabilistic terms. We tend to see the interactions of the tree or the table more obviously in closer proximity or when looking at their smaller scale concentrated boundaries. Nevertheless, these are part of larger and larger over-lays of bubble boundaries and complexities of interrelationships.

In terms of Eastern logic, our all pervading sense of Self, or knower, arose out of a centered concentration on the object. To define any specific thing, be it concrete or abstract, involves a process of delineation, whereby focused attention is primarily concentrated on the object, as opposed to, or isolated from, its ground. To the precise extent that we attempt to make the object more clear and distinct, we simultaneously cause its ground to appear more and more vague. This procedure continues until such time that the entire universe is conceived of as consisting of isolated entities hanging, as it were, in space.

We can only know the tree by its surroundings. That is to say, the conscious pattern of thought processes is sorted out by being focused out from an infinite pattern of awareness. The infinite elements of an environmental field must be divided into relatively simple, defined elements and relationships in order to enable them to be focused upon.

Simplified elements perceived in an environmental field or field of awareness are manifested to us in various communication cues. This simplification "does not ordinarily occur to us because we naively suppose that things are what we see in the first place, prior to the act of conscious attention. Obviously, the eye as such does not see things: it sees the total visual field in all its infinite detail."[4]

Adapting the above field concepts, creative and material proces-ses which are traditionally separated from each other can be seen as the same. If man's creative facilities were found to be of a structural rather than metaphysical nature, the often misleading term, "creative," would have to be replaced by, as Whyte[5] says, the more general term, "formative," in reference to the structured processes which create new forms. However, if it is found that matter is "creative," then this term, too, would have to be changed.

B   Environmental Communication Components[6]

Environmental field communication components can be classified in the following manner. In literature, just as letters are combined into words, words into sentences, sentences into paragraphs and so on, in environmental communication individual point-objects, point-events, or point-associations become grouped into lines, lines into planes, planes into volumes, etc. As a piece of space unfolding its structure is preceived not only as a series of discrete independent units placed next to each other in a mechanical, additive manner possessing a shape, structure, and identity of its own, but also as an integral part of a larger structure on a larger scale and higher order of interrelationships. That is to say, in a line consisting of $n - 1$ points, $A, E_1, E_2 \ldots E_{n-1}$, when you add a new point n (which in isolation has been identical with the points in the set on the line) to the set, now not only does this point become different (take on a different value) from what it was in isolation, but it also changes the structural properties of every single point on the line relative to its position on the line.

In regard to the definition of basic units or data, I do not think there exists any predefined conception of set units. Reality is a continuous flow of energy, with no breakdown. This is also Saussure's view when he rejects "the position that these are given 'objects,' 'things,' or 'substances.' "[7] He particularly emphasized set relationships. A definition of perceptual boundaries for such units in various scientific theories is only in conceptual form and for practical purposes.

There are some similarities between the unit types defined here for environmental communication, namely objects, events, and associations, and those defined in semiotics, namely icons, indices, and symbols.

Before I spell out environmental communication units, let me introduce some of the characteristics of the former entities as a comparative frame of reference.

In terms of hierarchy and added complexity beginning from objects to events to associations, one may see similarities among the above three types of environmental communication cues and three types of signs defined by Peirce, icons relative to objects, indices relative to events, and symbols relative to associations, the form of each being more complex than the preceeding one.

In Peirce's theory those signs whose relation to their objects depends on mental association are called "symbols." "If the sign signifies its objects solely by virtue of being really connected with it, as with physical symptoms, meterological signs, and a pointing finger, ... "[8] He calls such a sign an *Index*. "A sign which stands for something merely because it resembles" it is called an *Icon*.[9] He further specifies that "the icon is very perfect in respect to signification, bringing its interpreter face to face with the very character signified."[10] It is obvious that this is not necessarily true in the case of an index and far from true in the case of a symbol. Peirce has also argued that in any logical process we must use a "mixture" of icons, indices, and symbols. "We cannot dispense with any of them."[11]

To classify environmental phenomena, three major entities (cues), objects, events, and associations or environmental communication units, become the building blocks of environmental communication theory.

1. *Objects*, representing the material world, are especially seen within tangible boundaries.
2. *Events*, representing deeds, are defined as activities or behavior. They could be described as changes of state (either substantive or structural behavior) or disposition of matter (objects) in space and/or time. Such changes are accompanied by a charge of discharge of energy. Anger is reached through one's state of charge against some other state of the environment. Anger would disappear if the change of the state of the environment favored the person's expectation, or if a type of discharge of energy on his part could move him to rest.
3. *Associations* are provided by similarities and differences observed among objects, events, or their combinations in the space-time environment. The perceptual world is known through these associations and identified as sets of objects and events. Having identified, classified, and segregated among these object-event associations (in the shape of objects and events) as social objects or social behavior, we have created norms or a value system, i.e., what is "good," "bad," "desirable," "undesirable," etc.

We call these types of entities in the environmental field *symbols*; symbols represent any form of association, idea, concept, meaning, thought, attitude, etc. Symbols thus have comparative qualities in character. They are object-even patterns carrying certain values based on their space-time appearances or associations. Due to nature, these entities may or may not occur in any specific location but rather in the person's mind. These associations can be identified with Peirce's view, "the infinite number of triadic relations."[12] Associations are the source of all man's conceptions, just as are symbols in Peirce's theory. " 'All logical thought' " is an "operation upon symbols consisting in subsituation...."[13] Associations are such operations comparing various space-time object-events. "This process of refering back may change from phenomenon to phenomenon, and the type of rule (or convention or attitude) that allows one to correlate a given presence to a supposed object or concept may assume different forms."[14]

The following statement about the characteristics of signs in Peirce's theory shows them to be identical to their relevant environmental cues. "Symbols are not genuine signs; indices are signs degenerate in the first degree; icons are signs degenerate in the second degree. A symbol sufficiently complete always invokes an index; an index sufficiently complete always involves an icon."[15]

Our three types of cues can be classified into two major categories, "entities" and "relationships" or "elements" and "linkages." The first two, namely objects and events, which occur in some locality are called "formative elements;" the third type, namely associations as a product of the mind, assuming some kind of relationships not necessarily relevant to any location, are considered linkages.

The following are other conceptual definitions concerning environmental communication fields:

1. *Field.* The totality of the environment, physical and nonphysical, tangible and intangible, where the state of every single entity is conditioned by its structural relationships to the totality of entities and not conditioned by any predefined past or future states is considered "field."[16]

2. *Reference Points and Coordinate Systems.* Field theory requires no preconceived coordinates as a reference system, rather it calls for relative and changing coordinates drawn relevant to the

change of various states of field activity. In the creational sense or in external space-time, this moment is known as and is the origin or reference point for the past and future. Its activities are bubble to this reference point. In visual terms, a coordinate system could be assigned to wherever the observer's eye moves, the center of the cone of vision becomes the reference point. In other words, wherever on the scene (visual information matrix) the eye chooses to focus becomes the reference point and thus the origin of the coordinate system. There is no fixed, predefined value for any point; it is like music where you set an arbitrary base tone and tune different instruments on that common keynote.

Visual fields could be closed systems consisting of a set with limited boundaries (e.g., a painting) which could be fitted into a matrix $m \times n$. In this case the coordinates, or reference points, predetermine the size and boundary of the object (unless the object is not meant to be seen at one glance).

On the other hand, open-ended environmental fields do not have beginning or end. Thus the reference points are relative and drawn at wherever the eye moves. In this case, the visual threshold and field dimensions would be, and are, very much defined relative to the observer's distance from the object and the nature of the object or environment.

To construct or analyze a three-dimensional model of the environment, the principle of the geometry of space is applied. Points make lines; lines make planes; planes make volumes. Five major principles are involved:

1. As discussed in chapter 4, the units are not necessarily assembled in an additive molecular way. They might overlap, vary in intensity, etc.
2. The organization of the coding system is hierarchical in nature: an architectural element, a building, an urban segment, etc. are all hierarchical components of a unified system that appears in different forms, scales, and functions in an integrated whole.
3. The value of each code is relevant to the structure of its relation to the rest of the system or, in other words, to the position or disposition of this code to a network of other elements of the total system.

4. For practical reasons we use sequential spatial process in adding up point-units to lines, lines to planes and planes to volumes. That is to say, just as in creating musical notations or writing manuscripts, we too formulate a sequential coding system into a spatial one.
5. Although the human mind sees a number of things simultanously, owing to our incapability to reproduce such systems, we also use temporal sequential processes to reconstruct environmental communication systems. "An architectural object of whatever size and complexity is 'addressed' by routines of behavior which unfold over time and which often are sequentially situated in groups of space-cells composed in three-dimensional aggregates. The linear or multilinear geometry of behavioral episodes are, as it were, 'mapped into' the multidimensional geometries of architectonic objects."[17]

To be more specific, events, due to their nature, follow the sequential process of time. To be able to deal with the other two types of cues we arbitrarily construct them in temporal sequences too.

C. ARCHITECTURAL COMMUNICATION FIELD[18]

The human environment is part of a larger and more complex cosmic order. Our perception of our surrounding environment can only encompass a supercomplex world seen in systems of similarities and differences identified as message systems. Originality and redundancy of certain objects and events and their interrelationships gives each object or event a unique contextual meaning.

The formulations of such meaningful objects and events are a product of culture; i.e., the ways we use them and how we adapt them to our needs, desires, and value systems and vice versa, in other words, how we adapt to them. Our cultural evolution is a representation of this two-way process. "No human society exists without artifically reordering its environment—without employing environment formation (whether made or appropriated) as sign-tokens in a system of visual communication, representation and expression."[19]

"Every human society communicates architecturally. The component units of an architectonic code or system consist of contrastively-opposed formations in media addressed to visual perception. Distinctions or disjunctions in material formations are intended to cue culture-specific differences in meaning in a manner precisely analogous to other semiotic systems such as verbal language or bodily gesturing."[20]

Every communication system then is a system of codes where every code relevant to these three different sets of cues relates to differences in communicated meanings. The code system varies relative to types of cues; i.e., objects, events, and associations, e.g., in material form, color contrast, texture, material, shapes, etc., constitute the coding system. Yet the same differences might relate to sociocultural and behavioral differences and relevant associations. Thus an environmental communication system is a coding system comparing and thus communicating the associative values of a world of objects and events relative to their associations to a space-time network of objects and events and their combinations.

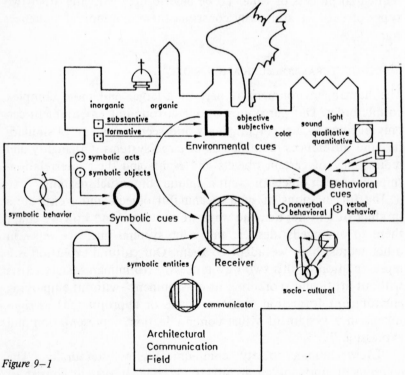

Figure 9–1

Architectural Communication Field

Environmental or architectural communication field following figure 9.1) is what we experience around us every day; it is divided into the following elements:

- environmental cues consisting of the environmental field object system,
- behavioral cues consisting of environmental field event patterns, and
- symbolic cues consisting of environmental field associations; i.e., ideas, concepts, meanings.

9.3 Environmental Transformation Techniques

With changes in philosophy and attitude toward cosmic pattern and order, man creates new tools and techniques which enable him to describe his conception of new patterns. In the recent development of man's view of his world, Set theory and its derivative, the new mathematics, became a cornerstone. This in itself became the foundation of many other branches of mathematics and the foundation for linkage between two major branches of *a priori* knowledge; i.e., mathematics and logic.

A. HISTORICAL DEVELOPMENT OF MATHEMATICAL TECHNIQUES

As just discussed, the world is composed of complex combinations of numerous subsets consisting of environmental cues, behavioral cues, and symbolic cues. Man has always been involved in some form of representation, analysis, and reorganization of these entities; he has invented new methods and techniques to improve these endeavors.

Man's knowledge and experience in the areas of the pure sciences and technology have improved tremendously over the past one hundred years.

New techniques available to man have further enabled him to present his views and share his concepts concerning cosmic order and the surrounding environment with others. Among these new tools are Set theory, Boolian algebra, projective geometry, probability, computer sciences, etc.

Before getting into concepts of probability, which are widely used here in environmental communication Field theory, we shall briefly introduce some of these mathematical techniques. Such an introduction would not involve any deep discussion of any part. Rather the idea is to familiarize the reader with the relevant notions.

With the change in man's philosophies and attitude toward cosmic pattern and order, man creates new tools and techniques which enable him to describe his conception of new patterns. In the recent development of man's view of his world, Set theory, the new mathematics, became a cornerstone. This in itself became the foundation of many other branches of mathematics, and the foundation for linkage between two major branches of *a priori* knowledge; namely, mathematics and logic.

Geometry is another important part of man's *a priori* knowledge, the theories of which have accumulated throughout history. Apparent in the history of the Western world is the fact that the Greeks were the first to use geometry as a logical concept. After this initial stage, Euclidian ideas and concepts of geometry are the most outstanding views in written history reflecting man's attempt to describe the universe in geometrical terms. During a long period of Western world history Euclidian geometry was the means by which man in an *a priori* manner related himself to the cosmic framework, using the Euclidian coordinate as a means by which he could orient himself in space.

Then came non-Euclidian geometry which totally questioned the foundations of Euclidian geometry. All in all, the new philosophic strain of thought, the whole question of the nature of truth, the order of the universe, the ideas of causality, and the problem of relativity were new challenges to man, and interrelated. Geometry, as a method of description of the dynamic process of the physical universe, whether the patterns be those involved with objects or events, becomes significantly different from that which Euclidean geometry had assumed. It is the author's belief that for the most part in architecture we still use the Euclidean views of geometry as a means to describe the spatial pattern, whereas knowledge has developed far beyond this stage. It is to be noted that at this moment in history one should expect *a priori* knowledge and structure of logic not only to bring building components together, lay out planning structural grids, or organize space, but rather to bring out the total object-event patterns of human experiences.

Today we must look at all the possible means and techniques which man has at his disposal to see which mathematics of geometry is most convenient and useful and should be used for various purposes. In any quantitative studies of spatial or environmental nature, it is desirable to be able to describe the forms with some mathematical precision. Thus it is reasonable to use one of the available techniques.

Application of these techniques is based on two major viewpoints. One is concerned with the study, analysis, and presentation of relationships within the representations themselves. The other is concerned with the relationships *among* these elements. There are three mathematical ways of introducing the fields of environmental properties which are discussed here.

Man's knowledge and experience in the areas of pure science and technology have tremendously improved over the past one hundred years. The new techniques available have enabled him to present his views and share his concepts concerning cosmic order and his surrounding environment.

B. CLASSIFICATION OF TRANSFORMATION TECHNIQUES

Following are three sets of techniques currently used in the representation and analysis of space: "Geometry of Space," "Structure of Space," and "Order of Space." Before getting into the third category (order of space) which is widely used in this theory of environmental communication field, we will briefly mention the other two.

i. GEOMETRY OF SPACE

The first set of techniques is concerned with the geometry of space—how points come together to make lines, lines to make planes, and planes to make volumes, described by techniques such as *Set theory* and *projective geometry*.

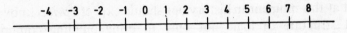

Figure 9–2
Set of Integers

Set theory,[21] in a mathematical set: one can begin by naming a number of units of a fixed length along a line. The line should be extended indefinitely in two directions—positive and negative. Now we have one universal set of integers, which we can call Z. If one wants to combine the two sets, we call this operation the union and intersection of sets, denoted by ZUB.

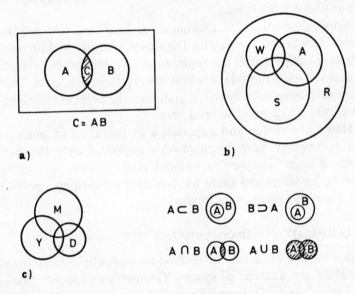

Figure 9–3
Major Notions in Set Theory

Sets can also be interesting, which is denoted by $Z \cap B$. A set which is contained in a universal set is called a subset. A number of units combined end-to-end make up a component. So far the elements discussed exist along a line in one dimension, but we may extend the idea into two and three dimension without difficulty. Mies Vander Rohe based many of his buildings on a rectangular and modular grid. One example was the Illinois Institute of Technology in Chicago which was set out entirely on a 12' by 12' grid. This method of organizing architectural space within a matrix of integrated cubic modules is one used by some architects with aesthetic effect.

R = set of all rooms in a building
W = subset of all rooms which must have windows
A = subset of all rooms which must have full air-conditioning
S = subset of all rooms which need a high level of insulation

In conventional algebra an expression such as $A + B = C$ contains two kinds of signifiers. The variables A, B, and C represent numerical values, while the symbols + and = refer to mathematical operations such as addition, equalization, and so on. An expression in Boolean algebra may look very similar, but often the letters represent simple statements or logical premises while the mathematical symbols refer to operations in logic, such as "and," "or," and so on.

Consequently, Set theory is a branch of logic. The diagrams illustrate its generic concepts.

In fig. 9–3.a, the rectangle represents a universe of discourse, a set of all possible statements concerning the topic in question, whereas the circles represent subsets of this universe, individual statements A and B, which are being compared, combined, or otherwise manipulated to give a third statement, C, which is represented by the shaded area.

The theories of real functions and predefined concepts of order are used in Set theory as a means of obtaining particular relationships. The concept of dimensions in the ordered linear continuum is one of them. The theory of probability is basically developed on the framework and methods originated in Set theory. Topology also depends a great deal on the concepts of Set theory.

Projective geometry. [22] When we project an elevation to give an angled view of it in such a way as to map parallel lines, we make what is called by mathematicians an *affine transformation*; that is, a transformation having an affinity with, or a likeness to, the original. Architects frequently use affine transformations in which the lengths of vertical lines and those parallel to the horizontal, rectangular axes are preserved. Such a projection is isometric. In mathematical terms, this is not strictly true since the length of

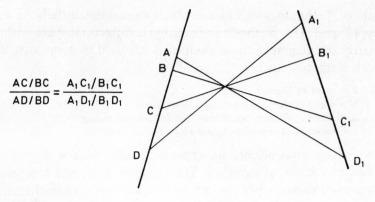

$$\frac{AC/BC}{AD/BD} = \frac{A_1 C_1 / B_1 C_1}{A_1 D_1 / B_1 D_1}$$

Figure 9–4

Projective Geometry

lines not parallel to the principal axes are not preserved. An isometric drawing must not be confused with the mathematical isometric transformation for which all lengths are preserved. However, while an isometric drawing is an example of an affine transformation, it is not typical: in general an affine transformation does not preserve lengths, only parallelism. The above equation is known as the cross-ratio: it is fundamental in the development of projective geometry and the theory of linear transformation.

Another application of Set theory in architectural presentation occurs when one uses matrixes and vectors to represent major points of elements of the physical environment.[23] Application of these techniques enable architects to store information relevant to such sets in computer memory, use it whenever necessary, and transfer it to different localities, and finally, use it in any form of combination of comparative analysis.

Following is an illustration of a descriptive geometry of a set of windows, M and N.

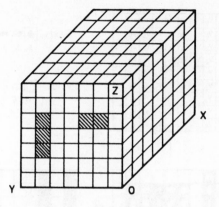

Figure 9–5a

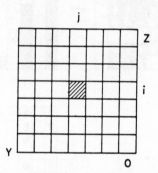

Figure 9–5b

Vertical & Horizontal
Vectors:

$\begin{bmatrix} 1 \\ 5 \end{bmatrix} = V_1$ $\begin{bmatrix} 5 \\ 1 \end{bmatrix} = H_1$

$\begin{bmatrix} 2 \\ 5 \end{bmatrix} = V_2$ $\begin{bmatrix} 5 \\ 2 \end{bmatrix} = H_2$

$\begin{bmatrix} 3 \\ 5 \end{bmatrix} = V_3$ $\begin{bmatrix} 5 \\ 3 \end{bmatrix} = H_3$

$\begin{bmatrix} 4 \\ 5 \end{bmatrix} = V_4$ $\begin{bmatrix} 5 \\ 4 \end{bmatrix} = H_4$

$\begin{bmatrix} 5 \\ 5 \end{bmatrix} = V_5$ $\begin{bmatrix} 5 \\ 5 \end{bmatrix} = H_5$

Figure 9–5c

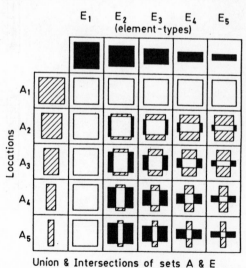

Union & Intersections of sets A & E

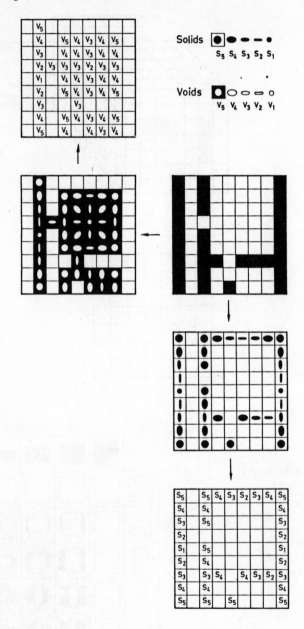

Figure 9–5d

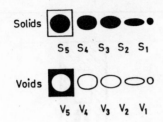

Figure 9–5e

Figure 9–5f

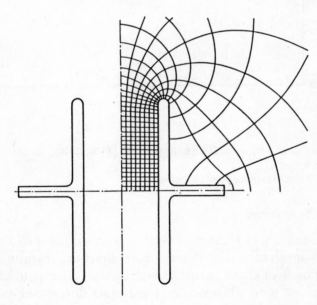

Figure 9–5g

Sets and Their Combinational Properties

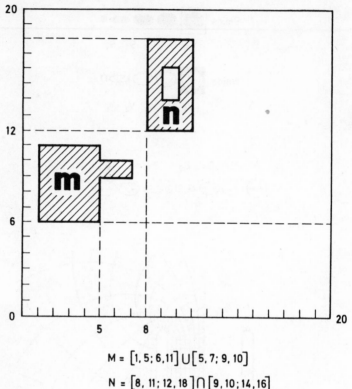

$$M = \left[1, 5; 6, 11\right] \cup \left[5, 7; 9, 10\right]$$

$$N = \left[8, 11; 12, 18\right] \cap \left[9, 10; 14, 16\right]$$

Figure 9–6
Sets and Descriptive Geometry of Environment

ii. STRUCTURE OF SPACE

The second set of techniques used in representing spatial characteristics involved routes (lines), their direction, magnitude, and
major points of characteristic change (nodes). That is to say, this
technique is used when localities and exact dimensions and location of parts of the environment are not focused on, rather the
structural components, major lines, and their interlocks, are
looked at.

Topology and *theory of graph* are two of these techniques.
Topology and Theory of Graph. Topology is the mathematics of
position and of distortions which deals with properties of objects
which are so fundamental that no amount of distortions will alter
their relationships.

Just as there is a relationship between the number of vertices and edges of a graph or tree, so there is a fundamental relationship between the corners (versigo, V), the sides (edges, F), and the faces (F) of a regular polyhedron, or three-dimensional solid.

If we make a cube or any other simple polyhedron out of thin rubber we could cut out one of the faces and fold the remainder flat out on a plane surface. The shapes would be distorted, but there would be the same number of vertices and edges and each plane would still form a polygon, but there would be one plane less. It has, in fact, become a planar network or graph.

When surfaces are distorted in this way, one enters the field of topology. A plane, square sheet of rubber can be stretched into a circle, a triangle, or any other polygon, a C–shape, a U–shape, any shape, which does not involve cutting or joining two ends that were originally free.

It is not possible to form a sphere from a plain sheet of rubber, but if one started out with a sphere, it could be distorted into a cube, a tetrahedron, or any other polygon, but not a cup; a cup has a handle which contains a hole. So to form a cup one would have to start with a Torus, a doughnut, or the shape of a car tire.

The essential point in topology is that each part of the original figure corresponds to one point, and one point only, of the figure to which it is transformed.

Conventional architectural and engineering drawings have a long history, and practitioners should be able to duplicate these conventional methods by using computer aids. Graphical output may be generated by computers in several ways.

Application of Graphic theory to analysis may be found in geography. Hagget has used it under the heading of "Locational Analysis," where he has classified the use of graphs in four classes: First, models with single paths, which are concerned with optimum paths where movement cost varies widely over different parts of the route. Second, models of networks without circuits, which are named "trees," where one starts with a single vertex A, and from this draws edges to several other vertices A_{12}, A_{13}, ... etc. A number of trees may be placed together to form a forest, and the various arcs in each tree are called branches. There is a single arc connecting any pair of varieties. Thirdly, we have models with circuits, which is an arc that returns to its starting point. And fourth, models of cellular networks which are concerned with the relationship between the sizes of animals and their forms.

In architecture and planning, to present properties of spatial human activity systems, the use of mapping techniques is sometimes employed. This is done as follows: different information sets are used to present various characteristics of such properties; e.g., information regarding the volume, surface, edge, or other major elements of environmental components. Another example could be the human activity system or movement pattern with which it is associated.

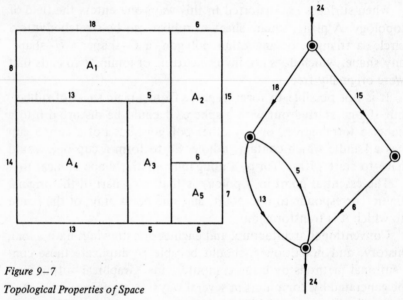

Figure 9–7

Topological Properties of Space

The application of the concept of *field* in this theory deals with topological properties of both tangible and intangible space (solids and voids). That is to say, field concepts are used to denote topological relationships between elements of the environment—in the case of a house, which room is located next to which, which rooms opens to which room; in other words, how each point within each field space (i.e., room) relates to others and so on.

To follow an example given by Lionel March,[24] suppose a_1, $a_2 \ldots \ldots a_n$ are the horizontal walls, with b_1, $b_2 \ldots \ldots b_n$ the vertical walls of a building with grid structural mumbers. Let us assign a value of 24, corresponding to the plan width, to the top and bottom members and 22, corresponding to vertical length, to the far east and west portion of the vertical outside walls. Associated values to the width horizontally are 24 (18 + 6) and 6 and 18 (13 + 5) and 24 (13 + 5 + 6). As discussed earlier (field model), this graph shows similarity with the physics of electricity or "electrical networks."[25] Architecturally speaking, these techniques provide us with new tools for planning and design. They help explore possibilities of relative position dimension and shapes of rooms and spaces which could be combined into a given area.

iii. ORDER OF SPACE

The third set of mathematical techniques used in the representation of properties of the environment is not concerned with either of the above two properties of the environment. Rather it is concerned with the *order* of properties of environmental field; i.e., it is interested in their regularity and randomness. Thus this technique assigns points to activities and then tries to analyze the probabilities of occurrence of various characteristic points of the environment. A communality of groups and clusters of points brings down the vast number of points to manageable sets. For event patterns with changing characteristics and location, Set and Graph theory, statistical mechanics, and Information theory are used to measure the properties of such field order.

Unity harmony and proportion, rhythm, structure, composition, form, even truth and virtue, are all qualities or aspects or the order of environmental communication, which can actually be the subject of the representation of such techniques. We refer to the structural relationship or arrangement of parts or elements. To plan or design is to organize, arrange, or give order or structure to the parts.

In the physical and natural sciences, various applications of the theory of probability are used as an analytical tool to identify patterns of behavior or phenomena under investigation. Principles of this same theory are also used to measure properties of relevant phenomena.

In contrast, in the classical theories of the physical sciences (Newtonian) described by classical mathematical theories, such measurements are not fixed and absolute; rather they are relative and probabilistic, conditioned by phenomenal circumstances, as well as the observer's views, conditioned by uncertainty principles.

Another well-defined set of theories widely used to measure order in random patterns are Information and Communication theory, described in chapter 4, These theories base their foundation on principles of probability. However, the application of quantitative methods in the social sciences has always been questionable. Nevertheless, the theories of probability are widely used, particularly in the area of the behavioral sciences. The precautions over the use of such methods are mostly related to the idea that man's behavior is not solely material in nature and cannot be measured by quantitative methods. The following are two examples of such techniques developed on the basis of the principles of probability and Information theory to measure random and qualitative properties of environmental communication space—order of space.

9.4 Originality and Probability Methods[26]

For the measurement of order of space two techniques are proposed in this book, namely, Originality and Probability methods. The following are the general descriptions of the two models. For more detailed Planning application, please see the case example provided in Appendix I.

A table has been prepared with environmental "element-types" (j) located horizontally in columns and environmental "locations", (i) arranged vertically in rows. The number of each element-type j in a given location i is x_{ij} and is entered in its relevant place on the matrix(A_{mn}).

Elements (E) Boundaries of any element (object or event) can be defined as simple and bubble. Based on predefined criteria, simple elements can be defined as architectural elements (doors, windows, walls, ceilings), construction components (bricks, walls, columns, doors, windows), or finally, geometrical elements describing pure and nonassociative objects, let us say one inch by one inch of an elevation of a building (or *lxlxl* inch of the volume). An element (object or event) is something which occupies a location.

An elements bubble boundaries could be defined as a hierarchy of boundaries having originated around a predefined simple element (or element-unit in the case of geometrical elements); that is, the first order of a bubble boundary of repetitive mosaic cover of a floor is an imaginary boundary covering nine ceramics with the original ceramic in the center. The second order is a boundary covering twenty-five ceramics, also with the original ceramic in the center. Since objects, and especially events, overlap, bubble boundaries represent the potential (or most probable) size and intensity of an object or event (activity). The higher the probability of occurrence of a point within a bubble boundary of an activity, the smaller the relevant bubble. Overlaps of hundreds of hierarchies of bubbles, concentrated around each activity, in say a house, justify their final location and size.

Locations (*L*) Location, similar to elements, could be defined in two ways, "simple" and "bubble." Simple locations are the entries of a superimposed matrix on, say, an under elevation design of a building (or relevant entries in three-dimensional terms). Whatever sets of elements fall within one square area of a matrix overlayed on a given elevation, plan, section, etc. of a building is given that box's identification (*Aij*) as its location. This matrix is called location matrix. Locations must not be confused with elements, i.e., objects and events.

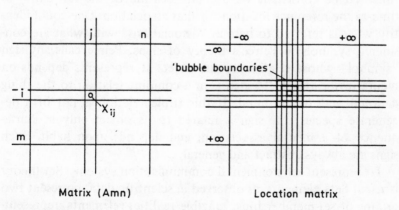

Matrix (Amn)   Location matrix

Figure 9–8
Matrices and Distribution Properties of Space

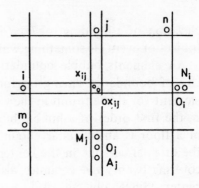

Bubble locations   Originality matrix

Figure 9–9
a) Location Matrix and b) Originality Matrix

Location "bubble boundaries" can be defined as hierarchies of boundaries having originated around a predefined simple location unit. Identical entries of location matrix are called relevant "location type."

Objects and events are identified in specific localities whereas associations only take place in man's mind. Thus to identify an object or event we refer to its "address" location in three-dimensional location matrices.

To identify association we use certain arbitrary localities, since in fact one element of an association is the starting point of a set of triadic relations which might happen to go back and forth in time. To be consistant we use the location of the last entity in time as the reference location for that association. One could identify what is referred to here as "associations" with what are considered symbols in Peirce's theory of signs. Peirce calls any sign "symbol" whose relation to the object it represents depends on mental associations. "A sign is in a conjoint relation to the thing denoted and to the mind. If this triple relation is not of a degenerate species, the sign is related to its object only in consequence of a mental association, and depends upon habit. Such signs are always abstract and general. . . . . ."[27]

To represent environmental communication systems, Set theory is used. Sets elements, as observed in scientific data, represent two groups of set-memberships: tangible realities (elements) represented in a finite set of finite sets having resulted from the combination of a set of finite sets.

The first group of sets shows elements, that which is observed in such physical realities as geographical characteristics, e.g., streets, houses, building parts, etc.

The second group of sets shows that which is observed in a set of sets of linkages among space-time entities within an assumed artificial boundary called bubble boundary, a boundary which is defined based on the certain probability of occurences (magnitude, intensity, and kind) of certain activities of a system.

Atkin, in his mathematical *Structure in Human Affairs*, has given a thorough analysis of such set relations when he discusses the structure of an institution, such as a university, via a mathematical relationship of its set of members and its subset, committees.

He uses *q-analysis* as a method of analyzing the university decision-process structure through the organization of its finite set of administrative committees, councils, and members' activities. This he sees to be true due to the fact that there is a correlation between a set of individuals serving in various committees and a set of university activities and its individuals. He says, "Every organization, institution, business, political party, or what-have-you, demonstrates the occurrence of relations between finite sets."[28] Although the apparent finite sets of tangible events (individuals and spaces and masses) are easy to define, the infinite set of intangible activities are not. These activity systems could be defined within hierarchies of bubble boundaries based on certain criteria. Examples of such criteria are the intensity of interaction of its members in a given location, greater or fewer number of members' participation in an activity, the nature of interaction among members within a given boundary, etc.

Bubble boundaries are used to define the domains of activities of object and tangible entities in a similar way. Built environment and its objects are also considered unstatic entities occurring in space-time patterns relative to man's desire. Thus they occur in certain patterns relative to man's conception, activities, and value system. Just as you can find various individuals in various space-time localities based on the structure of human affairs (sociocultural), you can also find objects in similar structural frameworks relative to human activities; e.g., in a library a specific book can be found within a specific probabilistic bubble boundary defined in the organization of the library shelving system. Or in architectural design, certain objects, motifs, or elements can be found in the structure of design perceptions; i.e., in any design if there is an organization and structure tying together all the subcomponents, there should be a way to predict the locality of certain elements at certain locations. In final words, relative to diversity within unity and legibility within resistability of random patterns of dynamic forms and functions of an environments.

The use of Set theory here suggests that environmental properties should not necessarily be measurable in the traditional sense of the word, but rather in that sense which is identifiable in set-membership.

Any set of objects or events demonstrates the occurrence of relations between a set of finite sets. To build a theory or mathematical model is first to identify specific sets among other sets or elements, or among a hierarchy of elements, sets of elements, set of sets of elements, etc., then find a mathematical relation among selected sets and unidentified sets of sets. "It is in the study of such relations that we shall find a great deal of basic structure" or "multidimensional structure."[29]

No doubt finite sets representing finite real elements are readily conceived because they deal with boundaries within reach of the intellect. But the boundaries of intuition can be analyzed by means of the structural analysis of combinations of sets.

"Cantor originally defined a set S as any collection of definite, indistinguishable objects of our intuition or of our intellect to be conceived as a whole."[30]

Originality analysis or *q-analysis* can not only be used for understanding the underlying structures of intangible activities and human value systems (event-associations). It is also helpful in the recreation or reorganization of their existing structures. When you undo an unknown complex structure, the very fact of understanding its mechanism better equips you to recreate its model structure. Planning and design endeavors are nothing but reorganization of systems of sets of objects, events, and associations. In his design approach, Christopher Alexander has used methods based on the same principles, reflected in *Notes on the Synthesis of Form and in Community and Privacy*.

"Originality." The originality (*Oij*) of an element-type *j* in a given location-type *i* is based on the frequency of occurrence of that element-type in the relevant column, relative to the frequency of occurrences of other element-types in that location-type, and is calculated by multiplying (*xij*) to the total number of element-types *j in location i—(Ni)* and divided by the total number of element-types *j* in the total system (*Mj*).

More complex definitions of originality can be defined and calculated; e.g., "sequential originality" which is a hierarchical originality of proximity or bubble originality.

If we rotate the location matrix (say by 45°), the originalities of each element in any new entry of the rotated matrix could be conceived of and calculated in similar fashion. A matrix with each of its entries covering a set of originalities (vertical, horizontal, and any number of desired rotations) calculated in this way is called an originality matrix.

$$o_{ij} = o_{X_{ij}} = \frac{N_i}{M_j} \, X_{ij}$$

"Probability." in matrix (*Amn*), for any given entry, two types of probability can be defined:

1. In a given environmental system, the probability of occurrence of element-type *j* in location i, conditioned by the total number of all element-types present in location *i*, is calculated by the division of the number of element-types *j* in location *i* by the total number of all element-types present in location *i*.

2. In a given environmental system, the probability of occurrence of element-type *j* in location *i*, conditioned by the total number of element-types *j*, is calculated by the division of the number of element-types *j* in location *i* by the total number of all element-types *j* in the system

$$(1) \; p_i = p_{X_{ij}} = \frac{X_{ij}}{N_i} \qquad\qquad (2) \; p_j = p_{X_{ij}} = \frac{X_{ij}}{M_j}$$

or based on Information theory formulas.[31]

$$P_{(i)} = - \sum_{j=1}^{n} P(i) \log P(i)$$

$$P_{(i,j)} = - \sum_{j=1}^{n} \sum_{i=1}^{m} P(i,j) \log P(i,j)$$

Like originality, if we rotate the location matrix, the probabilities of each element in any new entry of the rotated matrix is calculated in a similar way. A matrix each of its entries covering a set of probabilities is called probability matrix.

Originality and probability indices are designed to measure the uniqueness of a given element-type[32] in a given location (simple location, bubble boundary location), location type, or total system (the environment under consideration). Originality and probability indices are designed to measure the "unique value" of a given kind of element-type within a location, location type, or total system in relation to the full range of element-types available in an architectural environment. Their value therefore depends on the complexity of the system (the higher the number of element-types the more complex the system) and frequency of use of that element (the greater the frequency the more industrially oriented and less unique that element). In other words, indices assign more value to an element-type located in a location-type with many other varieties of element–types, than to an element-type repeating itself in isolation. The concept of originality or uniqueness is a measure of the exceptional qualities of a component of a system relative to the total system.

9.5 Design Rationale–Axioms

To outline a theoretical framework for environmental communication design, we need to simplify design objectives and criteria into a much smaller number of relatively known facts and principles. In other words, we should come up with design axioms. These axioms should be complex, universal, and incompatible. They should contain the totality of life forms or total environmental fields. To formulate such axioms, we shall define the total environmental field as systems of objects and events and their interrelationships. The following is an elementary sketch of axioms in environmental communication. Let us postulate that this set of axioms covers all environmental interactions, or any patterning and repatterning in the environment which can be explained.

A. Similarities and differences in structural patterns of matter in space-time provide us with identified *"objects."* Transformation of matter constantly gives us a different set of objects. Objects are not isolated artifacts; they are the interrelated configurations of patterning of matter.

B. The above dispositional properties, as well as transformation, provide us with another set of entities called *"events."* An event is a state of change in matter and/or environmental setting, either in location, time, or form (structure).

C. Such entities and their associations provide us with sets of messages: probabilistic, ordered-disordered patterns carrying information and thus communication. There are three sets of message systems—environmental, behavioral, and symbolic cues.

D. Man receives such communication messages in two manners—conscious or subconscious, objective or subjective, rational or nonrational.

E. The pattern of subconscious behavior, similar to the behavior of matter, is probabilistic and random, measured by the laws of entropy and the pattern of conscious behavior by centropy.

F. Man needs to maintain a sociobiological equilibrium between himself, the environment, and components of the environment. Such equilibrium is reached through interaction with surrounding environmental components by reordering or restructuring patterns of the environment.

Global equilibrium of the total system is achieved through integration and superimposition of a great number of many partial equilibriums produced by its sub systems; i.e., through structure of structures or order of orders.

The complexities of such overall environmental equilibriums are so great that they cannot be explained in a work of this magnitude. Actually, human knowledge in various disciplines tries to deal with the scope of such an endeavor. In this type of approach the ideal is to sketch the general overall picture of interactions among these varieties of interrelationships.

We are going to outline a few notions of such equilibrium in visual terms. Regarding the provision of axioms, suppose that the following assumptions are based on rationals earlier discussed.[33]

Law of balance—It is assumed that human visual function necessitates the presence of certain balance with regard to the occurrence of visual entities in any given visual field. That is to say, because of the psychological symmetrical nature of the human body, as well as man's frame of reference, he constantly tries to balance his field of vision and thus needs to perceive a balanced composition in environmental compositions.

Law of rhythm—It is assumed that in any field of environmental communication, provision of the repetition of elements creates continuity and flow of spatial continuum, as well as human activity patterns, and thus its presence is essential. In other words, each point in a visual field at any time is necessarily part of a rhythmic sequence of space and time in order to be in accord with the overall space-time natural rhythmic pattern.

Law of climax—It is assumed that in any field of environmental communication the presence of climax is essential in order to correspond to the cyclical pattern of life forms. Climax is produced by repetition of certain patterns in a rhythmic manner, building into it a new and accumulated pattern, thus changing the order from a simpler to more complex pattern system. Moreover, the sociobiological nature of man provides him with needs and desires; reaching for such needs necessitates interaction with the environment. Such interaction does not have a constant pattern. Rather it carries on some of the variation created by the factors and sociobiological climatic orders of cosmic behavior referred to above; as well as new added diversity which is reached through the combination of interaction overlays of other individuals interacting with and in the same environment.

Law of good proportion—It is assumed that in any field of environmental communication, provision of "good proportion" is essential. That is to say the properties of any environmental field are not and should not be considered accidental, rather they are based on certain functional and aesthetic necessities. Thus the originality of elements should be in responce to the provision of good proportion. In other words, each point in a visual field at any time is part of a hierarchical set of cosmic objects and functions. Thus it is necessarily read as part of a system of proportions. This law emphasizes the aesthetic quality reached through the use of integrated interrelations of elements and their harmonic proportions to each other and their function.

Law of functional expression—It is assumed that in any field of environmental communication, all functional properties and aesthetic qualities must be coordinated and correlated. That is to say, originality or probability matrices prepared for certain given architectural fields for various functional organization, as well as aesthetic expressions, should coincide and correlate.

Thus the world seen to us today via Einstein's concept solely of energy patterns supercedes the biofragmentation of the material and nonmaterial world. In such a world the underlying forces involved in functional justification of various forms are no different from the making of the physical appearance of an object. There is no difference between the internal and external forces at work in shaping a rock, plant, animal, or human being. In visual terms any single appearance of any form best serves its purpose or function.

Law of harmony—It is assumed that in any field of environmental communication, unity within diversity is provided through the harmonic order of all the above mentioned principles. That is to say, an originality or probability matrix prepared for all various factors should be harmonic in order. Thus it becomes obvious that although rhythm and climax are described as opposite functions, they are also the same and even reinforce opposite characteristics. In other words, climax, which presents a unique and original situation in a given field, gains its intensity through application of rhythmic order.

Man sees various phenomenal patterns in very complex overlays of balance, rhythm, climax, functional expression, proportion, and harmony. The nature of such a conception is derived from diversity within unity.

9.6 Environmental Communication Models—Concepts

In sections 9.1 and 9.2 we stated that the major dilemma in environmental planning and design is that the characteristics of its four constituent components—conscious, subconscious, organic, and inorganic—are different and even opposite. While the conscious and rational regulates and directs, the subconscious and non-rational, and even madness, enriches, man's total environmental experience. So in formulating any conceptual framework of design policy, this very point—the opposite nature of the characteristics of human experience—should be the first to be taken into consideration. In this regard, McHarg has also discussed the concept of evolution and cosmic order. In his words, "The conception of creation as movement from lower to higher order has its antithesis in destruction, the reduction from higher to lower levels. Evolution is then seen as a creative process, regression as reductive."[34] Or as he expresses in the following quote, "The cosmography has now linked creation with the increase in order in a system, and demonstrated that this is the path of evolution, that the antithesis is destruction, the path of retrogression consisting in the reduction of order from higher to lower levels. Both creation and destruction are seen to have descriptive, distinctive attributes."[35]

To deal with environmental communication field in the form of analysis, presentation, or planning and design, one can expect many different ways of joining the above four sets of parameters. On the basic of the purpose of analysis, presentation, or design, many different routes and combinations of techniques and methods can be used.

In building a model, the application of our six major axioms, i.e., rhythm, climax, balance, proportion, fundamental expression, and harmony, confronts us again with the problem of contradiction between various axioms. That is to say, rhythm and climax, two characteristics of aesthetic order, run in opposite directions. The first satisfies the desires of rational, logical, and technologically-oriented man, and the second satisfies the desires of individualistic, subjective man. Would this mean to satisfy these two opposite axioms, should we do opposite and controversial things,

or would it mean that the two are built-in complementary mechanisms of nature formulating the principle of diversity within
unity and counterbalancing one another, as well as the above cosmic order? With an affirmative answer to the last question, this is
how we anticipate the six axioms to relate to environmental order.
As presented in Fig. 9–10, the two sets of statements regarding
rhythm and climax show opposite directions in the process of
creating order. While rhythmic process assumes presence of repetition of certain elements and events and seeks a higher degree of
such presence, the climatic process assumes presence of random
pattern highlighted by an originality and uniqueness of elements
and events and seeks a higher degree of such foregrounds in the
midst of relevant backgrounds.

Historically, criteria for formal aesthetic judgement have been
balance, rhythm, proportion, symmetry, etc. With the exception
of symmetry, these criteria are used for organic judgement, although with a difference.

I personally reject any relation between the formal symmetry of
human physical appearances and sociopsychological structure and
perception.

Our aesthetic perception goes beyond only the physical properties of objects and their appearances. They are also rooted in
meanings having resulted from the nonphysical world of value
systems. The dynamics involved in the domain of aesthetic perception deal with a complex interaction of sociophysical, as well
as associative properties.

If there is one thing this author advocates it is that beauty is
manifested in opposite life forces, in contrast, in randomness, in
originality, and in variety, as well as in similarities, in repetitions,
and in rhythmic order. These characteristics run in opposite directions from those criteria for formal aesthetic patterns to the extent
that they even disturb them in order to make an aesthetic pattern.
Deviation from expectation is a major part of life and thus aesthetic performance. How could it be ignored in formal performance
aesthetics? Diversity and unity are the two key concepts in
aesthetic function. For some aestheticians formalism is a means of
unity, but unfortunately at the cost of variety.

To present this law of opposites with the concept of General
Systems theory, it can be said that while maximization of original-

ity and climax result in an increase of random patterns, and consequently increase in entropy, they influence the rhythmic function in producing reverse and opposite functions which decrease entropy. In other words, by production of opposite functions, an increase in rhythmic patterns controls the tendency toward destruction created by high entropy having resulted from increase in originality.

Before I discuss these six axioms I must state that the use of these concepts in this context differs from their historical usage. Although the historical notion in each case has been accepted, their application is different. The difference lies in the historical use of these concepts in a "formal" manner whereas I use them in an "organic" way, formal being rational-regular and organic being nonrational-irregular aesthetics. Whereas classical architecture is aesthetically formal, Gandi's work and some of LeCorbusier's works, such as Ronchamp, have organic qualities.

The first axiom is concerned with set relationships in part logically balanced by rational judgement where elements appear where they are expected in balance and symmetry, whereas the second axiom totally starts with a different premise; i.e., irregular forms do not leave any room for the logical mind to use them as a reference point of expectation and thus judgement.

The principle of differences signifies the existence of information. Similarities, rhythm, and regularities not only establish a positive coding system toward their own recognition, but also denote a negative coding system underlying the irregularities. The regularities become a ground, letting the irregularities stand out, be modified, and specified by the regular or rhythmic occurrence of repeated patterns. Each irregular code uses one or more regular relationships (repeated, rhythmic patterns) as its frame of reference to present itself to our perception.

Two sets of features or properties of an environmental communication system which simultaneously reinforce one another, or become the source of the creation of one another, are the variant or law of opposites, similarities and differences, regularities and irregularities, feminity and masculinity, etc. It is in the intersection of these pairs of features where any information or communication, including environmental communication, is born. (Fig. 9–10)

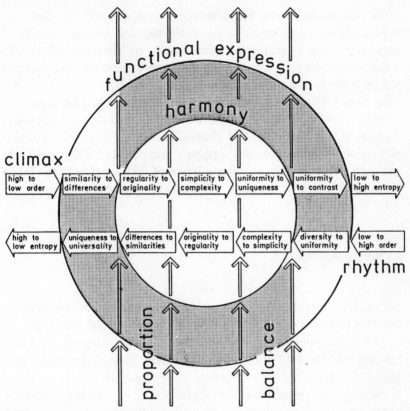

Figure 9–10
An Environmental Design Model

Rhythm. The law of rhythm necessitates direction from lower to higher order, differences to similarity, complexity to simplicity, diversity to uniformity, uniqueness to universality, originality to regularity, and finally, high to low entropy.

Climax. The law of climax necessitates direction from a low to high number of element-types, similarities to differences, simplicity to complexity, uniformity to diversity, regularity to originality, universality to uniqueness, and finally, low to high entropy.

Balance and Proportion. As well as being part of the above two sets of order (rhythm and climax), these four principles seem to be controlling factors on these sets as well; the principle of proportions and balance have both control among the components of built environment and between these components and their natural setting. Too much or to little rhythm in any part of a harmonic environment creates imbalance. By the same token, too much or too little diversity, originality, and climax is also controlled by balance and proportion.

Functional Expression and Harmony. These principles check all sets of parameters against one another, especially the opposing factors of, e.g., rhythm and climax. Harmony searches for diversity within unity through ordered complexity. Functional expression controls the interdependence of different layers of interaction between subfunctions and layers of various systems.

9.7 Sample model-Sketch

To sketch roughly the proposed environmental communication theories and techniques into a model, we may do the following:

a. Let us assume that a site is defined; then its three-dimensional boundaries could fit into sets of different three-dimensional matrices. Suppose we could define an exhaustive set of possible element-types considered for application, for example, use of break on facade elevation (N), as well as a module or location unit (U) (application of the dimension of break or other common units). Subsequently, we also form other matrices described in the theory, i.e., probability and originality matrices.

b. Let us assume that the mind could see rational and *a priori* relationships in simple linear order. That is to say, rational mind works when conscious attention is focused on certain things and infinite field is broken down into easily "thinkable" units.[36] This could be accomplished in two steps, first by breaking the totality of intuitive forms into subcomponents and into simple forms and relationships and, second, by screening out some of the peripheral details of the whole to make it fit into simple comprehensible shapes and relationships, or "thinkable" units. In other words, the mind can only contemplate one thing at a time. If we consider language as a representation of the structure of the mind, it reflects the structure of the mind, conscious and subconscious. The mouth, as a physiological instrument, is not capable of dealing with infinite dimensions of mental activities. Although gestures and other means of behavioral cues such as gesturing with the face, hands, and body are used to add to the limited activities of the tongue as an attempt to deal with the complexity of linguistic expressions, physically they act linearly and produce a series of signs in sound sequence and one at a time. That is to say, the conscious pattern of thought processes is sorted out by being focused out from an infinite pattern of awareness. The infinite elements of an environmental field must be divided into relatively simple, defined elements and relationships in order to enable them to be focused upon.

This could be done in two steps: first, by breaking the totality on intuitive forms into subcomponents and into simple form and relationships; and second, by screening out some of the peripheral details of the whole to make them fit into simple comprehensible shapes and relationships.

The simplified elements focused on in an environmental field or field of awareness are manifested to us in environmental cues, behavioral cues and symbolic cues.

c. Let us assume that to succeed in coping with the above mentioned problems and assumptions is to be able simultaneously to see each element of a form against all others. Considering the functioning of the mind, i.e., to see single patterns in a linear manner or to transform the language of the mind into computer language, we can do the following: assume a matrix overlay on a visual field, pictorial scene, or considered site.

   i. Let all the points (entries) of each element-type (column of the matrix) be seen and compared together.

  ii. Let all the points (entries) of each location-type be seen and compared together.

 iii. Let rotation of the matrix to new situations, as many times as necessary (up to 360°), cover all the elements of the matrix to enable each entry to be seen against all other elements through a vertical, horizontal, and diagonal vector and in a linear manner.

 iv. Let each element of the form xij (each entry of the matrix) be seen and compared to all the other elements of the form, as a common element of vertical elements (relevant column), a set of horizontal elements (relevant row) which runs through that element and a set of diagonal elements (relevant diagonal entries). Let there be a possibility that all the other columns and rows could replace this row and column by a shifting process of all the rows and columns.

On each cross section one could adapt some kind of sequential aesthetic order, i.e., rhythm, balance, harmony, etc. This sequential order based on combinatory permutations, linked to aesthetic predication would then be checked against and correlated with all other cross-sections for attainment of "optimum order" throughout each subsystem and total system. Implication of hierarchical structure throughout the system simplifies the process by identifying a higher order of originality to higher classes of elements and vice versa.

v. Let the objectives set forth for the design of coordinate systems be based on relative and moving coordinate systems where the origins of x, y and z are not fixed but, as in music, originate where everyone sets them up. That is where the eye chooses to focus or a relevant object in mind is located. The measurement originates from this point in all directions. Value scale moves along with the reference point. There is no fixed value for any point. Whatever point your eye chooses as a reference point sets the reference for other points.

vi. Let us assume that the sole purpose of any coordinate system is not to plot, locate, or describe individual entities, but rather to show the interrelationships of sets of simple relationships at one time and simultaneously. Considering the second characteristic, let the proposed coordinate system target the relationships where the binary digital system of discrimination, stored in either the mind or the computer as its extension, sets and compares complex forms in a combination of certain sets of simple linear relationships in which every single element in any form is seen in relation to all the other elements of that form.

vii. Assume that the proposed coordinate system does not follow the traditional Newtonian universal coordinate system with absolute homogeneity of distribution of its entries, but rather is conditioned by the above relative coordinate system with a variable density of properties. That is to say, properties are more "concentrated" in centers of concentrations where attention is focused and vice versa. Let us also consider the entries of the new coordinate system to be bubbled from certain origins. In such a system an object is not identified by certain preconceptual associations, but by its structural properties in space-time where hierarchies of bubble concentration within its boundaries are highly intensive. Let the same principle be true of events. Activities are known by their order and space-time structural properties, where concentration of such properties on lower orders of bubble hierarchies is increasing. Thus an object's or event's boundaries do not end at their traditional boundaries, but rather decrease in intensity.

d. Granted that the described matrices would be formed and based on proposed coordinate systems, the design objective is to reach the best combination of entries on a three-dimensional coordinate system of a given matrix—to shift all three sets of entries to all other locations, vertically, horizontally, and diagonally, as much as needed to find some optimum combination. Such an optimum combination, or order, could be found through the fulfillment of certain axioms by using various techniques, such as originality or probability.

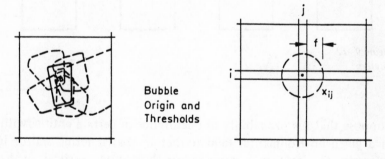

Bubble
Origin and
Thresholds

Figure 9–11

Bubble Boundaries: the Thresholds of Activities

e. To seek what could be optimum combinations or "harmonic order," let us start with a very easy problem—a simple function, i.e., a visual field—and use originality or probability techniques and the previously defined six visual axioms. Optimum combination could be found by the provision of certain optimum functions through certain programs; e.g., linear programming, transportation models, etc., for maximization of originality (columns, rows, and total system) or probability, etc., for a given function(s) such as rhythm and climax, while considering other axiomatic functions as constraints.

For the present let us use the principle of harmony as an overall objective factor and prepare programs toward the maximization of climax factors (i.e., maximization of originality or probability), on the one hand, and rhythm of composition, on the other. Programs for this maximization will be prepared based on two sets of constraints; that is, one set will be geared to the principle of balance and the other to proportion. Functional expression would be used as a coordination check list for running a number of various functional matrices to check for correlation among overlays of various factors and systems. The following are two simple examples of rhythm and climax.

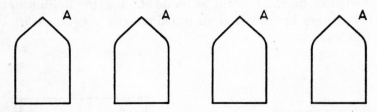

Figure 9–12
Rhythm

Suppose that the probability of occurrence of certain entities within a given environmental field (either in spatial terms and/or in reference to time) on a given vector (horizontal, vertical, or diagonal) repeats itself. At this moment we say that occurrence is rhythmic. Windows in regular arrangement on a facade, or regular column arrangement in a given plan, are rhythmic patterns. Any rhythmic pattern constitutes an order containing the following characteristics. First, interval (spatial or temporal) is the time or space distance between two similar elements of a repetitive set of entities of a given field. In the above figure the sets of points representing each arch are repetitive sets and the distance between individual elements of all sets (point A) is the rhythmic interval. Second, the repetitive properties of rhythmic order include the set of elements which repeat themselves (set of points which makes each arch). Third, a rhythm could be a combination of several overlays or combinations of different information produced by various communication sources. Fourth, a resonance is coincidence of the repetitive element or two or more of these overlays of rhythmic order. Fifth, in the case of overlays of several rhythmic orders, when the resonance does not happen, either regularly or randomly but with an increasing intensity and highlight, the highest intensity and highlight reached is called climax.

Climax

Climax is a built up uniqueness or originality of a state within a field. Characteristics of a climatic state in a given field are the following: First, climatic states are not separated from their field. Although they might be a figure relative to ground (total field), they are inseparable entities integrated in a total field. Second, it is only through a ground or ordered reference framework, often rhythmic in nature, that the climatic state is intensified. Let us say that in music, while a climax is a unique state you are taken to, your steps to such a state are the result of pushing and pulling resulting from a combination of various rhythmic order. Third, a climax, by nature, follows a cut or void. That is to say, the empty state following or around the highest climax, together with the peak of that climax, makes the highest contrast in the similarity and differences observed in a given pattern. Fourth, climatic orders are neither regular repetitive nor chaotic patterns, but rather hierarchical or ordered random patterns. Thus, in either case, familiarity with the lower sets of climatic orders sets the expectation of higher and higher climaxes, and finally, a drop or change of such expectation. Fifth, while repetition and rhythm were said to be a step toward climax, diversity and complexity are also necessary for higher originality and, thus, richer climax. Finally, irregularity built into regularity gives climax. Sixth, the highest contrast between two sets creates discontinuity and cuts—black next to white. Regular increase or decrease of contrast creates direction. This rhythmic order could lead and integrate sets of random entities toward regular hierarchical climaxes, and finally, create sets of climaxes or a climax system.

Note to chapter Nine

1. Karl Popper, *Logic of Scientific Discovery,* Hutchinson, London, 1963.
2. P. Parsons, R. Bales and E. Shils, "The Dimensions of Action-Space," in *Working Papers in the Theory of Action.*
3. D. Mortensen, *Communication: The Study of Human Interaction.*
4. Alan W. Watts, *Nature, Man and Woman,* Vintage Books: Random House, New York 1958.
5. L. Whyte, "His Creative Activities" in *Accent on Form,* p. 17.
6. A.T. Minai, "Cultural Change: Man's Concept of Nature and Total Environmental Communication," paper for *World Congress on Black Communication,* Nairobi, July 26-31, 1981.
7. Saussure, quoted by M. Singer "For a Semiotic Anthropology" in *Sight, Sound, and Sense,* p. 216.
8. Charles Sancers Peirce, quoted by M. Singer "For a Semiotic Anthropology", p. 216.
9. *Ibid.,* p. 217.
10. C. Peirce, quoted by Max H. Fisch, "Peirce's General Theory of Signs" in *Sight, Sound, and Sense,* p. 44.
11. *Ibid.,* p. 51.
12. A. Rey, "Communication vs. Semiosis: Two Conceptions of Semiotics, in *Sight, Sound, and Sense,* p. 102.
13. M. Fisch, "Peirce's General Theory of Signs," in *Sight, Sound, and Sense,* p. 42.
14. Umberto Eco, "Semiotics: A Discipline or an Interdisciplinary Method?" in *Sight, Sound, and Sense,* p. 74.
15. C. Peirce, quoted by M. Fisch, "Peirce's General Theory of Signs" in *Sight, Sound, and Sense,* p. 47.
16. K. Lewin, *Field theory.*
17. Donald Preziosi, *The Semiotics of Built Environment,* Indiana Univ. Press, Bloomington & London, 1979.
18. A.T. Minai, "Communication Field Theory A Conceptual Architectural Model."
19. D. Preziosi, *The Semiotics of Built Environment,* p. 1.
20. Ibid.

21. Lionel March and Philip Steadman, *Geometry of Environment*, M.I.T. Press, 1974, p. 9.
22. *Ibid.*, p. 23.
23. *Ibid.*, p. 89.
24. *Ibid.*, p. 12.
25. *Ibid.*, p. 13.
26. A.T. Minai, "Measuring Human Activity Systems in Esfahan: Originality and Centrality," *Ekistifcs*, vol. 240, Nov. 1975, pp. 323-327.
27. C. Peirce quoted by M. Singer in "For a Semiotic Anthropology" in *Sight, Sound, and Sense*, p. 216.
28. R.H. Atkin, *Mathematical Structure in Human Affairs*, Crane, Russak & Co., Inc., New York, 1974, p. 17.
29. *Ibid.* p. 14.
30. *Ibid.*, p. 8.
31. A. Moles, *Information Theory and Esthetic Perception*, pp. 21-23.
32. A.T. Minai, "Planning Human Activity Systems in Esfahan Region: Originality and Probability Model," presented at *ACPA Annual Conference*, Washington, D.C., October 24-25, 1981.
33. A. Watts, "The Infinite and the Finite," a chapter in his book *The Supreme Identity*, Vintage Books: Random House, New York 1972.
34. Ian McHarg, *Design with Nature*, Doubleday and Co., Inc. Garden City, New York, pp. 119-123.
35. *Ibid.*
36. K.G. Denbigh, An Inventive Universe, George Braziller, New York, 1975.

10. Communication Approach in Environmental Design Education

10.0 Introduction—Abstract

This chapter deals with environmental design education within the theoretical framework developed throughout this book. At the turn of the century an historical change in man's view of nature and universal laws took place which now requires a new educational orientation and attitude. This change was universally experienced throughout most of the disciplines. Physics witnessed a breakdown of the mechanical view of classical physics. In biology the *ad hoc* dualism of life principles was replaced by the law of integrated wholes. In the social sciences new philosophies regarding society as a total unit rather than a composite of collective individuals were formulated. Finally, in the arts, Cubism, Futurism, and Constructivism viewed the universality, multidimensionality, and objectivity of the art form.

It is argued that these changes were not fully reflected in architectural attitudes and education. In comparing medical education with architectural education it is pointed out that although both are professional disciplines, medicine has branched into professional practice, as well as research-oriented scholastic activities, whereas architecture has failed in this latter respect. The author suggests that a communications approach to architectural education be adopted. In using this method architecture could benefit from, 1. a commonality of theories and methods throughout various disciplines, 2. unification of the physical and nonphysical, qualitative, and quantitative aspects of the environment, and 3. the advantages of technological advances and information systems.

After this theoretical sketch, five types of graduates (research oriented, generalists, professionals, specialists, technicians) and four types of architectural Schools (comprehensive, professional, specialized, local) and their proposed orientation are defined. Finally, in Appendix II, Farabi University is referenced as a model for the new architectural education.

10.1 New Horizons in Architecture

The architecture of tomorrow will become more and more remote from simply constituting artifacts shaped by craftsmen based upon their subjective views. Directly and indirectly, its many dimensions will be determined by various disciplines and will involve the sociocultural, psychological, physical, biological, and economic factors formulated by other sciences. It will be greatly altered by the four major universal component characteristics—organic, inorganic, conscious, and subconscious. Sociocultural, psychological, economic, and political factors affect the formation of nonmaterial messages that are consciously and subconsciously communicated, while the natural and physical sciences determine the nature of its materiality, and finally, the pure sciences, technology, and cybernetics formulate the role of rationality in determining the properties of such formations, and the face of the built environment.

So it is the contribution of all four areas of human experience and knowledge which can help formulate a theoretical structure useful in molding the total human environment. Although each discipline might emphasize a special angle from which the total environment is viewed, all would nevertheless search for the common goal of a better understanding of complex structures of the interrelationships of environmental components. The various disciplines offer techniques and methods, each colored relative to the view of a particular discipline, revealing aspects of the complex configuration. At the same time, the pure sciences and technology, operating research, cybernetics, Information and Communication theory offer techniques which may be common to all disciplines.

Let us look at environmental experience and its meaning via communication and information concepts, and within field concepts. The world as known to us today is a complex dynamic field of interactions in which each particle, each element, is totally integrated into the whole. Any change in its state of being is conditioned by the state of all the other parts of the system. Thus it can be said that each particle carries as much information as the whole.[1]

In taking this view, architectural space is not to be thought of as geographical boundaries of a sum total of its particles, but rather the materialization of total human activity patterns, including physical, natural, and sociocultural flows of energy-events.

All purposeful actions are based on the possession and use of information, and architecture is no exception. Every human act is considered a drama which is played within a spatial context. The two (the act and the space) must be harmonized with each other, and it is the architect who should have an understanding for the drama and mastery of creating a harmonic spatial environment to fit a drama.

The creation and arrangement of sociocultural space by means of architectural order is a basic mode of cultural expression manifested in symbolic forms—either objects or events, an important part of human adaptation to the natural and social environment, signified in behavioral and psychological forms. Altogether it constitutes what could be called architectural communication fields of interactions. With such an orientation architecture could be defined as a dynamic flow of all material and nonmaterial matter-energy event patterns. Architecture is an "action space"[2] in which each point-particle (energy-matter) has certain unique properties conditioned by the structuring properties of all the points of the total field. The "action space"[3] created is activated by "hidden-dimensions"[4] having resulted from cultural attributes, as well as the sociopsychological and economic values of its users.

So the study, teaching, and practice of architecture should be based on an understanding of universal laws common to all disciplines involved in environmental planning and design where the synthesis of intellect and feeling, quality and quantity, material and nonmaterial, and finally, conscious and subconscious factors is guaranteed. Architecture is a harmonic symphony emerging from the rational and nonrational, having blended them into a meaningful order.

Within such a communication system, information is transmitted via *ordered-disordered pattern systems messages*. Against the laws of *entropy* and *centropy*, ordered-disordered patterns are measured as *information* or noise, meaningful or meaningless, and the messages are shaped through behavioral, environmental, and symbolic cues.[5]

The messages an architect creates and conveys are a continuous, simultaneous part of the total environmental communication system and are originated and received with a certain coding system common to both the creator and the user.

Thus information received by users of a built environment, unlike that of the intentions of its creators, is the outgrowth of first-hand experience conditioned by the dynamics of its environmental message system, as well as the receivers' field of immediate preconditioning. Hence perfect transformation from intentions to received messages is impossible and thus irrelevant. An educational system given to the imposition of a conventional fixed and rigid message system (style) is also irrelevant. Such an attitude in education should be replaced by the concept of simultaneity of field interaction and messages. The education of tomorrow's architects should be based upon this simultaneity, probabilistic, and random behavior or field environment.

The architect of tomorrow must develop sensitivity and alertness in order to be able continuously to interpret the rapidly-changing environmental information system, and to have the ability to create new messages, not based on conventions of the past, but relative to its spatiotemporal field circumstances. The problem of change, movement away from what we are used to, conditioned by that which we do not know and are unable to see, is that for which we are constantly searching. We seek new methods and means of incorporating our traditional ways, i.e., conceptual attitudes. Being so conditioned by our past, our search for the new is, in fact, a misconception. To deal with the problems of today and tomorrow we must not use today's technology and scientific means of solving the problems of yesterday; we must start with a basic search, not redefining but rather formulating new problems. We do not need to waste our energy and resources in delving into past deeds. In scientific terms, we must utilize such energy in dealing with our thought processes on a higher level and providing them with the capability to fuse with subconscious behavior or feeling and emotion.

The environmental communication system, which includes each individual (creator, builder, user), is part of a continuous process of bewildering communication patterns which can characterize future architecture. The language or message system used in such architecture is neither individual imaginary creation alone, nor mere rational, academic, or professional convictions produced by historical machinery or dictated by the material sciences. It is a new language fused from both the views of the arts and sciences and thinking and feeling. The architect of tomorrow, familiar with both languages, must be armed with new attitudes and logic capable of encompassing all the factors formulated by the human sciences, as well as all the potentials inherent in the vast capabilities of technological developments and the electronic and cybernetic revolution. He must stand for his own individual contributions and messages which are unique, not because his are necessarily better or superior to others, but rather because the information they carry has resulted from unique space-time environmental field communication.

The superiority of such an experience is not measured in isolation but, like field properties, is measured against the structure of total field properties incorporating the input of total field entries; i.e., all behavioral and environmental inputs, as well as their associations.

The architecture of tomorrow should reach for values and messages having arisen from interaction among processes involved in academic education, the professional realm, and many social activities where the continuous feedback process allows for crossfertilization and correction, thus maintenance with reality.

10.2 New Rationales in Architectural Educational Approach

In a previous chapters we defined architecture as environmental communication. We have also said that an environmental communication field consists of a combination of sets of components: objects, events, and associations. In utilizing a communication approach in education we must deal with its organization and subsystems; i.e., we should teach environmental components, as well as the ways they come together. Relative to the nature of the above three sets of components communicated to us via a system of three sets of cues – environmental, behavioral, and symbolic –

three types of mental transactions, as well as interaction between instructors and students, are expected and essential.

Furthermore, with this orientation, we would also be dealing with three types of education which necessarily operate on three levels of abstraction relative to those characteristics.

The first type of transaction involves physical realities or objects; hence perception of shape, form, and physical context are the main part of the educational process. The second type of transaction deals with activities and events. Events are a manifestation of some change of state in the environmental system where an understanding of human behavior and other life form is the main target of the educational process. The third type of transaction deals with associations—all possible mental conception products of a combination of all the above mentioned transactions, or one's description of such forms, both in space and time where abstract thinking and developments are the targets of the educational process.

Based on the nature of their speciality and in relation to the functioning of the mind, various disciplines have emphasized either one or a combination of these transactions. Physical and natural scientists, involved with physical objects, are mentally conditioned by certain behavioral functions and behavioral patterns. Finally, mathematicians deal with concepts and the intangible properties of thought processes. Each group's perception is conditioned by its own views and experiences.

Based on the nature of the three types of environmental communication components just discussed and the relevant mental transactions sketched out above, there are three realms and domains of intellectual intercourse, experience, and knowledge:

i. The realm of concrete and physical realities. This realm of man's intellectual activity constitutes the common body of both the sciences and the arts. The specialist deals with defined problems and answers. Unlike the third realm (the realm of abstraction), few fundamental questions are raised in this realm. The attitude is, "I do not need to confer with vague spirits, or mistake my own voice for that of Nature. I can ask Nature definite questions and get definite answers. Any questions that are indefinitely formulated or do not give definite answers are not valid or interesting. I make formulations from these answers and project my conclusions into the unknown, where I can discover hidden facts of Nature."[6] For this group, specialization is the basis of classification, problem identification, and thus problem solving. Moreover, fragmentation of the totality of human activities, experience, and knowledge is shifted into area disciplines.

ii. The realm of rationalization of behavior, reason, and logic. This realm of man's intellectual activity constitutes that portion of world experience and knowledge which he uses in establishing predefined man-made norms, regulations, policies, laws or any verbal activities related to the characteristics and interrelationships of objects and/or events defined as "norms," "ideals," "right," "wrong," etc.

"There is a world, and me in a world and me observing myself in a world. I classify things, qualities and actions in the world and in me so that I can order everything."

Definition, delineation, classification, comparison and judgement are some of the basic characteristics of this group's activities. In the realm of reason and logic the isolation of objects and events, standardization, comparison, and judgement are the common orientation. The totality of life experiences is merely seen as the interpretation and implementation of standard rules, norms, and judgement.

Herbert Lynden reports that the current education selection process puts more emphasis on the verbal than spatial abilities of students. He mentions that, "Tests for verbal demonstrations, numeracy/arithmetic and English have positive value for linguistic subjects but a very negative one for much of science and nil for mathematics, natural sciences and mechanical-technical subjects."[7]

Relative to this, some of the attitudes of most professionally-oriented students, among them architects and especially engineers, who combine their own majors with business administration, construction management, operation research, and even planning, can be explained. They are in search of elite administrative and management positions; they want to be politicians, rulers, academicians or simply want to have a greater possession of verbal knowledge and the capacity to demonstrate it. Nevertheless, as Lynden also points out, this attitude concentrated on verbal education distorts spatial reality. I frequently have a student with a professional degree in architecture who seeks my advice as to what specific aspect of planning he should go into. My answer is that, instead of being a planner, if you are good in architecture and have professional pride and enjoy what you do, you may take on planning programs and projects which reinforce your knowledge in terms of being a better architect, or else choose to implement your architectural background. However, do not aim to combine the two because it is most probably impossible to be good in both.

iii. The realm of abstraction and association. This realm of man's intellectual activity incorporates the highest level of abstraction in both the arts and the sciences. There are no set norms or values, no set examples, not even a common frame of reference. You do not find labels of artist or scientist, etc. There an individual, regardless of his discipline, is an ocean of random patterns in which he can, periodically, make some sense from among these patterns and represent it as his own observation and interpretation.

"I find that the further I ask questions, the less and less the world seems like a giant machine. I even find it difficult to ask the right questions and the answers often baffle me. I find that the answers are always in the frame of reference to a world which I myself have created through centuries of observation with the cosmos and with all the single events that I choose for study."[8]

For this group there is no subdivision; everything is interrelated. The structure of physical and biological life forms, the structure of sociocultural behavior, the structure of musical compositions and the structure of numerical order and organization all have a common ground. Nothing exists independently without interdependence.

In architecture, as in other professions, we need graduates who have the ability to synthesize these realms or else disciplines within each of the three realms; we need architectural engineers who can deal with buildable realities and concrete issues of electrical, mechanical, and structural engineering; we also require graduates who can fight it out in the midst of other human activities in order to market their creation, manage it, prove it, and defend it against the other activities absorbing the same resources: building managers, construction documenters. And finally, we need those who break the ground into a new realm of human activity and experience: the utopian, the abstract thinker, the artist, mathematician and musician who look into new relationships.

To educate these three groups of people we deal with different domains of human knowledge, different techniques and methods and, finally, different personalities to teach and be taught.

As a result of rapid dispersal of knowledge resulting from information explosion in the 20th century, especially in the last thirty years, technological development, particularly electronic advancement, put man in the midst of a tremendous amount of information regarding the total cosmic pattern and order.

In order to classify, identify, and understand these random, probabilistic life forms and the expansion of man's experience and knowledge, man should have made the most possible use of all the three above mentioned mental potentials and their utilization in relevant educational systems. Without doubt, at this point in the history of man's mental development, contributions of associative mental processes and their relevant education play a great role. In other words, through the development of this aspect of mental behavior man has been able to free himself from the limitations of his bodily and mundane surroundings and enter into the timeless and spaceless world of electronics. The disassociated role of educated man is increased awareness; he is involved with greater magnitudes and space–time distances. Thus the more expansive this range of interaction and involvement, the greater the scope of reality versus expectation and possible differences. Compared to a modern literate man, a primitive inhabitant whose world is small and isolated would never face such varieties of information and choice.

It is in architectural education and other disciplines which deal with the totality of life patterns that the dichotomy between various forms of input and information, especially qualitative and quantitative, verbal and spatial values, can be critically vast and in contrast, and thus the need for associative means of transaction of these forms becomes obvious.

Architectural education today is primarily geared toward the first, not the last, two characteristics. Consequently, this education belongs to yesterday rather than to the age of electronics and mass communication. Any educational attitude aimed at any isolated space-time experience or tied to any select group or the elite is irrelevant. The challenge of today's architectural education is simply to use to a maximum extent associative forms of knowledge as a synthetic means of integrating the input of various disciplines. The challenge is not to fill the student's mind with a gigantic and ever-growing number of object types and specifications, but rather to demonstrate how he can reach for them through a systematic process. The challenge is to oppose the mere teaching and repetition of facts which are quite irrelevant in today's life. The challenge is to be able to see and use a vast variety of information, which may even be in opposition, and develop the ability to join and synthesize this information.

The new electronic and cybernetic revolution requires persons who possess the ability to deal with "associative" forms of knowledge and information. This can be considered "abstract intelligence" which deals with a multiplicity of dimensions and relationships, overlaps and interlocks of function behavior, spaceless activities and functions, random and probabilistic information, and dynamic feedback interactions.

This type of ability is in contrast to both verbal ability and "concrete intelligence." Whereas a person with verbal orientation, say a lawyer, acts in accordance with conventional rules and regulations or conceptual contracts through which he demonstrates his views and verifications, an engineer, though equipped with concrete tested information, emphasizes experimentation tests and profiles. However, an associative thinker, systems analyst, designer, or programmer has to have the ability to gather every bit of information on different levels, deriving meaning out of various combinations of such inputs. I think that tomorrow's environmental planners and designers must have this ability; the synthesis of environmental factors can no longer be accomplished on the basis of a designer's subjective views reflected through the tip of his pencil on his sketches made at the studio drawing board. We are probably in consensus that this is exactly what the good architect of the past has done. He gathered all possible information and stored it in his memory, information he had acquired formally or informally experienced as a member of the community. Then, in designing, he actually manipulated this information as his pencil moved around on schematic design paper. Yet is it possible for today's architect to retain such a multitude of bits of information in his mind; is it possible to retain information derived in part from your awareness of being a member of a community; or is it possible to be the supreme master and demand other disciplines to feed you with information, letting you, the master, make the final decision? The answer to all of these questions is negative. Without the help of new electronic tools and their relevant human attitudes, it is impossible to be instantaneously in command of all required information. As in the cultures of the past, you cannot be a part of a society by virtue of your daily living experiences and knowledge. You must keep up with a gigantic amount of information to be able to be the de Vinci of your time. This is due to the fact that today social structure is based more on conventional formal rules and regulations than subconscious attitudes and feelings as reflected in past sociocultural structures. Let us say that the amount of ever-increasing norms, standards, rules and regulations which you should adhere to as an architect increases to such a point that the de Vinci of no time would be capable of memorizing them.

"Associative" conceptualization and ability is going to assume increased importance in abstract and analytical fields such as the theoretical physical sciences, mathematics, computer sciences, systems analysis and operation research. After associative concepts break the frontier of knowledge and are transformed to levels closer to the body of knowledge, both verbal and spatial inputs are supportable means for their presentation.

Verbal and spatial types both have their own vocabulary, method and orientation, as well as shortcomings. In analysis and reasoning, verbal types use the power of language and its jargon to prove their hypotheses while spatial types use different sets of stylistic clichés, including physical representation, whether it be drawings, models or real objects and life forms.

However, associative conceptualization deals with concepts of relationships such as unity, harmony, proportion, rhythm, structure, composition, and forms.

10.3 A Proposed Architectural Education System

As outlined in the first part of this book, the basic historic change in the physical sciences and man's view of nature in the early 20th century is one from atomism to structuralism. In abiding to this change in education, not only man's attitude in viewing nature and its components should be changed, but also academic philosophy and orientation, academic organizational framework and, finally, education methods and techniques. The change is from isolated fragmentation to structured parts within complex totalities. In General Systems theory, this view is generally referred to as system's approach. In this book it is suggested that this method used in environmental design education and environmental design, as architecture, be defined as communication.

Within this proposed definition, the totality of life and thus environment is a complex megasystem having resulted from the integration of very diversified complex systems, either physical or nonphysical. The structure of the total megasystem is then "the structure of structures." Thus it is wrong to look at the subcomponents of the total environment either from a vertical subdivision point of view(disciplinary approach) or a horizontal subdivisional point of view (scale oriented approach—interior design versus architecture versus planning). It is the continuity of life forms and their activities which require continuity of environmental design and planning.

As illustrated earlier, relative to the nature of the environment, the process of making form is also a dynamic one involving change in a set of instantaneous decision points over space and time. In other words, it is the pattern of decision points over space and time which illustrates this process. Teilhard de Chardin's point of view in this regard seems highly significant for he suggests that, "The different branches of science combine to demonstrate that the universe in its entirety must be regarded as one gigantic process, a process of becoming, of attaining new levels of existence and organization, which can properly be called a genesis or an evolution."

In adapting the definition "environmental communication forms and formation process" to architecture and the planning and design of the environment, one does not necessarily need to follow the traditional disciplinary approach and scale breakdown. Rather the environment should be seen as the structure of energy patterns (social, political, material, physical, etc.) toward a "reduction of tension."

It can be said that the recent cooperative attitude of most branches of knowledge has brought about quite interesting and fruitful results. It became known that a separation into categories, even at the level of the arts and sciences, was considered undesirable. It was realized that everything is tightly interwoven and interrelated and to look at parts of the system without consideration of the total system's behavior leads to the breakdown of what we started with.

It has become more and more apparent to us that the Eastern philosophy of man and nature, whereby we are a part of nature, is more in accordance with today's philosophy of knowledge than that of Western Christianity which recognized man to be on the top and above the pyramid of creation. Like Eastern attitudes, this view of knowledge regards destroying nature, of which we are a part, as the same as destroying ourselves.

The total explanation of animal behavior, including man, is not due to just which animal is being studied in isolation, but also how he interacts with his environment and the total socioeconomic system of which he is a part, how he changes it and adapts it to his needs, and also how he is being changed and adapted to his environment to fit in with its determinate factors.

Science has learned that although it is through intensive study that knowledge is broadened, the specialist usually concentrates on details at the expense of a more inclusive structure, a structure which holds together the parts of the entire system. Unless these specialized disciplinary approaches are integrated into a total comprehensive whole they are meaningless. Likewise, in contrast to previous emphasis on a single disciplinary approach in education, the present trend should aim toward interdisciplinary programs. The disciplinary approach of 18th and 19th century education cannot hold ground against the expansion of interdisciplinary programs in which the environmentalist could be trained not only to perceive artifacts as mere personal expressions, but also in terms of their other inherent dimensions. At this moment, I even doubt the value of our past experience with the interdisciplinary approach. Thus far the practice has been geared toward a collection of disciplines or a collection of courses from various disciplines rather than adherence to a common point of view, a unified denominator or overall theory and method as is suggested in this paper; i.e., environmental communication. Thus he should be trained to evaluate objects on the basis of their sociocultural aspects, as well as their intrinsic nature and structure. In other words, he should be taught to be sensitive to the fact that whatever message he wishes to convey is, in part, dependent on his own unique personal need to express his inner urges and also, in part, dependent on social factors and the laws of physical substances and structure inherent in the nature of matters address-ed in the natural sciences, as well as technology. Without a perspective based on a knowledge of all disciplines, the environ-mentalist could never hope to produce more than a one-dimension creation viewed within the confines of one aspect of human experience. The key is diversity within unity, moving from a single disciplinary approach to diversity gained from many disciplines. "Unity" is derived from a generalized body of knowledge and "diversity" from taking into account the views of numerous disciplines.

Thus any structure of the environment or its by-products that are planned or designed in the future will be created not by uniformity but by the integration of a vast number of varieties of hierarchical components organized in hierarchical order. The governing agent of such gigantic systems is "information flow."

Such systems are open systems which bring in information or energy from outside the system in order to move the system toward its "purpose." This is how the parts of the system are put together to achieve its purpose.

Architecture and its methodology of creation can be considered associative systems and purpose-generating systems carrying be-havioral, environmental, and symbolic information. It is a language of communication through behavioral, environmental, and sym-bolic cues or, as was concluded in the first chapter, architecture is a manifestation of cultural messages, architecture is communi-cation, and communication is culture.[9]

On these grounds, architectural education must shift from instruction in techniques for the answers to emphasis on the processes by which answers can be found. It must deal with exploration for design concepts and solutions, discovery of relationships and behavioral patterns, invention of new technique and methods and finally, ability to formulate new communication systems and messages. The new architectural teacher should either be a generalist and inquire into the characteristics of the total environmental communication system, or a specialist and deal specifically with one area, possessing a general understanding of total system behavior and the role of this particular area to the whole.

As a generalist, a teacher should himself know and be able to familiarize students with the total environmental communication system behavior, the objectives and contributions of each subdiscipline, their assumptions and hypotheses, potentials and limitations, methods and techniques, similarities and differences in approach and, finally, introduce students to the systematic approach of synthesizing the total input of various disciplines and also synthesizing techniques, methods, and theories which do not necessarily contrast with the opposing views brought in by other subdisciplines. This involves theories which are capable of integrating qualitative and quantitative measures, as well as unique and universal, individual and social, rational and nonrational values.

As a specialist, a teacher should know and relate to students the very detailed knowledge of his discipline, its methods, theories and principles. He should get students involved in experimental, practical, and actual working experience. In this breakdown, some traditional design studio activities can also be considered a subject of the specialist. That is to say, the role of synthesizing various subdisciplinary contributions and architecture should not necessarily be executed in the traditional way and through traditional means of presentation (drawings). The synthesis and integration of various inputs has to be accomplished through a method common to all disciplines which are involved; it must have a unifying language.

In a given design problem such as a housing complex, hospital or factory, the common dialogue between various disciplines involved in design should not necessarily be in the form of drawings. Although the final shape of a building will be a physical form, it will not necessarily be used or function in the manner the "architect" has imagined and printed or painted it to be.

The computer as a tool is a common denominator. I cannot predict that computer method will be commonly used in various disciplines, however the computer as a tool will surely be a common means of notation, memory storage, calculation and presentation. Growing knowledge and experience put into the development and use of probability, Information and Communication theory and principles has the potential of being a common method.

Concepts such as unity, harmony, proportions, rhythm, structure, composition and form can be shared by various disciplines in explaining the characteristic behavior pattern of lie forms, environmental communication, and even truth and virtue.

Information is communicated through a range of specialities and abilities, through the social sciences, natural sciences, physical sciences, pure sciences, psychoanalysis and anthropology, systems analysis and operations research, etc. However, each input is conditioned by disciplines which having neatly categorized the totality of life and environment in terms of their own domain, deliver their solution as if there were no other disciplines.

To outline further the proposed education system in concrete terms, I first define four types of Schools, then five types of graduates needed by society, and, finally, show how these two groups should correlate and respond to one another in such processes as structuring the School and designing their curriculum in order to provide the relevant and necessary education.

a. School-type classification
Based on the availability of disciplinary resources, human resources, and size and location, Schools could be classified into the following groups:
School-type 1—Schools within universities with a full range of disciplines related to architecture;
School-type 2—Schools solely geared to professional and practical output;
School-type 3—Schools with very specialized orientation; and
School-type 4—Local Schools with limited resources.

b. Categories graduates needed

Graduate-type 1–Practical-oriented professionals–capable of undertaking a project in an architectural office.

Graduate-type 2–Research-oriented scholars–interested in phenomenological issues which confront architecture. There is not a direct correlation between researchers and academicians. Academicians could be from a range of various categories, as could researchers. They could confront a wide range of issues, be they professional, technical, or geared to basic or applied research.

Graduate-type 3–Generalists–having a broad background spread out over various disciplines related to architecture. Their prime concern is answers to broad issues confronting architecture. Although they could become educators or researchers, they would not be quite as effective in any specific problem-solving-oriented project in an architectural office.

Graduate-type 4–Specialists–focusing their attention on a specialized subject area. This does not necessarily have to be professional or practical; it can also be technical or in the area of academic or research activity. The specialization classification could be made based on: subject matter, building type, or technologically-oriented building industries.

Graduate-type 5–Technicians–draftsmen being a good example of this type of graduate. However, this is not the only qualification, level, and capacity. Other qualifications exist and there is a great potential for expanding the number of technicians skilled in other technologically-oriented subjects, such as computer or building industries.

c. How to educate categories (b) in School-types (a)

A glance at the above sets of School-types and graduate-types classification might seem to be no different from existing types. The difference is not that much in the names of Schools, degrees, courses, etc., but rather in how the total system and its components are structured and organized; how subcomponents are built into total programs, how complexity is reached from simplicity and vice versa, how unity is derived from diversity and, finally, how the total educational system responds to life forms and patterns and society.

To optimize the total educational system, each unit should set its objectives as a complimentary function to the community, as well as the total educational system. The filtering process of past educational systems within which each School tried for elite output, anticipating that the market would alter the supply into lower levels, does not work anymore. The market today is interested in specific persons with specific training fitted to its own needs. These Schools which try for the best of everything are doomed to failure.

As earlier discussed, I do not believe that students should waste their energy in the pursuit of becoming specialists in a few disciplines. They should either be specialists in one area, or generalists involved in a cluster of disciplines. However in providing for the needs of society, educational institutions should concentrate their efforts, providing a range in magnitude and quality of generalists and specialists. They should change in their endeavor to educate "leaders." That is to say, the objective should not be the production of educational elites. Supposedly less-advanced students, or the "left overs," generate a greater volume of social needs, which are studied by the professionals. The objectives should be formulated in the reverse.

How to structure Schools?

i. Type-one Schools should be fully organized in the total university structure, vertically and horizontally (levels of academic affairs and discipline areas). Traditional sectorial education orientation does not fit the needs and requirements for this education. The isolation of departments or even Schools from the rest of the university or borrowing courses is not enough to fulfill the objectives of this type of education. The isolation of departments or even Schools from the rest of the university, with borrowing of faculty or sending students to other Schools for necessary courses, is not enough to fulfill the objectives of this educational system. In the next section, a model is sketched out for Farabi University which falls into this type of educational system.

Programs designed for these types of graduates should contain a full range of subjects varying in disciplines such as philosophy and logic, the social sciences, the natural sciences, the physical sciences, engineering, operations research, computer sciences, and technology, etc.

Given that a School in this category has resources in specialized areas they should give specialized programs high priority.

ii. Type-two professional Schools should try to utilize professional practice in the real world as a subsidiary to their educational capabilities. Like students in the Schools of medicine, students in type-two Schools should spend much of their time working with real problems in the real world. The problem-oriented approach should be tried, and the studio should be used as a forum to bring in every input from any discipline into a specific problem at hand. The student is not helped as much by isolated cases in different disciplinary areas. A program for these types of graduates should be treated as a forum workshop closely related to some type of practice. After a very few introductory courses any information brought to the forum should be geared and related to real and tangible design problems. No practical course such as structure, mechanical equipment, etc. should be taught in isolation, but rather in the context of workshop problems. Various specialists dealing with problems in the forum should have face to face collaborations, as they do in architectural offices.

iii. Type-three Schools with highly specialized resources should target their energy or specific areas of specialty with a small number of students working on special problems characterizing this system. These Schools are leaders in the innovative problem-solving approach to the frontiers of knowledge and experience in their specialty.

iv. Type-four local Schools should by no means try to compete with Schools of the other three types. They should either undertake responsibility for giving general and introductory knowledge to the students, preparing them to move on to the other Schools, or they should furnish them with technical skills.

		School-types			
		comprehensive	professional	specialized	local
type of education	professionals		×	×	
	research oriented	×		×	
	generalists	×			
	specialists		×	×	

Notes to Chapter Ten

1. A.T. Minai, "Communication Fields. A Proposed Definition of Architecture," unpublished paper.
2. T. Parsons, R. Bales, and E. Shils, "The Dimensions of Action-Space," in *Working Papers in The Theory of Action.*
3. T. Parsons and E. Shils, *Toward a General Theory of Action.*
4. E. Hall, *The Hidden Dimension.*
5. C.D. Mortensen, *Communication: the Study of Human Interaction.*
6. Herbert Lynden, *A New language for Environmental Design,* New York University Press, 1972.
7. *Ibid.*
8. *Ibid.*
9. A.T. Minai, "Cultural Change: Man's Concept of Nature and Total Environmental Communication."

Conclusion

In conclusion I should say the plan for this book was to develop a theory of environmental communication. Initially, I intended to cover the total perspective from philosophy to implementation in a single book, but as time passed and the volume of material grew, I decided to extend this endeavor into two books: first, *Architecture as Environmental Communication* covering the philosophical and theoretical framework leading to an application of this theory; second, *Environmental Design as Aesthetic Communication* covering a full range of application of the theory.

As you may have already noticed, this book was not written with the intent of being included in *Approaches to Semiotics*. After the final manuscript was proposed to Mouton for publication, it was decided that it be placed in this series.

Before I begin the conclusion I would like to say a few words about the relationship between semiotics and communication. If you recall, prior to the Indiana University Conference on Paralinguistics and Kinesics there was no general agreement as to whether communication, semiotics, or semiology was a fitting term for a field "which in time will include the study of all pattened communication in all modalities. . . . "[1] As Milton Singer explains, although there was considerable argument for and against the use of each of these terms, upon the suggestion made by Margaret Mead, the name "semiotic" was accepted as the title of this conference. This term was adopted by Prof. Sebeok who implemented this series, entitling it *Approaches to Semiotics*.

I think argument still exists, and I accept Morris's breakdown of "communication" into the three following classifications:
1. communication in general which covers "any instance of the establishment of a commonage, that is the making common of some property to a number of things;"
2. sign communication considered as "the arousing of common signification by the production of signs;" and
3. language communication "when the signs produced are language signs."

In comparing that which was discussed throughout this book with the definition of semiotics given by Sebeok, communication and signification, or Eco's definition of signs as "something that it is not itself,"[3] it is obvious that a common ground exists between semiotics and communication as used here. The emphasis has been placed on the general notion of communication rather than signification, which is a product of man-to-man communication. The reason for this emphasis was to deal first with the broader scope of man's relation to his total cosmic environment, and then scale down to specifics. While communication deals with any exchange of information, signification deals with those exchanges of information which have been signified.

So here we deal with a wide spectrum of communication where an object, event, or association stands both for itself and something else. There is no way to distinguish between sets of behavior, "a kind that communicates and a kind that does not communicate."[4] Signification only distinguished those communications which are intentional. A stop sign made in a transportational context has been formulated to signify only one particular message, and it was thus forced to relay that message and nothing else. Although sometimes necessary, this rigidity has no place in environmental communication and architecture. As expressed by Louis Kahn, an architectural piece is not created as a symbol. The designer can merely hope that it will become a symbol; i.e., if man interacts with the intended message it becomes a symbol.

Of course it should be noted that Sebeok's idea of semiotics and its domain of activities regarding communication expands far greater than that which we have just mentioned, particularly when he talks about his generic coding system where all living forms are seen through a "biosemitic" communication process. Although he himself specifically deals with signification as a bio-element of semiotics, in this case it seems that signification takes a different form and semiotics a much broader scope. Thus considering this scope of semiotics, any communication could be considered semiotics. Whether we use the above definition of semiotics given by Sebeok or the broad definition of communication which I have used throughout this book, both deal with one common concept and that is the observation of interrelations, interconnections, and relevant information representing universal structures, whether they be social, psychological, physical, or biological Information which each genetic cell carries or exchanges in order to secure continuity and integrity of the system it represents we term communication.

This book, covering the content referred to above, began with some notions which have inspired me throughout my architectural development. Here I would like to mention what these notions are and then, what I hope to have accomplished in this book.

That subject which has always been the greatest challenge in my architectural education is aesthetics, not the "formalistic" aesthetics included in the general course curriculum in architectural history or theory which deals with various styles, but phenomenological aesthetics which is broad in scope and perceived as the unity of cosmic order, whether that unity be seen by an artist or a scientist, whether it be an order in the sociocultural structure of a given society or a pattern in a physiobiological part of nature.

Throughout this search for aesthetic order in works of architecture I must confess I have always rejected a large portion of available literature which deals with aesthetic expression in works of art. The basic framework within which traditional aestheticians operate comes from two sources:

First, an aesthetician assumes a so-called "Western" orientation to knowledge, an orientation apparently having resulted from the Christian influence on the attitude toward man and nature classifying perceived patterns in nature and works of art as "good" or "right" in aesthetic terms or "bad" or "wrong" in nonaesthetic terms, an orientation which is built on conventional ideas of the past colored by subjectivity, beliefs, etc. and which leaves no room for objectivity and truth; i.e., aesthetics which applies not only to isolated individuals and products but to the overall process of cosmic order, including sociocultural, physical, and biological factors.

Second, an aesthetician uses the term *order* to express some logical or rationally-oriented perception of "reality" measured against some Cartesian frame of reference or logical and *a priori* analysis based on classical mechanics; e.g., he uses symmetry or "perfection" in geometrical form as a measure of "good form." This orientation does not leave room for random patterns and entropy, both of which, in my eyes, are the most valid criteria for aesthetic measurement; i.e., the aesthetics of wildness, madness, unpredictability, uncertainty, and rage for chaos.

Neither of the above two groups convinced me of the "rules" of what constitutes aesthetics. Rather to the contrary the claims of both seemed to me to be wrong. To me aesthetics is an interplay between order and disorder, rationality and nonrationality, consciousness and subconsciousness.

My search for aesthetics has led me to look for any principle on the basis of which I could account for a better understanding of the structural geometry of such ordered and disordered patterns of coordination between organisms and nature. Although convinced that all cosmic components are governed by the same law and are thus an inseparable pattern of interlocking systems of systems, I accept a disciplinary approach only as a means of classifying simple methods of analysis. In looking for such a pattern I have thus decided first to distinguish between elements involved in the activities of the mind and man's surroundings in nature, assuming there is a continuum of matter from the nonliving to the living where not only a distinction between the physical and metaphysical is impossible, but, moreover, a distinction between organic and inorganic matter, or in Rey's words where " . . .the human brain is related to the structure of the world as object—to human knowledge (which is the only possible meaning of 'world')."[5] I want to go further to see if behind these set-forth orders, which are after all man's perception of nature, lies a restless universe much more random, if not amasse, than that for which any mind might be equipped to comprehend.

In this regard, L.L. Whyte says, "But pulsation(s) when allowed to, go on and on, and the products of the ordering of morphic tendency are accumulated, while there are no persisting or accumulating consequences of disordering tendency."[6] He refers to "anthropomorphic" principles regarding an organism's cooperation with its environment where a continuous interplay between "morphic" and "entropic" activities maintains continuity of life processes. While morphic activities of organisms tend to build up orders, entropic tendencies disturb them. To me, this is the law of the beauty of life. The task of the aesthetician is to understand the underlying principles of such ordered-disordered patterns without any preconceived preferences as to subjective value judgements toward these characteristics: order or disorder. It is disturbing to see that no aestheticians use disorder (random pattern) as a criteria for aesthetic judgement. It is even more disturbing to see that even people like Whyte, an advocate of the concept, are preconditioned by the history of human knowledge. That is, while he illustrates the role which disorder plays in an organism's organic balance with nature to sustain life, he fails to give these patterns any credibility. Rather he takes it for granted that an ordered pattern presupposes some perogative. As he says, "So the morphic tendency has a remarkable privilege over the entropic: it leaves cumulative records, while the entropic has nothing to show for itself, being merely a randaizor or disturbing agent."[7] He himself states that these ordering and disordering tendencies are interrelated. "In organisms the ordering tendency needs its apparent antagonist in order that cycles may be completed, and the life processes continue. Life, if interpreted as the ordering principle, needs its antagonist if it is to emerge and to persist."[8]

As a matter of fact, the two sets of characteristics are complimentary to each other; i.e., each necessitates the existence of the other, not to oppose one another in the Helgelian philosophy of dialectic processes, but as states of the pendulum of life. In communication terms the total system at any space-time situation is necessary to the ordering principles of structuring messages, while a haphazard principle disturbs this set of formalized pictures in order to search for a new set of "abstractions."

Let me use the art of dancing on a rope in gymnastics as an example to reinforce this concept. The art of dance is the constant recreation of forms chosen from among the two sets of force patterns: one "undesigned"—and undesirable—gravity forces considered "disorder" which the dancer fights against, and the second "ordered," force patterns initiated by the dancer to balance the other. Here art is created by an interplay of these two sets which are both conditioned and in the process of conditioning one another. We do consider the first set of forces to be an unwanted, hazardess part of the pattern, yet in taking away this set art would not exist. Moreover, both of those sets follow the same rules and laws. It is only in our segregation that one or the other is desired. These views regarding the principle of order and disorder hold true in every art form or aesthetic experience, whether it be architecture, dance, or music.

The question confronting the development of any theory of aesthetics is then related to the characteristic behavior of these two sets of coordinative conditions which actually determine all organic behavior, including the features of its various units: form, function, and location at any space-time circumstance. One of the most important concepts related to the functions of any organism is so-called "vital surplus," or what makes life forms perform functions. This is actually a result of the interplay among the above mentioned sets of coordinates. As Whyte says, "The presence of the vital surplus implies that the total processes in organisms are not merely life-preserving, but life enchanging, not merely adaptive but formative and sometimes creative."[9]

Accepting the notions of random pattern as a part of aesthetic form and experience, I then had to see where they originate and how they perform in the human mind. Assuming that random patterns are not a behavior function of a rational, logical process of thought patterns, I had to restate the high historical values attached to the intuitive function of design activities and look for their origin, particularly in the subconscious mind. Thereafter I illustrated the role of subconscious activities of the mind and intuition in the creation of aesthetic forms.

In addition to the subdivision between mind and nature, I made another classification between those activities of mind formulating thoughts and emotions or rational and intuitive responses.

Having adapted a great deal from "scientific methods," it may occasionally leave the impression that I advocate quantitative methods and "problem solving."[10] However when it comes to the consideration of unknown boundaries of scientific knowledge regarding the intuitive aspects of man and his "hidden dimensions" of subconscious behavior, I tend to borrow from Carl Jung who values unconsciousness to the extent that he "saw it as the very source of consciousness and held that we begin our lives with our unconsciousness. . . ."[11] He further argues that conscious mind "grows out of an unconscious psyche which is older than it, and which goes on functioning together with it or even in spite of it."[12] And finally, he "implies a link between the individual and humanity as a whole—in fact, in some sense, between the individual and the entire cosmos—that cannot be understood within a mechanistic framework but is very consistant with the systems view of mind."[13]

In this respect Carl Jung's concept has been adapted; i.e., "psychological patterns were connected not only causally but also acausally. In particular, he introduces the term synchronicity for acausal connections between symbolic images in the inner, psychic world and events in the external reality."[14] Capra points out that the same view is practiced in the concept of "particle physics, and physicists are now also making a distinction between causal (or 'local') and actual (or 'nonlocal') connections."[15] He suggests that the "patterns of matter and patterns of mind are increasingly recognized as reflections of one another, which suggests that the study of order, in causal as well as acausal connectedness, may be an effective way of exploring the relationship between the inner and outer realms."[16]

With regard to the concept of distinct differences between rational and intuitive modes of the mind I have shared Geoffrey Vickers' approach. He emphasizes the conformity of the two modes, a conformity which would also connect them to the word "aesthetic". He states, "My thesis is that the human mind has available to it at least two different modes of knowing and that it uses both in appropriate or inappropriate combinations in its endless efforts to understand the world in which it finds itself, including its fellow human beings and itself. One of these modes is more dependent on analysis, logical reasoning, calculation, and explicit description. The other is more dependent on synthesis and the recognition of pattern, context and the multiple possible relations of figure and ground."[17]

He further argues that the first one manipulates the components with consideration to their contextual relationships, whereas the second involves both identifying and creating contextual mosaics without respect to individual components. Both of these processes, rationality and intuition, are essential in any mental activity. Whereas the rational process is capable of "reproduction and description," the intuitive process is not.

Furthermore, in this work I have tried to view architectural reality as the essential "interrelatedness and interdependence" of all phenomena whether they be in the physical, biological, social, cultural, or psychological realm.

In this attempt I have sought to develop a conceptual framework which formulates a new environmental paradigm rooted to already existing disciplines, a paradigm which views architecture as environmental communication or a network of interconnections among that which various individuals or disciplines view as disciplinary attributes of that unity called man and his environment. In physical terms this is actually in tune with the new trend of development in the physical sciences, namely "chance and necessity,"[18] on which Erich Jantsch bases his theory of "the recognition of a systematic interconnectedness over space and time of all natural dynamics."[19] This he sees manifested due to the openness of the universe's dynamic systems and subsystems, creativity, and change. As to the application of this universal principle to man, the concept sees man as a part of this total system without any separation between sociocultural and natural systems. Within such a framework we are not the "helpless subjects of evolution," but rather "evolution" itself. That is, at each state numerous levels of evolution, self-organization processes, "take over from random developments, if the proper conditions become established, and to accelerate or make possible in the first place the emergence of complex order."[20]

This is the exact concept or process Capra says has come about in physics; i.e., gradually bringing about "a network of interlocking concepts and models and, at the same time, developing the corresponding social organization." As he states, this type of attitude toward reality leads us beyond traditional disciplinary views "using whatever language becomes appropriate to describe different aspects of the multileveled, interrelated fabric of reality."[21]

To this end I have adapted systems approach to environmental communication, viewing man's total environment as sets of integrated wholes, "relationships and interactions," which instead of focusing on sets consisting of specific elements or component subsystems, emphasizes the structural properties and organization of its concepts. "The features of order, manifested in the particular form of a structure and the regular array and distribution of its substructures, are no more than the visible index of regularities of the underlying dynamics operating in its domain . . . "[22]

Within the above perspective architecture has been defined as environmental communication, a network of interaction: (a) between the designer and the users, through the designer's "intended messages," (b) between man and the material world through the observation of messages read in similarities and differences structured in matter either in the form of "object systems" or "behavioral patterns," and finally, (c) between man and his past and future through his association with all of the above forms and functions in immediate and distant space and time, and memories and their compilation in culture.

To define aesthetic patterns in assumed communication systems I have used the principles of Information theory which assumes information as a measure of order and disorder or uncertainty and thus the random characteristics of pattern performance in an environment. Information theory is used not only as a measurement of communication messages, but also as a common means of identifying order in various characteristic component patterns of nature.

Order and disorder can be explained in Whyte's words: "the universe displays a tendency toward. . .order, which I have called morphic; in the viable organism this morphic tendency becomes the tendency towards. . .the search for unity which gave rise to religion, art, philosophy, and the sciences."[23] In his words, "like 'random,' in a fundamental analysis of self-contradictory concepts."

What I have termed "the law of opposites" is the essential constituent of an aesthetic function or, as explained earlier, all communication arts including the performing arts—event patterns—(games, dance) or environmental arts—objects patterns—(plastic arts, architecture, etc.) are produced as interplays of ordered-disordered patterns. In Whyte's words, "To an open mind, unprejudiced by past or recent theories, there appear to exist in the material universe two great, and apparently opposed, general tendencies, of which it is natural to regard all other processes as special cases: *A.* Toward dynamical disorder called 'Entorpic.' *B.* Toward spatial order called 'Morphic.'[25] The two tendencies contrast each other a great deal. *A* leads to fluctuation.

B leads to a structural equilibrium which provides a framework or reference point for future states or " '*A*' peters out '*V*' leads on." This process occurs when time has come for a system to change due to some circumstantial change whether temperature, pressure composition or whatever.

In this theory it is assumed that the very nature of possession of any sort of structural potentiality within any set of components provides that set or system with, in Cyril Smith's words, "structural inertia."[25] Due to and relative to the nature of this inherent structure there exist sets of interacting linkages among the elements of that system which would tie those elements, as well as the components of their environment, together. Such interlocking linkage systems or structures resist any deviation from "norm-structure" by any single part of the environment and its communication system. This holds true in our perception of the environment as well.

Based on the nature of the system, whether it be simple, complex, open, closed. . . , there would also be differences in the nature of the linkage system. The simpler the system or the more open the system, the more it leaves room for the possibility of incorporation of alternative arrangements. On the contrary, due to the complex history and multitude of memory messages-linkages reinforcing the structural system, in complex systems the linkages are so tightly knit and uniquely organized that less room is thus left for the occurrence of a loose happening.

Changing some of these structures, whether they be social, cultural, physical, or biological, appears to be easy. Yet, this is not the case because each part is an element of a chain process which not only ties that part of neighboring components but also ties them to each of its neighbors and so forth on down the line, and possibly to a greater and greater complexity of system. It could be that sometime in the past each single part, due to circumstantial necessity, had found some stable pattern and interlocking system and then after that the alternation of any single element without alternation of the totality of elements became impossible.

There are various levels of forms of order ranging from the universal level to atoms and subparticles. The type of order we deal with in architecture is that which is experienced in total human experience and communication, and that which is ordered-disordered.

Any human endeavor pertains to both realism and emotion. The degree of importance of the role of each of these two varies from individual action to action, from culture to culture and is based on the nature of the action as well. The history of architecture shows that architecture is no exception. Prak states, "The function of a building determines its form in a double sense. In a purely rational sense by requiring that it will be practical and will work; in an aesthetic sense by demanding that the felt emotional importance of the function finds some expression in architecture."[26] He further argues that "If 'function' is so defined as to cover both the rational and emotional requirements of a certain purpose, then all architecture is functional." Prak gives a "simplified" scale for a relative percentage of the role of rational and emotional elements in some building-types.

An architect's vocabulary is form and material used in a variety of shapes, texture, color, and an unlimited combination of contexts and configurations to communicate: to provide the physical-psychological needs of man, to respond to the sociopsy-chological structure of its users by giving a proper spatial context to human event-patterns (behavior) and to respond to the trust of memory expectation manifested in associations.

That artistic part of architecture which deals with feelings and emotions consists of the immeasurable, irregular, and random patterns structured in the hidden dimension of qualitative space.

"The meaning of Art is distinguished from the world of facts by its emotive qualities. The meaning of Art is primarily one of feeling: the works of Art are symbols of emotions."[27]

Architecture is environmental communication. Where architects act is not solely for the provision of utilizable space, rather it is a game, a game fighting for survival, the survival of the fittest, i.e., the survival of staying in the game, and the game is intercommunication with the surrounding universe for the best utilization of information systems. The architect to survive the game uses new objects and new possibilities for forming objects which could best fit space-time information systems which constitute all universal laws of the physical world, the whole of life form behaviors, and finally, those combinational properties summed up in man's ever-evolving memory. Architecture, the art of shaping life to its soul—ever continuously increasing accumulation of information—associations, an art which might be defined as "the dream of orientation of a humanity in search of its soul."[28]

Even in primitive art, which seems to be an abstract "schematization" of forms, art forms tend to be manifest in an abstract manner. However the shapes are more a symbolic representation of the inner feelings of the artist rather than any realistic representation. In the words of Abell, "Art shows then, not 'the appearances of things, but their 'true nature'."[29] Or as he further argues; in this art "The way of things is depicted, is . . . a symbol for an attitude towards reality, caused by external social circumstances. Things are painted rosy or black depending on whether the circumstances are experienced collectively as good or bad."

Notes to Conclusion

1. M. Singer, "For a Semiotic Anthropology," in *Sight, Sound, and Sense*, p. 212.
2. C. Morris, quoted by A. Rey in "Communication vs. Semiosis: Two Conceptions of Semiotics" in *Sight, Sound, and Sense*, p. 102.
3. U. Eco, "Semiotics: A Discipline or an Interdisciplinary Method" in *Sight, Sound, and Sense*, p. 74.
4. John n. Deely, "Toward the Origin of Semiotics," in *Sight, Sound, and Sense*, p. 1.
5. A. Rey. "Communication vs. Semiosis. Two Conceptions of Semiotics" in *Sight, Sound, and Sense*, p. 108.
6. L. Whyte, *The Universe of Experience*, Harper & Row Publishers, 1974, p. 81.
7. *Ibid.*
8. *Ibid.*, p. 84.
9. *Ibid.*, p. 83.
10. H. Simon, *Human Problem Solving*.
11. F. Capra, *The Turning Point*, p. 361.
12. C. Jung, quoted by F. Capra in *The Turning Point*, p. 361.
13. *Ibid.*
14. F. Capra, *The Turning Point*, p. 362.
15. *Ibid.*, pp. 362–363.
16. *Ibid.*, p. 363.
17. Geoffrey Vickers, "Rationality and Intuition," in *On Aesthetics in Science*, ed. by Wechsler, p. 145.
18. E. Jantsch, *The Self-Organizing Universe*, p. 8.
19. Ibid.
20. *Ibid.*, p. 9.
21. F. Capra, *The Turning Point*, p. 265.

22. Paul Weiss, quoted by F. Capra in *The Turning Point*, p. 267.
23. L. Whyte, *The Universe of Experience*, p. 40.
24. *Ibid.*, p. 42.
25. Cyril Stanley Smith, 'Structural Hierarchy in Science, Art and History," in *On Aesthetics in Science*, ed. by Wechsler, p. 37.
26. Luning Prak, *The language of Architecture*, Mouton & Co., Netherlands, 1968, p. 25.
27. *Ibid.*, p. 17.
28. W. Abell, quoted by L. Prak, *The Language of Architecture*, p. 23.
29. *Ibid.*

Planning human activity systems
Esfahan region: A case study

a— Rationale of the Originality Indexes
b— Rationale of the Probability Indexes
c— Building Models—Assumptions
d— Originality Model
e— Probability Model

This appendix reflects the partial results of a research project carried out in the Esfahan region[1] by the author at the University of Tehran in 1975.[2] The purpose of incorporating the project here is to provide the reader with a more concrete presentation of some of the concepts discussed throughout the book. Although architecture and planning objectives might vary in their substance and scope, they could both fall into a similar methodological approach. Here in the Esfahan regional Study the objective of the plan is to optimize the function of the human activity system. The same objective could also be formulated for an architectural design problem.

The initial objective of the research project was to study the impact of new industrial complexes on the sociophysical structure of existing regions. The Esfahan region was used as a case study since a new steel mill factory and a city of 300,000 population was being built—40 kilometers from Esfahan City. The research project was divided into three phases; namely, before creation of the steel mill, within the process of implementation, and after full-scale development. The research project was designed to yield three independent sets of results, as well as a comparative analysis of the three phases of development, and thus the assessment of the impact studied.

In view of the overall aim of the study on the influence of the steel mill complex on the sociophysical structure of the region, it was realized necessary to comprehend the spatial organization of

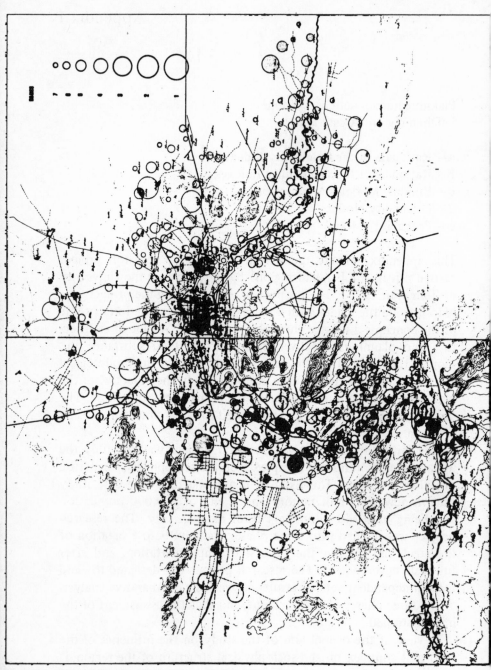

Originality Pattern of Settlements in Esfahan Region

economic and social systems on a regional scale. In other words, it was assumed that, in order to examine impact, we must have a conceptual model of the existing regional structure. Therefore, the development of such conceptual models was the goal of the first phase of the impact study.

Central Place Theory (hereafter CPT) provided an initial starting point. It postulates that because of the interplay of the two factors—the tendency of people to minimize their trip-taking and the difference in threshold markets/service populations for different urban functions—urban functions tend to arrange themselves in a recognizable and regular hierarchy. However two basic problems in applying CPT to the Esfahan region became immediately apparent. First CPT deals almost exclusively with commercial activities, whereas we are more interested in a comprehensive "sociophysical structure." Secondly, CPT assumes a uniform agricultural plain. Granted that modifications can be made to account for deviations from this assumption, the water scarcity and topography of the Esfahan region, and most of Iran, are so discrepant with these assumptions that it was decided to start with a more general systems theoretical approach and to consider the relevance of CPT within this larger framework.[3]

Furthermore, classical CPT deals essentially with urban functions and thus is concerned with settlements of over a certain size—in Iran, about 4000—5000 population. CPT postulates that urban functions tend to distribute themselves in a spatially-ordered hierarchy. This occurs because of the interplay of two factors. Different urban functions require different threshold service market areas, thus limiting supply. On the other hand, consumers tend to minimize trips by using the closest sources. The CPT hierarchy is a result of these two tendencies. Paul English, in *City and Village in Iran*, postulated the following hierarchy (although not using CPT directly): dominant urban center, regional subcenter, agricultural-weaving village, and small village/hamlet. Our study so far probably has enough data to support or reject this hierarchy and/or develop new models.

After deviations from the model being used for studying the Esfahan region were examined, CPT was modified for the extensions (geographically and functionally) to which it was being subjected.

To modify CPT the following measures were taken:

1) It is not only commercial activities for which the model should account, but all human activities. That is to say, all human activities are interdependent and thus spatially organized throughout the region.

2) The region should not be considered a continuous flow of activities (uniform plan), but a constellation of units (settlements) spatially organized into interrelated components of one system.

3) To build models which are not only descriptive in nature (like CPT) but could also be used as planning tools. Thus CPT modifications lead to the development of new models; i.e., Originality and Probability capable of maximizing some objective function in order to maximize the efficiency—subject to equity constraints (which are of a normative nature)—of spatial distribution of regional common facilities throughout the system.

These models were proposed so that hierarchies other than those measured by CPT could be examined: (1) originality or centrality model and (2) probability model—designed to measure such hierarchies; i.e., functional locations throughout the regional hierarchy.

This section focuses on the completion of the first phase of the project. The prime objective of this phase was to see how existing traditional regions (following a "natural" growth path without major outside forces) operate, and to understand the underlying socio-economic and natural forces holding the constituent elements of the settlement patterns together in the existing Esfahan region. The objective of this phase was also to build models capable of describing the patterning of human activity systems and of optimizing the distribution function of the system.

A systems approach method was based on the concepts developed in previous chapters adapted to identify the components of the system described as activities located in space.[4] The first step was to find a valid means of dividing the entire system into subsystems.

A major subdivision of the total regional system to subsystems was accomplished by isolating "natural" and "human activity" systems.

In arid regions, such as Esfahan, due to a scarcity of water resources and cultivatable land, the natural system tends to play the more important role in the development of the region. Under such circumstances factors related to the "natural system" shape the basic locational pattern of agricultural activities. The availability of water and basic locational pattern related to arable land play a determining role. The human activity system, on the other hand, though generally influenced by the natural system and its basic structural framework, is shaped by sociopolitical, economical, and administrative factors which organize its spatial distribution.

Following the analysis of each one of the subsystems, correlation analyses were conducted: (1) between the two systems, each considered as a whole; and (2) between the elements of the two, as an effort to measure the degree of interrelation of the two sets of components making up each system.

Of the two systems, the human activity system was the more complex. Outside the commercial facilities, most of the other common facilities were built by the government, and thus did not follow the demand pattern. This was in contrast to the spatial distribution of agricultural activities which fully correlated with the availability of water and land, themselves, and well correlated with population distribution.

Through correlation analysis, it was found that insufficiency and inefficiency in the distribution of common facilities have resulted from the dual functional role which the region is now playing. The common facilities are distributed according to two different patterns. One follows natural growth—that is to say, the traditional agricultural pattern—and the other follows a preimposed and planned growth pattern foreseen by the government, but lacking enough socioeconomic and political backup. In other words, the region in which agricultural activities and sociocultural activities, as well as common facilities, had followed the traditional man/land relationship is now facing problems created by the superimposition of activities whose spatial distribution follows a different logic (that of human systems).

It was thus decided that it would be useful to develop means by which one could correct the distribution of human activity system and common facilities so as to strike a balance between efficiency and equity considerations.

As stated earlier, this part of the project was to study the spatial organization of socio-economic systems of the Esfahan region. In other words, the development of conceptual models of the existing sociophysical structure of the region was the goal of the first phase of the project. Two models measuring the behavior of human activity systems were developed. The first model was termed "Originality"[5] and the second "Probability."[6]

Both models are physical studies of the locational processes which shape the sociophysical structure of the region. Each model consists of two parts. The first part of each is analytical and serves as a descriptive model; it aims at reaching a working understanding of existing urban and village systems within the region in terms of both a general theoretical base and a conceptual, and eventually quantitative, descriptive base.

Originality and Probability models are developed as such means. They are designed to analyze human activity patterns in general and common facilities distribution in particular. They are to measure their distribution efficiency and equity, as well as be used as planning tools to optimize the efficiency and, hopefully, the equity of such distribution patterns. This is accomplished by correcting the distribution of human activity patterns and relevant common facilities through providing proper location for new activities in a given niche. Of course, efficiency and equity are not necessarily achieved concurrently. Based on economy of scale, agglomeration economy (efficiency), increases in polarization of human settlement patterns, and relevant activity patterns, the more efficient the system might become. But the distribution of facilities thus obtained would not necessarily provide an equal accessibility to all users (equity).

a. Rationale of the Originality Indexes

ORIGINALITY MATRIX

A table is prepared with facilities located in columns and settlements arranged in rows. The number of each facility in a given village is entered in its relevant place on the table (Xij).

The multiplication of this number (Xij) by the total number of different facilities $(Mi$ sum of relevant row), in a settlement (i) divided by the total number of this facility in the whole region $(Nj$ sum of the relevant column), constitutes the relevant originality of a given facility in a given village. The higher the originality of a given facility in a given village, the higher the value of that facility for the total system.

Originality indices are designed to measure the uniqueness of a given facility in a settlement, in a settlement-type or in the whole region.[7] It also measures the uniqueness of a given village in terms of the variety of activities contained within and, therefore, the potential interactions between all the different facilities and services in the whole region.

The originality indices are designed to measure the value of a given kind of activity within a settlement in relation to the full range of activities available (or not available) within that settlement. They therefore assign more importance to a retailer located in a settlement with other retailers or government services, or any of the facilities under consideration, than to a retailer located in isolation (agglomeration economics). These indices take into consideration other components—the whole is really more than the sum of the parts. The name of the indices is derived from the General Systems theory concept of originality or uniqueness—a measure of the exceptional qualities of a component of a system relative to the total system.

b. Rationale of the Probability Indexes-The Probability Matrix

A table has been prepared with facilities located in columns and settlement types arranged along rows.[8] The order and type of each

No. of Facilities in Ech. Settlement type	No. of Settlements in Each Type	Settlement Type (No. of Facs. in Each)	Bath (Public) Barber	Teahouse	Inn Restaurant	Butcher	Retailer	Wholesaler	Water Supply	Power Distribution	Small-Scale Manufacturing	Confectionery Sugar MFG.	Power Supply	Bread Shop	Clinic	Primary School	Secondary School	Governmental Organizations	P.T.T.
			1	2	3	4	5	6	7	8	9	10	11	12	13	14	15	16	17
80	80	1							44 .56				1 .01			1 .01			1 .01
54	27	2		1 .03			3 .10		7 .22	1 .03	6 .20								
84	28	3	7 .25				3 .11		5 .18		2 .07		3 .11				1 .04		
112	28	4	10 .36				6 .21		6 .21	1 .04			2 .07	1 .04		8 .29			
60	12	5	6 .50			1 .08	2 .17									7 .56			
114	19	6	15 .79				5 .26		4 .21		3 .16		1 .05	10 .53					
217	31	7	21 .68	1 .03	1 .03		24 .77		2 .07		4 .13	1 .03	3 .10			20 .65			
264	33	8	28 .85	1 .03		3 .09	27 .82		4 .12		3 .09		2 .06			23 .70			
288	32	9	29 .91	2 .06		7 .22	30 .94	3 .09	4 .13	1 .03	5 .16		2 .06			31 .97		1 .03	
250	25	10	25 .10		1 .04	6 .24	23 .92		7 .28		12 .48		3 .12	1 .04		23 .92			
275	25	11	22 .88	1 .04		15 .60	24 .96	1 .04	7 .28	2 .08	12 .48		5 .20	4 .16	1 .04	24 .96		1 .04	
204	17	12	16 .94			15 .88	17 .10		4 .24	1 .06	14 .82		4 .24	4 .24		15 .88			
156	12	13	12 .10			8 .67	10 .83	1 .08	5 .42		10 .83		3 .25	4 .33	1 .08	12 .10			
196	14	14	14 .10	3 .21	1 .07	13 .93	14 .10		3 .21		13 .93		2 .14	3 .36	1 .07	14 .10			1 .07
135	9	15	9 .10	1 .11	1 .11	8 .89	9 .10	1 .11	6 .67	2 .22	9 .10		3 .33	5 .56		9 .10			
128	8	16	8 .10	1 .12	2 .25	8 .10	8 .10	1 .13	7 .88	1 .13	7 .88	1 .13	5 .63	7 .88	1 .13	8 .10			
68	4	17	4 .10	2 .50	1 .25	4 .10	4 .10	1 .25	3 .75	1 .25	4 .10		3 .75	2 .50	1 .25	4 .10			
54	3	18	3 .10	1 .33	1 .33	3 .10	3 .10	1 .33	.33		3 .10		1 .33	3 .33	1 .10	3 .10			
19	1	19	1 .10			1 .10	1 .10	1 .10		1 .10	1 .10		1 .10			1 .10	1 .10		
Probability Sum			13,241	1,465	1,087	8,592	13,143	2,036	5,740	1,820	8,834	4,90	4,558	4,091	9,55	13,481	1,036	7,1	8,4
			19	19	19	19	19	19	19	19	19	19	19	19	19	19	19	19	19
Probability Mean			.697	.077	.057	.452	.692	.107	.302	.096	.465	.026	.240	.215	.050	.710	.054	.040	.040

The Probability Matrix

Post Office	Mail Box	Revolutionary Corps	Medical & Vet. Services	Mortuary	Notary Services	Religions & Charitable	House of Equity	Village Council	Mosque	Storehouse	Co-Operative	Flour Mill	Food Prep. & Wholesaler	Tractor	Gelim & Weaving	Weaving Carpet	Spinning & Cloth Weaving	Probability Sum	Probability Mean
18	19	20	21	22	23	24	25	26	27	28	29	30	31	32	33	34	35		
		2 .03						4 .05	4 .05	9 .11		2 .03		9 .11	2 .03	1 .01		1.014	.029
	2 .06	2 .06				1 .03	1 .03	9 .30	5 .17	6 .20				6 .20		3 .10		1.618	.046
	2 .07	11 .39			2 .07	3 .11		11 .40	15 .54	8 .29				5 .18		6 .21		3.022	.086
1 .04	9 .32	10 .36				8 .29		17 .61	15 .54	5 .18	1 .04	2 .07		8 .29		2 .07		3.996	.114
	5 .42	9 .75				5 .42		9 .75	8 .67	3 .25	1 .08			2 .17		2 .17		5.061	.143
	7 .37	13 .66	1 .05			11 .59		13 .68	12 .63	4 .21		1 .05	1 .05	4 .21	1 .05	3 .16	1 .05	5.949	.170
	12 .39	22 .71		3 .10		20 .65		24 .77	28 .90	7 .23	4 .13	3 .10		3 .10		13 .42		6.967	.199
2 .06	20 .61	25 .76	1 .03	1 .03		32 .96		26 .80	33 .10	12 .36	1 .03	3 .09		7 .21	1 .03	7 .21	2 .06	8.000	.229
	16 .50	21 .66		2 .06		24 .75		30 .94	31 .97	14 .44	3 .09	6 .19	1 .03	6 .19		13 .41	1 .06	8.782	.251
1 .04	15 .60	17 .68	1 .04	1 .04		24 .96	1 .04	24 .96	25 .10	11 .44	1 .04	10 .40		5 .20	1 .04	10 .40	2 .08	10.000	.285
1 .04	12 .45	11 .44	2 .08	4 .16	1 .04	25 .10	1 .04	24 .96	25 .10	13 .52	2 .08	11 .44	2 .08	2 .08		9 .36	1 .04	11.000	.314
	8 .47	9 .53	1 .06	4 .24	1 .06	17 .10		17 .10	17 .10	8 .47	3 .19	10 .59	1 .06	1 .06	1 .06	12 .71	4 .24	11.940	.341
	9 .75	7 .58	2 .17	3 .25	1 .08	12 .10	3 .25	10 .83	12 .10	6 .50	5 .42	10 .83		2 .17	1 .08	5 .42	2 .17	13.129	.375
	10 .71	8 .57	1 .07	5 .36		14 .10	1 .07	13 .92	14 .10	12 .86	3 .21	10 .71		4 .29	2 .14	11 .78	4 .29	12.373	.354
	4 .44	5 .56	4 .44	1 .11		9 .10		8 .89	9 .10	8 .89	3 .33	7 .78		2 .22	1 .11	7 .78	4 .44	14.997	.428
	2 .25	1 .13	2 .25	8 .10	1 .13	8 .10	1 .13	6 .75	8 .10	5 .63	2 .25	8 .10	1 .13	2 .25		5 .63	3 .38	16.000	.457
3 .75	2 .50	3 .75	3 .75	3 .75		4 .10	1 .25	1 .25	4 .10	2 .50		3 .75		3 .75		2 .50		17.000	.486
1 .33	2 .67	2 .67	1 .33	3 .10		3 .10	1 .33	2 .67	3 .10	3 .10	1 .33	3 .10		1 .33	1 .33	1 .33	1 .33	17.763	.506
	1 .10			1 .10		1 .10		1 .10	1 .10	1 .10		1 .10		1 .10		1 .10	1 .10	19.000	.543
1,027	8,579	9,267	2,276	5,093	3,78	13,887	1,126	13,514	15,484	9,073	2,215	8,032	3,48	5,060	8,76	6,950	3,104	Probability Sum	
19	19	19	19	19	19	19	19	19	19	19	19	19	19	19	19	19	19		
.054	.451	.488	.120	.268	.020	.731	.059	.711	.815	.478	.117	.423	.018	.266	.046	.366	.163	Probability Mean	

The Probability Matrix

settlement is determined by the number of facilities present in each settlement. The number of each facility in a given settlement-type (Xij) is entered in its relevant place on the table. The division of this number by the total number of settlements in a given settlement-type (Mi the relevant row) constitutes the relevant probability of occurrence ($P Xij$) of a given facility (j) in a given settlement-type (i). The higher the Pij, the higher the value of that facility for that settlement-type and vice versa.

Probability models have generally been designed in this research to deal with understanding regional activity systems. They are used to measure the value of a given type of activity (e.g., facilities) within a settlement-type in relation to the full range of activities within that settlement-type, as well as the entire region. It would thus measure the potential interaction among all different facilities in each settlement-type and region. In other words, the value of a given facility in a specific settlement-type is the relative degree of the occurrence of this activity within a settlement in relation to the full range of activities available (or not available) within that settlement-type in conjunction with other facilities or government services (or any of the facilities under consideration) rather than to a facility located in isolation.

c. Building Models–Assumptions

In building both of the models, the following assumptions have been made. Although with the originality model we dealt with individual settlements, with the building probability model we dealt with settlement-types.

1) It is assumed that the table(s) reflect the originality (probability) of the facilities which were necessarily developed in accordance with the law of supply and demand.

2) It is assumed that the efficiency of the system implies the maximization of the sum of the originalities (probabilities). It is therefore more desirable to replace facilities with lower originalities (probabilities) for given settlements (types) by facilities with higher originalities (probabilities).

3) It is assumed that in a perfect situation in a region such as Esfahan, various facilities at certain settlement levels (size) should occur in an orderly fashion. Therefore, on this basis, the hierarchical order of the settlements can be established.

4) It is assumed that the facilities with low originalities (probabilities) are haphazard; meaning that their occurrences have been accidental. These facilities could be discontinued, in contrast to those facilities with high originalities (probabilities) which are of greater value and which should, therefore, be reinforced.

5) It is assumed that in order to formulate development policies, it is necessary to standardize the previously-mentioned haphazard patterns through the establishment of definite standards (number of facilities) for predefined settlement levels.

6) It is assumed that higher efficiency would entail the maximization of the sum of all originalities (probabilities) in the above mentioned table(s) given certain constraints.

7) It is assumed that the importance of each facility for each settlement (type) in the region is relative to its originality (probability) index. Therefore the occurrence of facilities with very low originality (probabilty) in a given settlement (type) is accidental and unnecessary.

8) It is essential to classify facilities relative to their originalities (probabilities) for different settlement-types and, in this way, arrive at standards for the classification of settlement-types throughout the region and also the country as a whole.

9) It is assumed that for population forecasts in given regions, a certain number of facilities can be estimated. Assigning these numbers to relevant columns of the matrix, it is assumed that given certain constraints, the originality (probability) model could distribute the facilities to those settlement-types which could maximize the sum of originalities (probabilities) of the total system.

10) It is assumed that in a given case the smaller the number of a given facility (*j*) in a given settlement-type (*i*) case of scarce facilities, the smaller the number of settlements in the relevant settlement-type. Likewise, the larger the number of any facility–type (*j*) in a given settlement-type (*i*), the greater the number of settlements in relevant settlement-types; i.e., the greater the spread of facilities and settlements.

d originality MODEL

(1) $o_{ij} = o_{xij} = \dfrac{M_i}{N_j} X_{ij}$

Division by N_j increases the influence of scarce facilities. Multiplication by M_i will emphasize the importance of supporting functions, as suggested by the theory of "agglomeration and efficiency".

The followings are originalities of settlement i and facility j in the total system. (2,3)

n = Number of facility types
m = Number of settlements
X_{ij} = Number of j-facilities in settlement i
N_j = Total number of j-facilities in the region
M_i – Total number of facilities in settlement i
$^o X_{ij}$ = Originality of J-facility in the settlement i
O_j = Sum of total originalities of j-facilities in the whole region
O_i = Sum of total originalities of all the facilities in the settlement i
A_j = Proposed total number of j-facilities in the region

(2)

$$O_i = \sum_{j=1}^{n} \frac{\sum_{i=1}^{n} X_{ij}}{\sum_{j=1}^{m} X_{ij}} X_{ij}$$

(3)

$$O_j = \sum_{i=1}^{m} \frac{\sum_{i=1}^{n} X_{ij}}{\sum_{j=1}^{m} X_{ij}} X_{ij}$$

Sum of originalities of all the settlements and all the facilities are: (4,5)

(4)

$$\sum O_i = \sum_{i=1}^{m} \sum_{j=1}^{n} \frac{\sum_{i=1}^{n} X_{ij}}{\sum_{j=1}^{m} X_{ij}} X_{ij}$$

(5)

$$\sum O_j = \sum_{j=1}^{n} \sum_{i=1}^{m} \frac{\sum_{i=1}^{n} X_{ij}}{\sum_{j=1}^{m} X_{ij}} X_{ij}$$

To optimize the system, given certain constraints, the total sum should be maximized. (6,7)

(6) $\text{Max} \sum O_i$

(7) $\text{Max} \sum O_j$

e probability MODEL

$$(1) \quad p_{ij} = p_{x_{ij}} = \frac{X_{ij}}{M_i}$$

Division by N_i increases the influence of settlements in the higher type, i.e., settlements with a greater number of supporting functions (larger i – smaller N_i)

The followings are probabilities of occurrences of settlements and facilities in the total system. (2,3)

$$(2) \quad P_i = \frac{\sum\limits_{j=1}^{n} p_{ij}}{n}$$

$$(3) \quad P_j = \frac{\sum\limits_{i=1}^{m} p_{ij}}{m}$$

n = Number of facility types
m = Number of settlement types
X_{ij} = Number of j-facilities in the type i-settlements
p_{ij} = Probability of occurrence of j-facilities in the type i-settlements
N_j = Total no. of j-facilities in the region
M_i = Total no. of settlements in the type i-settlements
P_j = Sum of total probabilities of occurrences of j-facilities in the whole region
P_i = Sum of total probabilities of occurrences of all the facilities in the type i-settlements
A_j = Proposed total no. of j-facilities in the region
c_i = Total no. of settlements in type i-settlements

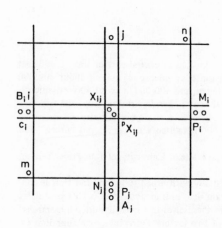

Sum of probabilities of occurrences of all the settlements and all the facilities are: (4,5)

$$(4) \quad \sum P_i = \sum_{i=1}^{m} \frac{\sum\limits_{j=1}^{n} p_{ij}}{n}$$

$$(5) \quad \sum P_j = \sum_{j=1}^{n} \frac{\sum\limits_{i=1}^{m} p_{ij}}{m}$$

To optimize the system, given certain constraints, the total sum should be maximized. (6,7)

$$(6) \quad \left\{ \begin{array}{l} \text{Max} \ \sum P_i \\[2ex] \text{Max} \ \sum P_j \end{array} \right.$$

(7)

It should be mentioned that having built the models, with the above objectives in mind, we found that by maximizing the sum of originalities or probabilities, as a means of optimizing the distribution of common facilities, the models had to some extent polarized the facilities into limited settlement centers, suggesting a growth pole type of development. On the other hand, to obtain equity especially in an agricultural regional function where man/land relation is necessary and important we had to insert some constraint on the model to secure the necessary equity and thus a balance. Although this will not be further discussed here, it will give the reader some ideas for further development of the models.

It is hoped that the paring of the two models could provide this complementary function and thus a balance between efficiency and equity. That is to say, where the originality model tends to polarize these activities, the use of a set of defined probabilities induced for certain functions in certain settlement sizes and functions could secure the necessary equity.

Notes to Appendix I

1. Esfahan region is a city-centered region located in central part of Iran–5,000 feet above sea level. The region is a river basin (Zayandehrood) area of about 800,000 inhabitants (400,000 in the city of Esfahan, and 400,000 in about 400 settlements, ranging from 100,000 to 60,000 inhabitants). Beside Esfahan City, the region is predominantly agricultural oriented. According to Iran's Ministry of Interior's definition, population centers over 5,000 inhabitants are considered "urban" and below that are "rural."

2. *Regional Analysis for Iran*, Asghar Talaye Minai, University of Iran Press, Tehran, Iran, 1974.

3. Furthermore classical CPT deals essentially with urban functions and thus is concerned with settlements of over a certain size–in Iran, about 5,000. CPT postulates that urban functions tend to distribute themselves in a spatially-ordered hierarchy. This occurs because of the interplay of two factors. Different urban functions require different threshold service market areas, thus limiting supply. On the other hand, consumers tend to minimize trips by using the closest sources. The CPT hierarchy is a result of these two tendencies. Paul English, in *City and Village in Iran*, (Madison, University of Wisconsin Press) postulates the following hierarchy (although not using CPT directly): dominant urban center, regional subcenter, agricultural-weaving village, and small village/hamlet.

4. See, for example, J. Brian McLoughlin, *Urban and Regional Planning, A Systems Approach*, London, Faber & Faber, 1969.

5. A paper on the first part of the originality model was published in *Ekistics* 240, November, 1975: "Measuring Human Activity Systems in Esfahan: Originality and Centrality."

6. A paper on the first part of the probability model was prepared for the Second International Congress of Architecture in Shiraz, Iran (24–30 September, 1974): "A Framework for Regional Analysis and Planning in Iran."

7. In a more detailed study, the indexes were divided into seven sectors or subsystems: workshops (including repairshops and handicrafts); social (local social interaction); health; education; agricultural and government supplied facilities; and commerce. From the gross distribution of these indexes, a seven-rank hierarchy was derived for each sector.

8. Settlement-type–all settlements with equal number of facilities fall into a settlement-type.

An educational system:
Case example

Farabi is a University planned and established in Tehran, Iran during the latter 70's. The author was involved in the early processes of conceptual development, planning, and implementation of the university which was the first of its kind, especially founded to provide training in the arts.

The prime objectives of the University were set:

1. to bring the arts to the focus of University activity and attention and to subordinate the other disciplines;
2. to treat the arts neither as a subjective treatment of artifacts as was the practice in some 17th, 18th, and 19th century European art academies, nor to treat artists as second class citizens as in the universities of the early 20th century, but rather to set art activities in the center and let other disciplines grow around them;
3. to question the dominance of Western orientation in the written history of the arts and attempt to enrich the body of Western knowledge drawing upon Asian and African traditions, while at the same time using Iran's geographical and sociological situation as a bridge between the East and the West;
4. to try innovative educational philosophies, methods, and techniques in the areas of environmental art and design, and the performing arts and communication.

In art schools and academies, the arts have traditionally been no more than activities arising out of individually oriented concentration, while in the universities, art activities have usually been pushed to the periphery. In response to this situation, the Farabi University system attempts to have environmental planning and design and the performing arts as the primary focus with a secondary emphasis on the sciences, arts, and culture.

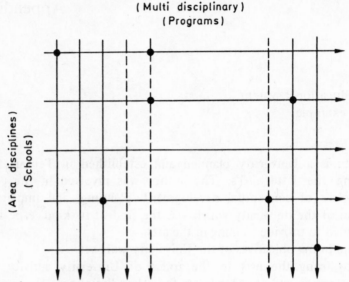

(Multi disciplinary)
(Programs)

(Area disciplines)
(Schools)

Diagram 1
Conceptual Framework of Farabi University

Although after the student rebellion of the seventies a few universities and Schools, including the Beaux Arts, questioned their past programs and converted to similar systems on an experimental basis, results of these innovations are yet to be evaluated. Following is a short description of Farabi University.

a. *The Farabi system.* In the design of the administrative organization of the university (see diagram 1), a matrix corresponds horizontally to the disciplinary "school clusters" (Area Disciplines) and vertically to the interdisciplinary programs (Multi-Disciplinary).

The difference between this system and traditional systems is that in contrast to the latter's sectorial organization of educational management, the matrix of this system integrates the total activities of the institution. Each school is not an isolated activity but, as a horizontal member of the matrix, it is a forum of some clusters of disciplinary activities through which all the vertical programs run. A School is not a closed system tied to the University system; it is a component of an open system that activates flows from one to the other through various activities such as "programs."

b. *Schools.* School clusters consist of five major areas of academic activity, as well as a broader School of Arts and Sciences, two areas of professional and practical training, and one art education institute (see diagrams 2 and 3):
— Plastic Arts
— Applied Arts and Industrial Design
— Environmental Design and Planning
— Music and related arts
— Communication and the performing arts
— Arts and Sciences (consisting of four departments: physical sciences, natural sciences, social studies, and pure sciences)
— Practical Music (Conservatory)
— Acting
— Art Education

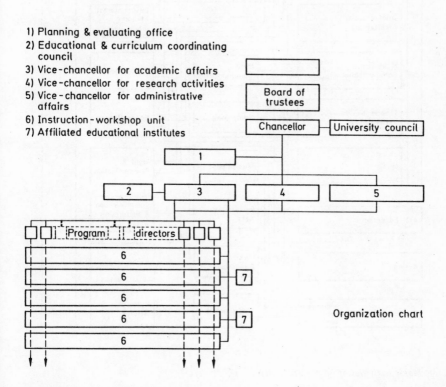

1) Planning & evaluating office
2) Educational & curriculum coordinating council
3) Vice-chancellor for academic affairs
4) Vice-chancellor for research activities
5) Vice-chancellor for administrative affairs
6) Instruction-workshop unit
7) Affiliated educational institutes

Organization chart

Diagram 2
Organization Chart of Farabi University

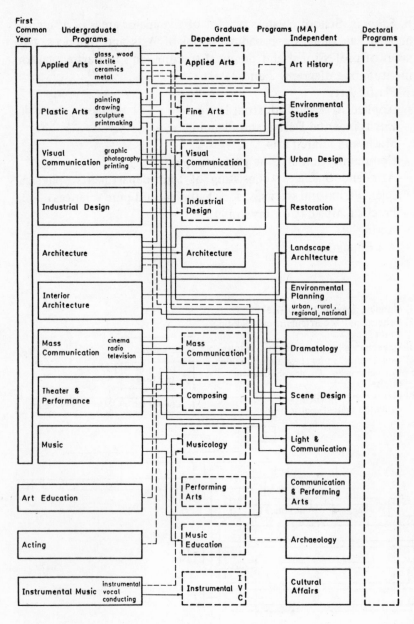

Diagram 3

Major Activities of Farabi University

These clusters attempt to fulfill such disciplinary objectives as the advancement of knowledge in each discipline via improvement of the faculty, more effective handling of disciplinary courses offered by the clusters, as well as those teaching and research materials related to these activities. Faculty promotions and appointments, in addition to course evaluation and control, is being effected through these clusters.

c. *"Programs."* The programs, however, are interdisciplinary–oriented, each program consisting of *x* number of courses chosen from different clusters and assembled as a package, bearing in mind the objectives of the particular program and its degree. Each program operates under the auspices of an interdisciplinary committee headed by a director.

d. *First-year curriculum.* The first-year program has been set for general study designed for all students entering the University, except those enrolled in practical-oriented courses.

In order to provide the student with a wide spectrum of knowledge as a base for environmental creation, the university first-year curriculum was designed in such a way that it could provide all students with a full perspective of human knowledge and experience. It is through introduction to a panorama of man's total historical knowledge and experience that a student can begin to understand the emergence of discipline areas, i.e., Schools and departments. Going through this program a student is expected to be able to make better choices in selecting his discipline area. The first-year program is not treated as disciplinary-oriented courses on various subject matter; it is, rather, organized as broad generalized themes into theoretical and workshop forums.

Part of the program contains five general themes (one morning a day) through which a student, before he selects a discipline area, is given a glance at man's total perspective of knowledge.

The first year curriculum then consists of seven major subjects including five theoretical courses taught on the basis of the following themes:

Man and Cosmos
Man and Society
Man and Nature
Man and the Arts
Man and Technology

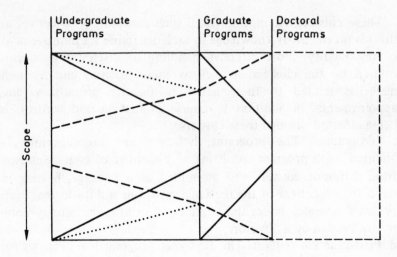

Diagram 4
Scope of Programs of Farabi University

In addition to five theoretical themes, there are two practical-oriented workshops: Workshop I—Basic Design (including the plastic arts, spatial design concepts using color, light, texture, etc.); and Workshop II—Sound, Motion (including communication, music, and the performing arts).

Studios are likewise not designed to practice on preconceived forms, shapes, concepts, and techniques, but rather to use the studio to explore ways of human expression. Thus these studio programs are intended to bring out whatever talent and potential a student might have. The attitude here is based on generic creation and design, and leads the student to believe that art and culture are to be felt and understood as patterns and processes of life forms and activities rather than artifacts produced to satisfy this or that "style", or conventions made by this or that school of thought.

This would serve as a means toward settling upon their major area of study and programs, discover their potentials and capabilities, obtain a general introduction to the sociology of knowledge, normalize and equalize their different levels of background, and act as an introduction to different programs leading to various degrees.

e. *Course breakdown and characteristics.* The characteristics of course breakdown in the areas of theory and workshop are as follows:

1. *Theory.* After the first year curriculum, the theoretical aspect of university programs still continue to be structured around those five general themes. In the second year, the theme man and technology transforms into areas of *a priori* knowledge, such as the pure sciences and technology, and in the third and fourth years it becomes technical courses of structure, mechanical equipment, etc. Man and nature also narrows in scope and degree of abstraction from the first to the fourth year. Thus it proceeds from general theories of organic-inorganic matter to ecological, climatic, and physiobiological factors, to strength of materials and, finally, to construction materials. In the areas of the social sciences and the humanities, namely, man and the cosmos, man and society, and man and the arts, the method is the same; i.e., to move from abstract general concepts in the first year to applied and concrete concepts as the student advances.

Nevertheless there is a strong difference in the treatment of the nonphysical sciences in the Farabi attitude. Whereas in the areas of acquired knowledge, i. e., the physical sciences, the pure sciences and technology, the chronological advancement of human knowledge and experience is important, in the human value system it is not. The reason for this is that in the evolution of history, due to a lack of communication between various spatio-temporal cultures, such value systems did not necessarily build upon each other. Specifically, the written history of the Western world does not fully represent cultures of the whole world. For this reason, at Farabi it was intended to study the arts and culture of various spatio-temporal origins rather than the chronological body of Western knowledge.

2. *Workshop.* Throughout various programs, workshops are treated as forums for ideas and for working experiences, to synthesize various points of view, different inputs brought in by different disciplines and specialities, and to unify these interactions in a problem-oriented project. In the first year, workshops are more abstract in dealing with conceptual ideas and images and become more and more concrete and applied as they advance. At the same time each workshop project is a unique experience complementary

to the total set of workshops each student must take. The workshop objectives are:

(a) maintenance of a close relationship with the tangible world and its physical potentials and attributes;

(b) maintenance of face to face close relationships between student-faculty, faculty-faculty, and student-student regarding various, even opposing, viewpoints;

(c) learning from doing;

(d) direct experience with the application of various tools and techniques and media via different communication channels—such experience would also imply *a priori* knowledge; i.e., the pure sciences, logic, and mathematics used in the creation of a harmonic order; and finally,

(e) alternative choices. It is believed that the more flexible the education system, the more it can respond to individual needs, potential, and talent. In aiming to respond to the needs, the University system allows for the following (see diagram 4):

(a) the system as differentiated among six academic clusters and three profession-practice centers where the centers deal with training oriented educational functions; and

(b) a student who wants to attain comprehensive knowledge and experience, whether he comes from a broad based undergraduate program (dotted line) or one of the practical oriented centers (broken line) has to follow the broken line in the graduate program and into a Ph.D. program afterwards

(c) A student who wants to attain a specialized degree at the end of four years follows the solid line.

(d) Those who either have a general-comprehensive undergraduate or graduate degree and what to get a professional master's degree follow the graduate solid line.